UNCOMMON MARKET

UNCOMMON MARKET

Capital, Class and Power in
the European Community

Stuart Holland

First published 1980 by
THE MACMILLAN PRESS LTD
*London and Basingstoke
Companies and representatives
throughout the world*

Typeset by
STYLESET LIMITED
Salisbury, Wiltshire

and Printed in Great Britain by
Billing and Sons Limited
Guildford, London, Oxford, Worcester

British Library Cataloguing in Publication Data

Holland, Stuart
    UnCommon Market
    I. European communities
    I. Title
    382'.9142   HC241 2

    ISBN 0-333-19707-0
    ISBN 0-333-27686-8 Papermac

To Jenny

Contents

List of Tables and Figures

TABLES

FIGURES

Preface

Lichtenberg once compared a book with a mirror, observing that if an ass looked in, how could a prophet look out?

This book is not especially prophetic. In the main it is analytical rather than prescriptive. But there is little doubt that some commentators will see in it another rationale for an anti-EEC case, based on prejudice of the kind which they themselves reflect, rather than on analysis.

Some readers will judge the balance of the argument for themselves. Certainly my view on the Community have changed over time, which is more than one can say of some of the self-avowed empiricists in the EEC question, for whom facts count little against the fervour of their vision, or illusion of *Europa über alles*.

In a real sense much of the argument is dialectical, stressing contradictions between aims and achievements, design and deeds. But it also is implicitly dialectical in another sense, that the counter vision of democratic internationlist and socialist community of European states must be based on recognition that this so-called common market is unequal and uncommon in character, bureaucratic in form, and at present tends to neutralise political power and disintegrate national economic and social structures.

Also, in a real sense, the argument is multi-dimensional — or, in the jargon of academics, inter-disciplinary. In this way it seeks quite consciously to integrate elements of economics and social and political thought into the analysis of Western European integration itself.

If the case as argued provokes on-going thought as a basis for action to change this uncommon market of the EEC it will have been worthwhile.

ACKNOWLEDGEMENT
My special thanks are due to Frances Richardson for research assistance with parts of this analysis. She is in no way accountable for its arguments or conclusions.

July 1979   STUART HOLLAND

Part One
Institutions and Instruments

1 UnCommon Pretensions

Superficially, the economics of Western European integration have been dominated by political factors. This is no more than should be expected. The political element in economic policy is not reduced simply by its translation to an international level. If anything it is increased, especially if issues of national sovereignty are involved. Besides, the main events of the formation and enlargement of the European Economic Community were more political than most international economic arrangements since the war. In 1961 the first President of the EEC Commission stated bluntly, 'we are not in business at all – we are in politics'.[1] Yet this was hardly a revelation. A political drive linked the formation of the European Coal and Steel Community in 1952, the abortive proposals for a European Defence Community in 1954, and the establishment of the EEC and Euratom in 1957. From the start political factors were stressed, not disguised.

The reasons were obvious enough. The Second World War was widely held to have owed its indirect origins to the unemployment of the post-1919 and post-1929 depressions on which extremist nationalism has spawned. It also had devastated major areas in the main Continental European countries twice in the lifetime of leading politicians. Its human and social costs encouraged a conscious break with the international institutions which had proved broken reeds when faced with the brutality of Fascism. For some Continental politicians this meant supplementing the United Nations with mechanisms which – at least in principle – would inter-lock national economies in such a way as to make a future war in Western Europe impossible.[2] New supranational institutions would be forged, with voting agreements which would bind even major states. Their terms of reference would be specified in detailed constitutions; their action initiated by independent supranational bodies, and infringements tried before a supranational court of justice. From small beginnings they would think big and for the very long term. A customs union would be extended to a common market, which itself would be only an intermediate stage in the integration of national policies in an economic union, possibly on federal lines paralleling the United States with a United States of Europe. In the 1950s Cold War tensions intensified the support of hard-headed men for what otherwise might have remained pipe-dreaming for Jean Monnet.[3]

Instrumental Economics
In other words, the role of economic *analysis* in the initial integration of the economies of the member states of the European Communities was

secondary. In fact economics was seen as instrumental. It was a means to primarily political ends. By the same token the role of economists and economic theory was relatively minor. Only a handful of economists were consulted in the drafting of the Coal and Steel Community's Paris Treaty, while economists and statisticians were specifically excluded from the drafting of the EEC's Rome Treaty.[4] In the House of Commons in August 1961, the then Prime Minister (Harold Macmillan) admitted that the Government proposed to apply for EEC membership without making the studies of the likely impact on particular sectors of British industry, and the 1966–70 Labour Government published its own estimate of the economic effects of EEC membership in February 1970 – nearly three years after its decision to propose entry negotiations.[5]

None of this need cause undue surprise. Governments are not elected simply to fulfil the recommendations of professional economists, and in international politics they cannot be concerned only with questions of economic policy.

However, the apparently secondary role of economists and economic theory in the founding of the European Communities should not disguise the fact that its originators drew on a prevailing ideology which was both economic and political. In essence, this was the ideology of liberal capitalism, or the assumption that the self-interest of enterprise could be harnessed in the public interest through a liberalisation of trade, capital and labour movements. The outspoken Walter Hallstein again, put the issue with typical bluntness in writing in 1962 of the dominant philosophy behind the Community treaties: As he asserted: 'since Adam Smith the arguments in favour of free trade have been refined and qualified by a very considerable body of economic doctrine, but the core of the theory still stands.'[6]

Walter Hallstein was right enough in one key respect. Although challenged by the Left, and by the increasingly State capitalist intervention of European governments, which no longer relied exclusively on the market in their attempts to harness private self-interest to the public benefit, the core of the liberal capitalist ideology hungover from Smith and the eighteenth century still stood, incarnate, in the Treaties of the European Communities. And that theory served a major political end in cementing and legitimising the capitalism which the United States had underpinned through Marshall Aid and NATO since the postwar settlement.

The unifying theme of liberal capitalist economic and political integration was clearer in the Paris Treaty of the European Coal and Steel Community than in the Rome Treaty of the EEC.[7] It partly accounts for the formally tougher powers of decision given to its supranational High Authority. The other main reason was the powers widely held necessary for the ECSC to cope with the trusts and cartels in steel. Giant heavy-industrial companies such as Krupp and Thyssen had acted in a thoroughly collusive manner in the first half of the century. But they had also been notorious for providing the Hitler Reich with virtually self-contained armanents industries. It is important to remember these general and particular factors in interpreting both the extent of the supranational powers given to the Coal and Steel High Authority, and the degree to which they later were allowed to fall into dis-use.[8]

Supranationalism versus Internationalism

However, the Rome Treaty itself, signed by the Six in March 1957, allowed considerable powers of decision to a nominally supranational body – the Commission – and provided for decision on Commission proposals by majority vote in the Council of Ministers (composed of Ministers delegated for particular decisions by the member states). The majority voting procedure, which could put even a major state such as France, Italy or West Germany in a minority, was intended to be legally binding. The procedure was also supposed to be progressive, with majority voting on the main aspects of further integration really beginning from 1966.

In this pretension to supranationalism the main Community Treaties went much further than either the General Agreement on Trade and Tariffs (with which they shared a common philosophy of liberalisation), or the European Free Trade Association, which was set up under British *aegis* after the failure of negotiations in the mid-1950s to establish an inner common market of the Six and an outer free trade area of the Seven later EFTA members.

The contrast between the provisions of the EEC Rome Treaty and the EFTA Stockholm Convention illustrates the point. The Rome Treaty envisaged three progressive stages from predominantly unanimous to predominantly majority voting. Its intended schema of stages to supranationalism can be represented as Table 1.1.[9] Significantly enough, as shown later, the main switch from unanimous international voting to supranational majority voting was supposed to occur in January 1966.

By contrast, the Stockholm Convention of EFTA was always predominantly and, it can be argued, realistically, international in character. It involved no pretension to progressive stages (see Table 1.2).

The difference between these EEC and EFTA arrangements was and

TABLE 1.1 The Treaty of Rome

	Total votes	Majority decisions	Percentage of total	Unanimous decisions	Percentage of total
Stage 1	82	27	32.9	55	67.1
Stage 2	73	32	43.8	41	56.2
Stage 3	77	43	55.8	34	44.2

TABLE 1.2 The Stockholm Convention

Total votes	Majority decisions	Percentage of total	Unanimous decisions	Percentage of total
43	17	39.5	26	60.5

remains crucial to the fortunes of Western European integration. In one sense, it is the difference between acceptance of an international framework in which joint action may reinforce national sovereignty, and a supranational framework which would diminish it.

As is well enough grasped, at least at the intuitive level, French policy under De Gaulle was to challenge the supranationalism of the Rome Treaty and Community institutions. In practice, De Gaulle's reaction was widely represented, with some justification, as the assertion of not only national interests but also nationalism within the Community.

Yet, as will be shown, De Gaulle's policy towards the Community was not entirely hostile. Until at least the mid-1960s it was thoroughly pragmatic. Moreover, it can be argued that the supranational institutions of the Community, founded in reaction to the last world war, and in part aiming — retrospectively and too late — to avoid it, have acted as an obstacle to feasible international action between Western European governments in the postwar period.

Irreversibility?

It frequently is not grasped that the mechanisms of Community integration are not simply those of supranational versus international institutions. In itself, supranationalism is a feature of US federalism, whereby the federal government has powers and funds which are different from and binding on individual member 'states'.

The basic difference between the European project of the EEC and other federal models lies in the nominal irreversibility of Community integration. In contrast with the principles of parliamentary democracy at national level, where nothing legislated by one administration is binding on the next (provided it can mobilise a majority), Community integration implies a series of *one-way* and irreversible measures, embodied in Commission decisions and directives, and legitimated by the Treaties themselves.

In a very basic sense, this is a reason why so many internationalists are opposed to Community supranationalism. They question whether one model of the economy and society, such as that enshrined in the Community Treaties, is relevant to the changing structures of the economy and society over time. They also challenge the right of officials, isolated from the political process through limited accountability, to determine whether such a process as reflected in the national (or regional) vote should be subject to a higher overriding principle of Community integration.

The contrast between such irreversible change at the institutional level of State or Community power, and the reversibility of political change at national level, is elaborated in Chapter 7. However, at this preliminary level, a specific contrast is instructive. For instance, it has become widespread knowledge that the Labour Party programmes of the 1970s argued the case for a 'fundamental and irreversible change in the balance of power in favour of working people and their families'. But such irreversibility itself is qualified by two main factors. First, the change would have to be supported on a consensus basis if it were to prove irreversible in the medium-term. Second, while its advocates might hope for such irreversibility through persuasion, the measures concerned could in both principle and practice be reversed, modified or amended by later Governments.

Neither condition obtains with the irreversible mechanisms of Community procedures, so long as (i) the present structures and procedures of integration are sustained and (ii) national governments find themselves unable either to reverse such procedures or withdraw from the Community because their effective economic and political dependence has become irreversible through integration itself.

Arguably, a Community Assembly with parliamentary powers should be able to reverse Community decisions taken at the level of the Council of Ministers, and also reverse Commission directives. But, in practice, the European Assembly has only limited powers. By article 144 of the Rome Treaty the Assembly can pass a censure motion on the Commission, but only with a two-thirds majority, rather than the simple majority necessary in, for instance, the British parliament. Also, the result of such a censure would be to sack the whole Commission. Thus the Assembly was originally offered an axe which it was unlikely to wield, rather than a scalpel with which to amend legislation in the more normal manner of parliaments.

Since the mid-1970s the Assembly has on three occasions initially opposed the Community budget, honing down its axe to scalpel size in the form of amendments. This followed a new procedure endorsed by national governments by which the Assembly could modify a budget when this did not involve an increase in total obligatory expenditure (introduced in the UK parliament on 8 December 1975). In other words, the Assembly could propose specific increases in the budget, but only with offsetting reductions to compensate for them. However, on each occasion the Assembly climbed down when the crunch came on the final reading, rather than oppose both the Commission and the Council.

Even if the Assembly does not pass the Community's budget, a so-called one-twelfth formula comes into operation, by which the Commission can spend one-twelfth of the previous year's budget each month for the next year. The system is biased heavily against the Assembly, which in practice so far has served more as a fig-leaf of democracy rather than a democratic institution proper.

Moreover, in principle, the Assembly has no power to modify the

Treaties of the Community itself. Besides, since they are mainly economic
and much more detailed than, for instance, the US constitution, this poses
a crucial political problem, For the Treaties of the European Community
idealise and thereby legimate the mechanisms of capitalism at a European
level. Their revision and transformation would mean little less than the
successful challenge of European capitalism itself.

Unjust Returns

The issues concerned can be related to an element in Community philosophy which, wherever possible, has marched in step with its founding principles: the aim of avoiding *juste retour.* Put simply, *juste retour* means
a just return. In other words, governments have sought to gain some kind
of equivalent return from the Community for what they have put into it.
Such a principle is anathema to federalists. This is not necessarily because
they see it as wrong in itself. But they see it as wrong now relative to a
federal Community which could ensure a just return over the longer term
to countries, regions, industries and social groups which may be disadvantaged in the short term in the approach to a supranational and federal
Community.

The idealism of such federalists should not be in question. But it is
fundamentally misplaced. It is as ideal, and as irrelevant to the needs of
the Community to date as the philosophy of liberal capitalism which has
underlain its founding charters. Put more directly, if the working of the
market mechanism were itself basically equal between countries, regions,
industries and social groups and classes, many political parties and governments would be more enthusiastic supporters of a Community which
sought to push through adjustments and accomodations today which gave
rise to a better tomorrow.

But the market of the Community is essentially a capitalist market,
uncommon and unequal in the record of who gains what, where, why and
when. Its mechanisms have already disintegrated major industries and
regions in the Community, and threaten to realise an inner and outer
Europe of rich and poor countries. And in part, such disintegration is the
result of the dominance of liberal capitalist policies which, for many
federalists — because they are enshrined in the Treaties — have the status
and relevance of the ark of the Community covenant.

One of the troubles with rejection of *juste retour* rapidly became clear
enough in practice. While, in theory, rapid progress to common policies
through harmonisation could in the long-run compensate individual losses
by gains, opposition to the principle of *juste retour* itself acted as an
obstacle to rapid agreement. Ideally, politics should be a matter of principle
in action. But in reality most politics takes the form of trade-offs between
different power blocs and interest groups. Some of these are overrepre-
sented, misguided or plain backward-looking. But others, such as the
regional and national pressures for more autonomy, or the environment

lobby, point to real needs for government closer to people themselves, or a liveable environment, which harmonisation policies legitimised by reference to treaties alone may either miss or actually frustrate.

In other words, opposition to the principle of *juste retour* has tended to demand not only unacceptable inequalities of treatment over the long-term, but has implied that the Community Treaties and the Community's institutions — especially the Commission and High Authority — have a better idea of what is just, and to whom returns should be distributed, than have governments, political institutions, trades unions or pressure groups. One of the clearest applications of such unjust return was to be the terms imposed on Britain, through accepting the Common Agricultural Policy as a condition of EEC membership. The switch from low-cost producers, and generally low prices for food products, to higher costs and higher prices through the CAP, represented a real welfare loss for British consumers which was not compensated by competitive stimulus, greater investment, higher employment in industry, or offsetting reverse transfers of funds.[10]

Granted the obvious inequality in the distribution of costs and benefits from European integration, it might well be asked why the advocates of integration itself did not adopt a more interventionist line, and favour positive discrimination in favour of the 'losers' from integration at a particular stage of the game. On grounds either of pragmatism or equity, it would have seemed a sensible course of action.

There is a comparison here between the limits of conventional integration theory and that of the conventional theory of economic welfare. According to the latter, a policy could be justified if its gains, overall, outweigh losses to different groups. But, in practice, eschewing such common sense, so-called welfare theory quickly moved from this implicitly egalitarian premise to more practical arguments which involved redistribution through growth — with less for the more advantaged and vice versa — rather than redistribution *per se*.[11] It was very much this latter principle which ruled in the Commission and lay at the root of the initiatives which it took to harmonise national policies in the first decade of the Community. While it had some force then, it has decidedly less in the 1970s when growth itself has gone by the board, and disparities are growing in income and product per head between major regions and areas, some of which are as big as member countries themselves.

Besides, as Ralf Dahrendorf strongly argued in two articles published under a pseudonym when he was still an EEC Commissioner, the principles of the founding Treaties of the Community, as interpreted by technocrats rather than politicians, tended to give a bizarre interpretation of priorities. Thus, he wrote,

Europe becomes increasingly bureaucratic [with] a craze for harmonisation . . . Whoever regards harmonisation as of value in itself very rapidly loses the ability to distinguish between important and unimportant, necessary and superfluous matters. More than that, he interferes with the principle of *differentiating* between regions and countries, and runs into the danger of creating a uniform Europe.[12]

Dahrendorf stressed that the combination of such crazed harmonisation with supranational pretensions had in fact prevented the Community from achieving quite practical gains in international action. He therefore endorsed and recommended the so-called Davignon formula which envisaged that member governments in the Community should meet regularly outside the framework of Community institutions. This summitry formula, supplemented by regular meetings of Ministers and Permanent Representatives (national ambassadors to the Community) has certainly tended to substitute for the Commission's formal initiative on policies, providing alternative vehicles for the expression of specific interests which would by overridden by harmonisation and *laissez-faire* driven to extremes.

On the other hand, institutional pragmatism in itself does not cope with the problem of the implicit liberal capitalist philosophy in the Community Treaties, and the extent to which this is increasingly divorced from the real needs of governments and economic policy. It certainly does not ensure that the 'negative' integration philosophy of 'thou shalt not' is supplanted by more relevant policies. Harmonising conditions for competition or creating a common currency does little or nothing to cope with the crisis of the Community in the 1970s, including the accountability of big-business power, a planned joint reflation of public spending and demand, or the re-establishment of full and useful employment. If anything, in these areas, the founding charters of the Communities are an incubus posing more problems than they solve.

Negative and Positive Policies
One reason is the predominantly 'negative' rather than 'positive' character of the Community treaties and institutions. They are strong on 'thou shalt not' but much weaker on 'we shall'.

Two main factors are responsible for this. At the institutional level, as already stressed, the supranational pretensions of the Treaties tend to obstruct pragmatic joint action between governments on an international basis. At another level, by drawing on the prevailing ideology of liberal capitalism, the Treaties and Commission are mainly concerned with *preventing* abuses to competition and the market mechanism rather than with *providing* a framework for joint intervention to achieve what the market itself cannot do.

The explicit economic rationales of 'negative' and 'positive' integration are analysed in more detail later (see especially Chapter 3). However, the 'negative' character of the Rome Treaty, in the above sense, emerges both from its major titles, which specify the four 'freedoms' of movement for goods, persons, services and capital (i.e. the three main stages of integration up to and including a common market) and also from the common policies which it specified should be agreed to by the member countries.[13] Basically, these amounted to (i) a competition policy to prevent 'abuses of competition' and 'distortions' in the competitive process; (ii) a common transport policy, and (iii) a common agricultural policy. These policies would be administered by the Commission rather than by the governments themselves through the Council. In addition, provision was made for the future harmonisation of certain national policies, and especially those which it was maintained would otherwise affect and distort trade between the member states, including indirect taxation on goods and services.

In other words, the Rome Treaty extended the common market for coal and steel of the Paris Treaty and laid the basis for an economic union. It did not, however, commit the member states to monetary union. The 'negative' integration philosophy emerges from the extent to which the common policies agreed in principle in advance were intended to ensure the removal of obstacles to the freer working of the market mechanism.

Apart from agriculture or industry, the failure in any meaningful sense to achieve a Community transport policy was a good case in point. As one of the three main policy areas specified for joint action in the Treaty of Rome, this sought essentially to remove barriers to carrying by private hauliers, and to restrict rates to a range with upper and lower limits, to avoid monopoly overcharging or undercutting as a non-tariff barrier. This two-pronged 'fork' was similar in character to the so-called 'snakes', or upper and lower limits for exchange rate changes, attempted with varying degrees of unsuccess in the 1970s. For twenty years Community transport policy has hardly moved beyond the negative philosophy of the forked tariff, save for attempts to maintain that national governments may not restrict the destruction of their roads and environment by giant lorries, and the attempted introduction of tachometers, or driver time-check instruments into cabs. The main thrust of the environment lobby of the late 1960s and 1970s seems to have passed it by, as has the scope for moving specified categories of Community transport from road to less polluting and much safer rail.

It might well be said that the Commission's transport policy has been so concerned with harmonising rear-view mirrors that it could not see where it was going. By the late-1970s, even one of the most pro-Market members of the British Cabinet, Transport Minister Bill Rodgers, judged that, the Nine's transport policy, had been 'preoccupied with trivia'.[14] Certainly, its proposals — themselves mainly negative in character — have prompted equally negative reactions from member governments. Commenting on this, Nigel Despicht has written that 'a negative attitude on the part of member states was often fully justified'; and it terms which very much parallel Dahrendorf's general judgement, 'Community institutions themselves were inadequate to the task of making common policies for long-established, technical but politically sensitive activities'.[15]

Granted that such policies gave rise to double negatives – in their conception and in the reaction of member governments – it is worth pointing out that the Rome Treaty was considerably more 'negative' and *laissez-faire* in character than the principal background document from which, allegedly, it sprang: the so-called Spaak Report.[16] This comparison is worth elaborating, since it is arguable that if the EEC had from the start embodied more of the real world philosophy of the Spaak Report, and been as pragmatic as the internationalist procedures of EFTA's Stockholm Convention, it could have raised less opposition across the political spectrum and, over the last quarter-century, might have achieved much more.

The contrast is clear in both the general analysis of the role of the market, and the role of State intervention. For instance, the Treaty stipulates that except in specified exemption cases

> any aid granted by a member State or through State resources in any form whatsoever which distorts or threatens to distort competition by favouring certain undertakings or the production of certain goods shall, insofar as it affects trade between member States, be deemed incompatible with the Common Market.

State aids of 'a social character' or to make good damage from natural disasters 'or other extraordinary events' were also allowed, as were 'aids to promote the economic development of regions where the standard of living is abnormally low', or where there is 'serious unemployment'. And, as with the Paris Treaty, a Social Fund was established to assist in the retraining of workers who had lost their jobs as a result of the impact of integration. A European Development Bank was set up to facilitate the financing of projects in less-developed regions, as well as 'projects of common interest to several member States which by their size or nature cannot be entirely financed by the various means available to the individual member States'.[17] Nonetheless, decisions whether or not to grant such exceptions to the Treaty's competition rules or to approve Social Fund expenditure were to lie with the Commission rather than the member states themselves. And the apprehension at the Commission's possible use of its powers was typified by Italy's insistence that it be allowed a special protocol or exception to the Treaty to permit it to implement the relatively low and anyway indirect intervention measures in favour of the development of its problem southern region in the Vanoni Programme of 1955.

By further contrast, the Spaak Report of 1956 had been about as 'positive' in character as most interventionists could have wished. For instance, it allowed that it was

> wrong to suggest that, when areas which have not attained the same

stage of economic development are suddenly joined together, the lower cost of manpower and the higher return on investment automatically assure faster progress of the initially less developed region, leading ultimately to the alignment of economic levels. On the contrary, as shown by the Italian unification experiment after 1860 and in the United States after the war of Secession, the gap may widen cumulatively if the basic conditions are not met by public means. Positive and collective action, on the other hand, benefits the more developed areas too, for they share in the enhanced economic activity thus created, and it prevents the pressure on their wages and standard of living which the connection with less developed regions might otherwise entail.[18]

A clearer statement of the 'positive' integration case could hardly have been desired. Why the apparent contrast with the Treaty?

Undoubtedly, one reason was the greater difficulty of establishing in advance in a legal document those policies which might entail 'public' action either at the national or the Community level. 'Positive' policies are harder to anticipate than 'negative' policies, which can draw on the already established language of the international vocabulary of GATT and other liberalisation agreements. Besides, the Treaty itself was drawn up in a hurry, partly to avoid the possibility that the forthcoming elections in France would mean either the election of a goverment which was opposed to European integration, or a government of a more distinctly nationalist character introduced to 'solve' France's main international problem at the time – Algeria. In other words, it was rushed through partly in the false hope of stopping De Gaulle.

But these were not the only reasons. From the beginning, West Germany was opposed to anything which scented of State intervention. The legitimation of the Federal Republic depended strongly on its differences from the centrally planned society over its eastern border. For Konrad Adenauer, as for Walter Hallstein – not only first president of the Commission, but also former West German Foreign Minister – it was important for the Federal Republic to regain a place in the sun of international affairs, but not at the cost of denuding herself of commitment to the dominance of a market economy and the competitive process.

In its early years the EEC tended to reinforce this impression that it was bent on submitting its member economies to a competitive rigour greater than most of them had ever known. One factor in this context was the entrusting of its competition division to Hans von der Groeben, an avid advocate of economic liberalism, determined to ensure that the Community as a whole should benefit from the fruits of the free working of the market mechanism. In the mid-1960s he wrote:

the Common Market is gradually divesting the Member States of the traditional instruments for influencing trade between Community countries: customs duties, quantitative restrictions, and limitations on the free movement of goods, services and capital . . . [But] it gives the Community and the Member States no powers to intervene directly in entrepreneurial planning and operations, which are to be coordinated through the play of the market and the price mechanism.[19]

Certainly von der Groeben gave every impression that he knew what he wanted to do and how he would get there. In 1959 he set about tackling what he considered unjustifiable levels of government aid in a problem sector — shipbuilding. However, both the French and the Italian governments drew his attention to the fact that shipbuilding was not simply a Community industry and that their own aid levels (averaging some 15 per cent of production cost) were minor in comparison with government assistance to the leader in the world shipbuilding league — Japan. They agreed to a formal reduction of aid to 10 per cent, but in practice quietly continued to grant those aid levels which seemed appropriate to them. The Italians in particular learned the lesson of this early experience of Commission liberalism, and therafter simply refused to inform the Commission's competition division of the effective aid which they were giving to their new concentration of steel production in the South, on the instep of the Italian peninsula, at Taranto.[20]

Legitimation in Question

Thus, in the Italian steel affair, the Commission came up against a wall of silence famed in southern Italy. The incident could be put down to idiosyncrasy. But, as with shipbuilding, the Commission was rushing in where most angels at least trod with care. By seeking to give substance to every letter of every sub-clause in the Treaty, as if nothing had really changed since Adam Smith, it showed itself insensitive to real needs in basic industry, regional development and — thereby — the distribution of income and employment. It was not simply a problem of legalism on the part of some Commissioners at the time, trained as lawyers, reaching for the Treaty whenever they heard the words 'State aid'. It was the relevance of the liberal capitalist ideology of the Treaties, and especially the Rome Treaty, which was in question.

However, much of the questioning was implicit rather than explicit. For one thing, most of the States comprising the original Six members of the Community were nominally liberal capitalist in character. Also, the three major countries were governed by parties or groups which were Centre to Centre-Right in political disposition. The fact that one, in Italy, was pursuing policies through public enterprise which in northern Europe would have put it to the Left of the social democrats, was not something which it wished to rationalise, far less advertise. The fact that another, in France, was committed to wide-ranging and detailed planning, with extensive State intervention through banking and finance, was both rationalised and advertised, with typical *panache,* but as introducing co-ordination and coherence into the market, rather than substituting it.[21]

Behind such factors lay the importance for the governments of the Centre-Right in the Community to distinguish themselves from the main parties of the Left. To stress that the market mechanism not only could be abused, but could itself aggravate structural, social and regional inequali-ties — as had the Spaak Report — could lay them open on their home front to challenge from Socialists, Communists or both. The opening of the EEC, which coincided with the first recession in economic growth since postwar reconstruction, was in fact seen by some of the signatories as a means of maintaining not only expansion, but also their own political hegemony. If they would not agree to a straightjacket, tied by lawyers in the Commission, some were aware none the less of the advantages of closer links with other governments of a similar political colour, and of an insti-tution which gave an economic underpinning to both NATO and the Atlantic alliance.

In effect, a key role played by both the Rome Treaty and the three communities of the 1950s — ECSC, the EEC and Euratom — was the legiti-mation of liberal capitalism, in form if not in substance. As Jürgen Haber-mas has pointed out, this need for legitimation and consensus support is especially important in plural societies precisely because they survive through consent rather than repression. And in such a system, the role of the market is not neutral. It assumes a double function: as a *steering mechanism* in the allocation of resources, and as an institutionalised *power relation* between the owners of the means of production and wage labour. As Habermas says, 'with the appearance of functional weaknesses in the market . . . re-coupling the economic system to the political creates an increased need for legitimation'.[22]

The creation of the European Communities performed such a role for Western European capitalism by taking the initiative, and for a while the virtual monopoly, of claims to internationalism. It appeared progressive and forward-looking at a time when some countries were either ashamed to look back or concerned not to look more closely at themselves. Such a claim has helped keep it on the agenda of governments despite their patent disagreements on essential features of the rate, nature and scale of integration itself. It partly explains why the European Left has been so divided over whether to seek to work through the Community, despite its explicitly capitalist rationale and unequal benefits.

Yet this process of legitimation for European capitalism, through the Community, poses difficulties. If the concept of Europe is to remain identified with Community Europe, the governments and institutions of the Community will need to be able to deliver more tangible achievements then its record to date. Monetary union, of course, would fill the gap left by failure to attain virtually any extensive common policy save that for agriculture. Yet monetary union has been difficult to approach, far less achieve. Even in the preliminary efforts at aligned currencies during the experiments with the 'snake' during the 1970s, it rapidly has become clear that some members economies are stronger than others, with an inner and outer group based essentially on West Germany and Benelux on the one hand, and the other countries on the other.[23] Also, the 'snake' revisited — in the form of the EMS of European Monetary System — got off to a weak start in 1978 with the exclusion of Britain, a hesitant late joining by Italy, and a French delay on the scheduled 'go' date of January 1979.

Meanwhile, as argued later, monetary union has increasingly been associated in the 1970s with *monetarism*. Economic union, which should be the fourth main stage of integration, and the ante-chamber to monetary and a federal system, has virtually gone by the board. The main test for the European Communities to date — joint policies to cope with the economic crisis of the 1970s — has been failed. Ritual declarations in Davignon-style summits have been made on the need for reflation and the re-attainment of full employment. But the Community is rent not only by cyclical unemployment, but a crisis of economic structures which it has shown no capacity to grasp. If monetary union is approached by an inner group of stronger countries, with mechanisms which impose deflationary restraint of public spending and credit on others, it may widely discredit this Community and its uncommon policies in the eyes of a generation which is either unemployed, under-employed or frustrated in fulfilling what it considers to be legitimate aspirations.

It is in such a context that the implicit philosophy of the Community treaties has been, and is likely increasingly to prove, a handicap to internationalists of Left and Right alike. For the progressive Right, the EEC's reliance on market forces and its basic antipathy to State intervention obstructs an intelligent framework for State capitalism at the Community level. Its assumed adjustment of social, economic and regional structures through the competitive process is unrealistic not only in a period when those structures are in strain or crisis, but even by the terms of reference of the classical economists, who never assumed as much. Making this point in the 1950s, Thomas Balogh presciently pointed out that even the free-trade area proposals of the time, by which an outer Europe would be associated with an inner Europe of the Six, constituted a scheme which was 'fraught with dangers for all areas of slower growth than Germany'[24]

For the Left, a capitalist market ideology in the EEC now strongly imbued with monetarism represents the danger of a reinforced dominance of private over public power. This constitutes a major threat when combined with the prospect of supranational powers granted to a European Monetary Fund. Few on the European Left wish to see the entire substitution of the market by central planning and State control. Yet many wish to see the dominance of social and public rather than capitalist and private criteria in the allocation of resources at Community level, and at present they see no prospect of achieving this through the present Community and its works. The issue need not be represented as that of no-market versus this market. It could be a socialised rather than privatised market in which common objectives and the public welfare predominated over uncommon divisions and private interests. One of the weaknesses of the uncommon market today has been its failure to achieve what the French socialist André Philip advocated in the year of the signature of the Rome Treaty, when he wrote that 'the market can be extended not by liberalisation but by orgaisation'.[25] In other words, it could be planned.

For the Left today, neither planning nor public enterprise are seen in themselves as socialist. It is also appreciated that both mechanisms can be used by the prevailing system, with unchanged class relations and the same dominance of private over public criteria. In other words, planning can be capitalist planning, and public enterprise can be State capitalist control of the means of production.

But fractions of both the Right and Left today might be able to make a more plausible case for working through Community institutions if more had been achieved over the thirty years since the founding of the Coal and Steel Community. If Community Europe had lowered its view from the stars which constitute its own symbol, and focused attention on specific problems of social, structural and regional inequality, it might have managed to avoid both irrelevance, and the charge that it is taking decision-making too far from where it counts for working people and the mass votes.

Such a case was plausibly made by André Marchal, one of the leading economists of the French structuralist school, in a detailed analysis of the limits of more ambitious Community integration published in the early 1960s.[26] But Marchal's case depended on an explicit international framework for Community action, rather than the supranationalism of its pretensions. And, like much else which could have been achieved at the Western European level since the war, it passed by default.

NOTES

1. Walter Hallstein, EEC Commission Press Release, 22 May 1961.
2. In announcing the aims of the European Coal and Steel Community in May 1950, the then French Foreign Minister Robert Schuman hopefully declared that 'the solidarity in production thus established will make it plain that any war between France and Germany becomes not merely unthinkable but materially impossible'.
3. One of the most important pressure groups has been Jean Monnet's Action Committee for a United States of Europe. See, further, Action Committee for the United States of Europe, *Statements and Declarations 1955–67*, Chatham House–PEP European Series, no. 9 (Mar. 1969).

4. Nora Beloff, *The General Says No.* (1963) p. 119. The claim is attributed to Pierre Uri, a close associate of Monnet's, and one of the drafters of the Paris Treaty.

5. (i) HMSO, *Parliamentary Debates, Hansard*, 2 Aug. 1961, col. 1489; (ii) *Britain and the European Communities: An Economic Assessment*, Cmnd., 4289 (HMSO, Feb. 1970).

6. Walter Hallstein, *United Europe*, (Oxford University Press, 1962) p. 31

7. *Treaty Constituting the European Coal and Steel Community* (Paris Treaty) (HMSO 1952); and *Treaty Setting Up the European Economic Community* (Rome Treaty) (HMSO, 1957).

8. 'Dis-use' rather than 'abuse' is an under statement granted the extent to which the ECSC Treaty did not later impede Community-sponsored cartels in steel during the crisis of the 1970s.

9. The analysis of voting principles in the Rome Treaty and the Stockholm Convention was prepared by Frances Richardson, formerly of Sussex University. For the text of the Stockholm Convention see *Text of Convention*, Cmnd., 641 (HMSO and European Free Trade Association, 1959).

10. Thus, in 1978 Labour Prime Minister James Callaghan could argue with reason that there was no question of Britain agreeing to monetary union while the overall bill to the country was unjust. See further (i) John Palmer, 'Britain's EEC's Bill on Brink of Doubling', *Guardian*, 13 Nov. 1978; and (ii) Hamish McRae, 'Callaghan Hits Out at EEC's Lack of Equity', *Guardian*, 14 Nov. 1978

11. For a typical conventional analysis of non-egalitarian welfare economics see Ian Little, *A Critique of Welfare Economics* (Oxford University Press, 1956).

12. Ralf Dahrendorf (Wieland Europa), 'A New Goal for Europe', originally published in *Die Zeit* nos 28 and 29 (1971) and republished in translation in Michael Hodges (ed.) *European Integration* (Penguin, 1972) pp. 74–87.

13. For emphasis on the four 'freedoms' of the Rome Treaty see Jacques and Collette Nême, *Economie Européenne* (1970).

14. *The Economist*, 23 Sept. 1978, p.66.

15. Nigel Despicht, *The Transport Policy of the European Community*, Chatham House–PEP, European Series no. 12 (Sept. 1969) p. 83.

16. Secretariat of the Intergovernmental Committee Created by the Messina Conference, *Report from the Delegation Heads to the Ministers of Foreign Affairs*, 120 F/56 (mimeo) (Brussels, 1956): henceforth referred to as *The Spaak Report*.

17. *Rome Treaty*, Articles 42, 77, 92, 95 and 123–30.

18. *Spaak Report*.

19. Hans von der Groeben, *Competition Policy in the Common Market* (EEC Commission, Brussels, 1965).

20. Avison Wormald, in Stuart Holland (ed.), *The State as Entrepreneur* (Weidenfeld & Nicolson, 1972) chapter 4.

21. Pierre Massé, *Le Plan ou L'Anti Hassard* (Gallimard, 1965).

22. Jürgen Habermas, *Legitimation Crisis* (Heinemann Educational, 1976) pp. 25 and 36.

23. For a chronology of the mixed fortunes of the snake see further Paul Fabra, 'Les négotiations sur le Projet Monétaire Européen, *Le Monde*, 19 Sept. 1978.

24. Thomas Balogh, in G.D.N. Worswick (ed.), *The Free Trade Proposals* (1960).

25. André Philip, 'Social Aspects of European Economic Integration, *International Labour Review* (Sept. 1957) p. 255.

26. André Marchal, *L'Europe Solidaire* (Cujas, 1964).

2 Claims and Compromises

Collision between the Monnet vision of a United States of Europe and De Gaulle's view of 'a Europe of nation states' from the Atlantic to the Urals was virtually inevitable. Finally, and almost overdue in some eyes, it came in July 1965.

There were several underlying issues. One was the Commission proposal that levies on agricultural imports, anticipated in the terms of the Common Agricultural Policy, should henceforth be paid to it direct rather than via the member states. This would have given it an independent revenue of sizable proportions by the standards of the time — equivalent to about £1 billion a year in terms of the then sterling exchange rate. In April 1965 the French delegation stated bluntly that the Commission proposals went too far, and overstepped the immediate practical issues of establishing a Common Agricultural Policy. In the first week in May, they repeated their case that there was no immediate need for financial independence for the Commission, recommended that the common policy for agriculture would be better focused on a plan for structural reform and competitiveness, and maintained that the Commission's budget should continue to be financed by national contributions.[1]

Clearly this isssue was important. It was not so much the size of the budget which was in question, since the French expected a net benefit from it. The issue, common to the struggle between national parliaments and executives, was who controlled the money and whether a single member state could withold its contributions if necessary. Behind this lay the further issue of how such a major decision would be taken. The Commission wanted to proceed by a majority vote in the Council of Ministers which could put France in a minority and result in her being overruled not only on the question of contributions, or the scale and distribution of the fund, but also on other matters of important national interest ranging wider than agriculture.

Challenge to Supranationalism

When the French found themselves in a minority on the Council, and faced with a vote in the European Assembly supporting the Commission position, they stalled during the critical period scheduled for the decision (up to 30 June 1965). On 1 July France withdrew its government representatives from Brussels and left its seat at the Council of Ministers unfilled. The result was to halt virtually any Council business and therefore

Community activity. A poker game of the first order was played for seven months, with the stakes involving the future of the EEC as a supranational experiment or an international confederation of a more traditional type. In January 1966 De Gaulle won outright. The member governments of the Community met at Luxembourg and agreed a declaration that from that date majority votes would not be taken on the Council in cases of 'important national interest'. Since that time, few majority decisions have been taken, although since 1975 an increase in the regional budget went through by default through failure to agree a majority rejection.[2]

In practice, January 1966 was a turning point in the Community's evolution. Though the enthusiasts for European integration have sometimes been reluctant to admit as much, the establishment of the practice of unanimous voting for several years translated the Community from a venture in supranationalism into an inner OECD with the incubus of a common agricultural policy. The scale of the reversal can be illustrated by reference to the range of decisions, set out in the previous chapter, which would have been taken by majority vote in the Council from January 1966 had De Gaulle not adopted the policy of the 'empty chair' from June 1965 and imposed the compromise of Luxembourg in January 1966.

For some visionaries, the Luxembourg compromise is the act of original sin whence stemmed the loss of a federal Eden and supranationalism. However, De Gaulle made considerable efforts to make possible a joint Community policy framework in wider areas than just agriculture during the period before the dramatic walk-out from the Council of Ministers in July 1965. His initiative in this respect is of major relevance both to the question of supranational *versus* international action in the Community, and to the opening stages of what was to become the ongoing saga of an industrial counterpart to the common policy for agriculture.

De Gaulle intended that France should remain in the Community on a *provisional* basis. The provision was that she would be compensated on the agricultural account for what she expected to lose in industrial competition with Germany. But behind this lay his concern to modernise the structure of French industry and to ensure that France took her place among the leaders of advanced technology, if necessary through joint Community action.

His aims here complemented his grand design in the political and military arena, for his vision of a Europe of nation-states from the Atlantic to the Urals was essentially non-Atlanticist: i.e. it rejected the premise of American political and military hegemony in Western Europe. Thus, during the early 1960s he endorsed the commitment of major sums of public expenditure to projects such as Concorde; Diamant, a rocket launcher with intercontinental capacity; the *arme nucleaire*, in the form of a French atomic bomb; the *force de frappe*, a government sponsored supersonic bomber force; and *Plan calcul*, the computer programme necessary for development and operation of the first three items in his nuclear arsenal following the US government's refusal to allow IBM to sell France its biggest range of computers.

While clearly enough opposed to the concept of a supranational European Community, De Gaulle was advised by senior officials that France could not undertake so massive an advanced technology programme without serious strain on other areas of scheduled public expenditure. Officially, the Fifth Plan for 1966—70 was supposed to designate priority public expenditure to housing, health and education, which had been relatively neglected in earlier plans. If the necessary choice of resource use did not appear the published version of the French Plan to be debated in parliament, it none the less did not need a crystal ball to see that *'grave social tensions'* could ensue from raising expectations in social spending while in fact pre-empting the necessary resources for an advanced technology and defence programme.[3] Only *Concorde* had a relatively established bilaterial funding and sponsorship, and even then it appeared likely to prove the only white elephant capable of carrying passengers at twice the speed of sound.

False Start in Industrial Policy

For such reasons, De Gaulle sanctioned iniatitives at Community level which could facilitate bilateral or multilateral joint ventures in modern and advanced technology. The need for some kind of initiative stemmed from the fact that prevailing legislation in the member states at the time reflected the conventional wisdom of anti-monopoly policy that mergers tended to be against the public interest, and should bear tax penalties. Early in 1965, the French pointed out that such tax barriers were outdated relative to the need for Europe to develop companies with sufficient international strength to survive British and American competition. They therefore proposed a statute for European Trading Companies which would remove double taxation and other barriers to Community transnational mergers, incorporated into national legislation and, where appropriate, municipal law.[4]

The Commission, in its enthusiasm to build the Treaty of Rome in at least a decade, if not a day, replied that the French proposal was welcome, but opposed the principle that it should have national or municipal status. Instead, they insisted on a Community statute to which member governments should jointly subscribe.[5] It was hardly what the French had in mind, on two accounts. First, there was the question of who gained the tax revenue concerned; and, second, where would disputes be decided? The French had made their proposal in part to recoup the sovereignty which they found seeping to foreign multinational capital. Losing potential tax revenue and legal jurisdiction over leading French firms opting for 'Community' company status was an unacceptable prospect. It could aggravate precisely the problem which their proposals were designed to help solve.

The difference of views continued through the spring and summer of 1965, and closer to the date of the walk-out from the Council on 1 July. Behind the French international proposal, and the supranational response proposed by the Commission, lay the deeper divide of the role of intervention in the industrial sector of the economy. With the indelicate touch characteristic of his intervention elsewhere, the then Competition Commissioner Hans von der Groben stressed the primary importance of competition policy and the free working of the market, as opposed to measures designed to promote mergers or restructuring. He also stressed that any dispute between companies and governments should be settled in the final appeal court at Luxembourg.[6]

Thus the differences between France and the Commission were both on institutions and on the ideology of intervention. Of the two, the institutional difference seems to have been the more clearly important, i.e. whether the proposed Company statute should have joint national or supranational status. In terms of ideology, both proposals were of a 'negative' integration character: the French wanted to break down or remove specific barriers to the working of the market on the assumption that this would facilitate mergers and concentration; the Commission (less realistically) wanted the same negative end on the assumption that equal conditions for competition would prove a competition between equals.

Meanwhile, the saga of the uncommon Company Statute dragged on. Partially deterred by the absence of the French from the Council, the Commission produced a further statement on industrial policy admitting the tax problems in mergers but at the same time stressing the applicability of the Rome Treaty's competition rules in Articles 85 and 86. They also confirmed French fears by arguing that the difference between national arrangements on merger taxation should be harmonised. They still held open the formal option of harmonising municipal rather than national law, but none the less recommended a supranational statute to be introduced by a convention between member states.[7]

In June 1966 the Commission hazarded another initiative but this fell on deaf French ears. By December that year it had formulated a draft statute, now incorporating proposals for a dual board structure including worker representatives, on the German *Mitbestimmung* or co-determination model — under pressure from the German TUC (DGB). The French were still not interested, and in 1970 were joined with support from a new quarter — the combined forces of the biggest trades unions in both France and Italy: the CGT and the CGIL. A committee established by these — mainly Communist — unions challenged the proposal in its form at that stage on two main grounds: (i) that it would strengthen monopoly power at the European level and (ii) that the Commission's proposals for 'European' works councils, backed by only a minority union representation of one-third on the supervisory boards of companies, would incorporate rather than extend the freedoms of the workers concerned.[8]

Thus, paralleling the differences between the French government and the Commission, there were now major differences on both instruments and ideology between the Commission and major trade unions. As argued later, such differences within what could nominally be considered a homogenous class group – i.e. organised labour – are typical not only of the problems confronting common policies in general, but also common class-based policies in particular. Different fractions of the same nominal class can and do contribute to fractured policies at Community level, especially where this reinforces fractures between different forms of capitalist state and national policy.

Certainly the proposals for a European Company Statute – the would-be instrument of a Common Industrial Policy – has remained fractured on precisely these grounds since 1970. Meantime, the Commission managed to come up with its first successful case – in 1971 – prosecuting a major company for 'abuse of dominant power', i.e. the much-vaunted terms of the main Rome Treaty Article 86 on competition.[9] But this case – against Continental Can – not only followed more than a dozen years of the Treaty, but still was limited in crucial respects. On the one hand, it remained 'negative' in character, rather than harnessing the power of private big business to 'positive' ends in a planned framework; also, the powers concerned were *ex-post* rather than *ex-ante*. In other words, the Commission could only tackle a problem arising from concentration once posed, rather than anticipating and preventing it.[10]

As the Community moved into the 1970s, and away from the decade dominated by De Gaulle, the issue whether industrial policy should seek to promote the merger of European versus US capital became more clearly focused. The so-called Colonna Plan of February 1970 was mainly concerned with how to counter American investment in Europe, and explicitly advocated merger promotion between European companies. Following concern at a number of takeovers in the electrical industry by Westinghouse, the Commission considered that it should be given the power to veto takeovers by American companies – a power which the French government had exercised when Westinghouse tried to take over Jeumont-Schneider. The Colonna Plan also argued that state aids and incentives should be allowed to be used to promote European mergers.[11]

But thereby the Commission was posed with a dilemma: concentration *versus* competition. It responded with a mixed package: elements of its traditional 'negative' integration policy (i.e. 'thou shalt not merge'), laced with aids and incentives to mergers. In principle, the attitude could have been coherent, with approval of mergers between medium-sized firms, and disapproval for the bigger league. But in practice there was little coherence in the approach, and the Commission's record on preventing major mergers was minimal.

This dominance of 'negative' integration philosophy also showed clearly in a parallel Commission proposal, echoed throught the 1970s, that free access should be provided by all Community firms to public contracts awarded by national governments.[12] Its basic unwillingness to ensure the dominance of public authority and intervention was also reflected in two measures which it proposed in February and October 1971: (i) so-called 'development contracts' in industry, in which initiative was left to the private sector, and (ii) a so-called 'marriage broker' agency for firms willing to wed rather than be obliged to go to the alter.[13]

In one institutional respect, the Colonna Plan was interesting. It amounted to a formula for co-operation between governments and the Commission rather than a supranational policy imposed upon governments by the Commission. To this extent it might be argued that one of the main lessons from the false start in industrial policy was being learned. On the other hand, such a pragmatic formula for what would have amounted to essentially *inter*national joint action was stressed by the Commission to be interim and provisional. After half a decade of talk it was still determined to push for a supranational solution to industrial policy rather than make limited — but possibly real — progress on an international basis.

This 'big bid' approach has resulted in the failure through the 1970s to achieve a common industrial statute worthy of the name, and thus a key basis for a Common Industrial Policy. Meanwhile, as opposed to the intra-sectoral aspects of the behaviour of firms, the Community was becoming exercised by the problem of inter-sectoral imbalance, including the decline of whole sectors of traditional industry, and the weakness of main areas of advanced technology. This showed at and after the Vienna Conference of April 1972, where discussions covered the issue of mergers and growth in small and medium-sized enterprises, but also ranged over the problems of steel, shipbuilding, non-ferrous metals, machine tools, textiles, paper, tele-communications, electronics and nuclear power.[14]

In short, it became clear that a major structural crisis was emerging in both the basic and advanced sectors of industry. In practice, this was caused by two main factors, which in the late 1970s are even more clearly pronounced: (i) technological unemployment through the substitution of capital for labour, and (ii) lost competitiveness *vis-à-vis non*-European countries, especially Japan and South-East Asia. Neither problem could be resolved by 'negative' integration policies of the kind embodied in the Rome Treaty and attempted through the Commission proposals for a European Company Statute. Technical progress, resulting in high produc-tivity capital and labour displacement, is a *result* rather than an 'abuse' or 'distortion' of the competitive process. Similarly, the greater competitive-ness of Japanese and South-East Asian products was based on a combina-tion of high productivity capital organised mainly in giant combines (in the Japanese *zaibatsus*) with labour whose wage costs (in South-East Asia) was as little as one-tenth of European levels.[15]

Similarly, granting an extension of nominal powers to European labour through rights to representation on supervisory boards (as embodied in the later Company Statute proposals) would hardly contribute to greater wage competitiveness if the representation amounted to any real influence, while the new 'competition' in South-East Asia — frequently including European multinationals abroad — was notable for its support of local regimes which banned or severely limited even basic trade union rights. If the ideology of competition dominant in the Rome Treaty were to be pursued to its logical conclusion, this would mean reducing the living standards of many European workers (at least in those sectors where there are modern multinational companies with comparable levels of capital efficiency or higher productivity located *outside* the Community. Yet, in turn, this would reduce effective demand through a lowered purchasing power on the part of the working class in the Community, prompting a further crisis of capital accumulation.

In essence, such a crisis *has* occurred in the mid- and later 1970s, in part through the restraint of overall consumption by cuts in the growth of public expenditure — and in some cases net cuts in real terms — following the monetarist reaction to the OPEC oil price increases and deflationary budgets. By the end of the decade, the industrial capacity of key sectors of the Community economy was underemployed to the tune of 20 per cent or more. Logically, in this context, the most appropriate policy *for* industry would be the joint reflation of demand through raised public spending and credit from surplus to deficit countries, combined with policies for both intra-sectoral restructuring of firms and inter-sectoral distribution of productivity gains through taxation.

Such policies, recommended to the Commission in 1976 in the form of the Maldague Report on Structural Factors in Inflation, would amount to both positive intervention and a degree of positive integration, feasibly within an international planning context relating at least the main aggregates involved.[16] But such 'positive' policies would have meant a challenge not only to the dominant 'negative' ideology in the Commission, but also to the main surplus country — West Germany. It would entail a change in attitudes and action on the role of public intervention in the economy. But this is unacceptable to those who — largely ignorant not only of Marx but also of Keynes — assume that the theory of Adam Smith remains relevant to economies and societies which happened to benefit substantially from a postwar boom two centuries after his time.

As a result, industrial policy in the Community today is schizophrenic. While still claiming to defend the Covenant of the Rome Treaty, it has bent its knee to Baal in the form of policies which amount to Commission-sponsored cartels in steel, protection for specific areas of textiles, and a host of further candidates for special exemptions from the provisions on competition prevailing in the texts of the founding fathers.[17]

The schizophrenia is specific and can be analysed. It represents a classic contradiction between a dominant ideology of competitive national capital operating in a Community framework, and a dominant basic structure of monopolistic multinational capital operating on a global scale. It symptomises the fact that while Community institutions attempting an unrealistic supranational model have not even managed to agree an effective joint Company Statute, multinational and international capital from Europe, America and Japan has managed to help disintegrate sectors of European industry by integrating its own operations world-wide.

The Commission's failure to achieve a pragmatic, joint national solution to the questions of a common industrial policy was an important but widely neglected background to the French walk-out from the Council of Ministers in July 1965. The French had come up with proposals which, if accepted, could have amounted to a degree of international co-operation which was less than the supranationalism sought by the Commission, but more than the talk-shop framework of the OECD or intermittent summits between heads of government.

Certainly the fact that the then President of the European Commission, Walter Hallstein, chose to act – in De Gaulle's words – 'as if he were a Head of State', rolling out red carpets for visiting dignitaries to the Commission, exacerbated the underlying issue of internationalism versus supranationalism. But the 'red carpet' affair was not decisive, nor was De Gaulle's attitude to the Community in other areas than agriculture either rigid or unpragmatic. His challenge to supranationalism was not simply the act of an aging Sun King, nor of a man whose 'certain view of France' happened to exclude everything in French-speaking Brussels.

The Agricultural Albatross
De Gaulle's pragmatism is partly indicated by the fact that, when he acceded to the presidency in 1958 during a period when the Gaullists were preoccupied with both constitutional reform and the Algerian question, he held a brief series of meetings to consider the simple issue of whether France should remain a member of the nascent European Community. It appears to have been argued by the relevant Ministers that the ten articles of the Rome Treaty relating to a Common Agricultural Policy (38 to 47) could be implemented in such a way as to compensate France on the agricultural front for any loss in industrial trade with other member countries, especially Germany. If they were, and if other French interests – e.g. for the franc zone countries – were safeguarded, membership of the Community need not be a net disadvantage for France (quite apart from its potential as an arena for French influence in Western Europe).

The detailed negotiation of the policy, product by product, spanned more than a decade. In July 1957, within four months of signature of the Rome Treaty, a general conference of the Six had been held at Stresa, at which the main principles of the policy were agreed. These were to include import levies, export subsidies, price support levels and an intervention fund – FEOGA (Fonds Européen d'Orientation et de Garantie Agricole). But it was January 1962 before FEOGA was established, November 1966 before the operation of a common market for olive oil, and July 1967 before the beginning of a common market for a wider range of products including cereals, pork, eggs and poultry meat, fruit and vegetables. In July 1968, sugar, milk products and beef joined the list. Tobacco and wine trailed along in April and June 1970. Fishing tailed after in February 1971. In other words, establishment of the main elements of the CAP took some one and a half times as long as the other main policy which the Community can at present claim to have achieved — the customs union.

Delay in getting it off the ground was not to prove the main criticism of the CAP. Many people, and some political parties, wished it had simply stayed there. This was for two main reasons. The first was widely held in Britain, but also expressed by Pierre Mendès France, a former French Prime Minister and a dominant influence under the Fourth Republic. It was the case against external protection, and in favour of a free trade area in which consumers would benefit from imports of lower-cost food.[18] The second main case against the CAP was its support of prices rather than support of production. The price-support system as applied in the CAP is not uniform, even in terminology. There are different *intervention, base, exclusion, indicative, minimum, reference, withdrawal* and *threshold* prices in the policy. But they all amount to intervention to assure a guaranteed minimum income to producers via general price support, rather than the 'deficiency payments' system obtaining in Britain before adoption of the CAP, which amounted to support for specific levels of production. One of the key differences between the two systems lay in the fact that, under CAP price support, the Community was obliged to buy up — through FEOGA — however much farmers actually produced.[19]

The infamous result has been the periodic 'wine lakes' and 'butter mountains'. The latter were estimated at one time as equivalent in weight to the total population of Austria. Part of this has been sold to the Soviet Union at a fraction of its real production cost.

In fact, although the lakes have certainly been deep, and the mountains high, the surpluses have not all been permanent, and have tended in several cases to represent a fraction of total agricultural production in the Community.[20] Also, while EEC food prices tended to be substantially higher than the lowest world prices in the 1960s, the situation was reversed in the mid-1970s through a combination of factors, including both world shortage and the so-called 'great grain robbery' (by which Soviet buyers managed to clean out a high proportion of US wheat surpluses).[21]

Nonetheless, it remains strongly arguable that the CAP is both economically inefficient and socially unjust. Its support costs are excessive, its consumer prices are too high, it acts as a disincentive to structural reform in farming, and its subsidies via price support fail to distinguish relatively rich from relatively poor producers. It guarantees no long-term gain for consumers who are temporarily advantaged by the 'green pound' formula. It does not even guarantee overall European self-sufficiency in food. The

EEC remains the biggest single market for US food exports, which themselves constitute the main factor balancing US payments. But it could well be argued that the most basic shortcoming of the CAP stems from its attempt to impose a common policy on highly uncommon agricultural structures in the member states.

For instance, in the mid-1960s, when CAP policies were beginning to come into effect, agricultural labour as a share of the total working population amounted to some 16 per cent for the EEC as a whole. But this included a variation from 6 per cent in Belgium, 8 per cent in the Netherlands, and 11 per cent in West Germany to 17 per cent in France and 24 per cent in Italy. The figures indicate different overall efficiencies in agriculture in the different countries – relatively high in Belgium and the Netherlands, low in France, very low in Italy, and intermediate in West Germany.

These global proportions themselves masked major differences between types of farming and different agricultural regions in the Six.[22] The kinds of farming included both differences in product mix and disparate forms of holding. Broadly, the dominant share of working population in agriculture – three-quarters – represented peasant family farming, or partial employment in agriculture, while capitalist farming, with the hiring of dependent labour, accounted for the remaining quarter. Such broad distinctions include other differences, with the form of agricultural exploitation ranging from mixed-product peasant smallholdings to large-scale capitalist specialisation.[23] To some extent, this coincided with major regional differences, e.g. between capitalist farming in northern Italy and north-central France, and peasant farming elsewhere.[24]

Certainly, this overall picture conceals a mosaic of differences in type of holding, type of tenure and type of production. A detailed breakdown of agriculture in southern Italy shows that there is no strict uniformity between the type of holding, kind of tenure, product mix and productivity. Specific factors, such as the proximity of part-time smallholdings to a major urban market such as Naples or Rome, to which products can be sold direct by the part-timers, appear to exert a major influence on productivity and income. There is no clear correlation between the size of a unit of ownership and productivity, especially when ownership conceals forms of tenure, such as the *mezzadria* or sharecropping system in southern Italy, which date back to the time *métayage* of France before the 1789 revolution.[25]

None the less, the anachronism of the CAP is shown by the fact that it offers the same or similar price support for production from virtually feudal, high-cost forms of farming as it does to highly modern, low-cost capitalist production. The system is socially unjust in the sense that the peasantry exploited by such forms of holding, or handicapped by antiquated farming techniques, gets a subsistence living, while the large-scale capitalist farmers of the developed areas of the Community make massive profits – frequently as absentee landlords. Economically, the system is inefficient

in the sense that the consumer is paying a price inflated to that level necessary for the subsistence of the least efficient producers in the system.

Failed Reforms

In 1968, Sicco Mansholt, then Commissioner for Agriculture, heralded
proposals for a reform of the CAP. His *Agriculture 1980*, known as the
Mansholt Plan, had the merit of taking a long-term structural view of agriculture in the Community, despite the discomforture which this caused
agriculture Ministers who were still congratulating themselves on their
achievement in getting the policy off the ground in the first place.[26]

The specific aims of the Mansholt Plan were (i) to reduce rising FEOGA
price support by creating (ii) larger farms warranting more capital investment, and (iii) improving marketing. This was the kind of statement of
good intention with which many interested parties could agree. The clout,
and potential dissension, was contained in the further specific proposals:
(iv) to take 5 million hectares of land out of agricultural production and
(v) to 'facilitate' the movement of 5 million people out of agriculture
during the 1970s by a combination of advanced retirement schemes, grants
and training schemes (Fig. 2.1).

In short, the Mansholt Plan aimed at classic rationalisation through the
accelerated reduction of small units. It was stressed that the plan was
'voluntary'. Its proposed compensation terms were substantial, even if not
dramatic. It was also stressed that anyway there would be a considerable
further reduction of the agricultural labour force without Mansholt. And in
fact, by 1975, agricultural labour as a share of total working population
was down to 8.9 per cent in the then larger Community of Nine.[27] This
partly reflected the low UK proportion, of around 3.5 per cent of total
labour, but also represented the continuing refusal of the young to follow
their parents into farming rather than seek off-farm employment.

None the less, Mansholt's proposals prompted strong resistance from
agricultural pressure groups, and only lukewarm interest from governments.
The publication within a year of the Vedel Report, commissioned independently by the French government, which largely paralleled Mansholt's
rationalisation proposals, was not sufficient to overcome the opposition of
the farm lobbies.[28] One general political factor was the massive social dis-
location which the reduction of 'small units' would actually involve. In
1966–7 there were 6.5 million farms in the Community. But, as already
mentioned, some three-quarters of them were relatively small holdings run
by family employment rather than wage labour. The average age of the
farmers themselves was around 55 years.[29] In other words, a shift of 5
million workers out of farming would have meant a major outflow from
the family smallholding sector. But this in turn would have meant the
social euthanasia of families whose way of life, as well as livelihood, were
tied up in small-scale farming.

In any event, the CAP was about to be sabotaged by new pressures re-

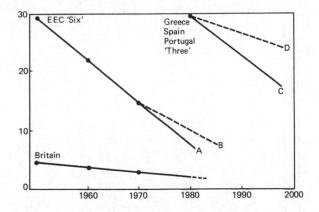

* % of total labour force
Key: A — Mansholt Plan target reduction
B — Estimated trend without Mansholt
C — Necessary reduction for applicant 'Three' to parallel original 'Six'
D — Probable lower reduction under different demand for labour

Fig. 2.1 *Agricultural employment* in the EEC*

flecting the uneven development of member economies. In August 1969 the French devalued the franc. In October that year the West German government floated the Mark, and introduced border levies on agricultural products without consulting Brussels. Within a week the Commission accepted the *fait accompli*, consoling itself in return with the statement of intention of the summit conference at the Hague, the same month, to advance the Community towards economic and monetary union. But from thereon, partly in response to the dollar devaluations of 1971 and 1973, most of the Community countries either floated, revalued or devalued in a succession of changing parities which wrought havoc with the concept of common prices for agricultural products. The case of wheat was significant. The only period in which the CAP achieved a common indicative price was that immediately following the initial price agreement, in 1967–9. Common prices had become a fiction between uncommon partners. The monetary compensatory accounts or MCAs (of which the 'green pound' is a part) were introduced, following West German measures in 1969 on a 'temporary' basis which, like so many exceptions to common policies, have proved a new rule. They were specifically designed to prevent trade from low-price to high-price countries, thereby undermining the concept of a common agricultural market.[30]

In 1972 the Council of Ministers adopted three recommendations for voluntary modernisation of farming on the lines of the Mansholt report four years earlier. One of the measures concerned retirement pensions. The others covered farm training and aid for modernisation in those cases

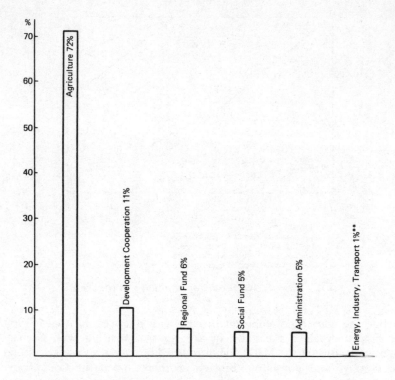

* Preliminary draft budget excluding reserves, repayments to
  members states and the administrative costs of Council of
  Ministers, Court of Justice and European Parliament, etc.
** Excluding Euratom

Fig. 2.2   *EEC: main distribution of resources (1980)**

where 'development plans' were submitted. Interestingly enough, the Commission's own press office admitted that 'in practice, the measures will lead to relatively few fundamental changes since most governments in the Community have moved towards a common position in their national farm modernization and social programmes'.[31] In other words, the Council decision was marginal and to a large extent cosmetic.

In 1980, as indicated in Fig. 2.2, the CAP consumed some three-quarters of total Community expenditure. This share reduces the other items of common spending to relative insignificance. In comparison with the giant Agricultural Policy, the Social Fund, Regional Fund, Development Aid and Energy and Research are dwarfed. The situation partly reflects the fact that Mansholt's hopes for a reduction of farm support, like his hopes for major structural reform, were not realised. His plan had envisaged that the cost of the CAP could be reduced by two-thirds from 2000 million units of account in 1968 to 750 million in 1980. In fact, ten years later, it had trebled in value.

It could well be argued, in one sense, that the CAP represents not only agricultural spending as such, but also the main part of Community social and regional support, since its funds subsidise literally millions of small-holders in the Community's problem underdeveloped regions who would otherwise be below acceptable income levels. By any standard of social concern for the aged, economically weak and relatively unadaptable work-force in Continental agriculture, this is a strong case on its own grounds. But the social benefits due in this sense should be met through a different agricultural policy if the wider social benefit to the consumer is also to be assured.

Such an effective reform of the Common Agricultural Policy would de-mand planning. In other words, it would mean integration not so much in the sense of creating a single market, as integrated structural, social and spat-ial policies. Such planning would need to relate change in agriculture to the distribution of employment between agriculture and the other main sec-tors of the economy – industry and services. It would entail income re-distribution between different social classes in agriculture – especially small-scale tenants and owner-operators, on the one hand, and large-scale capitalist enterprise on the other. In addition, planning in any real sense would need to integrate the regional distribution of employment and in-come to the spatial distribution of different agricultural structures.

Frustrated Common Planning

In fact the Community did begin a tentative approach to some kind of planning in the early and mid-1960s. If the proposals concerned had taken effect, they might at least have opened the way to effective planning in the longer-term. But such an initiative was frustrated by a variety of factors which illustrate the difficulties of planning for change within a capitalist power structure. In particular, the conflict between different ideologies as to the legitimate role for state intervention in nation-states which embody different experiences of the use and abuse of state power, frustra-ted Community planning itself.

The planning which the Community has attempted to date through four successive medium-term economic programmes has been frustrated by an equally important factor. Essentially, while nation-states have estab-lished varying degrees of legitimacy for intervening in the structure of the economy at home, this has been mainly in response to social and political pressures from specific sections of the main classes in national society – for instance, the management of small industrial and commercial enter-prises threatened by the concentration and centralisation of capital. Big business, in the phase of its multinational spread during the two decades following the creation of the EEC, has supported Community policies such as liberalisation of trade, capital and labour. But it neither needs nor is interested in supporting planning which would modify its freedom to decide what is produced, where, how and in whose interest. In other words, it has no interest in supporting Community planning where this changes the power relations between itself and the public authority rather than aiding and abetting what it anyway wants to do.

This is not to say that Community Europe could not achieve joint international planning of resources. But it does indicate that such planning cannot be achieved by blueprints and declarations of intent alone, irrespective of the basic structure of the economic and class forces in society. The very problems of planning at Community level arise substantially because of the unreadiness of liberal capitalist planners to admit the scale to which problems at the economic, social and regional level are caused by both capitalist integration and the mechanisms of capitalism itself. In particular the crisis of Community planning – even before the onset of mass unemployment and inflation in the 1970s – stemmed substantially from the limited 'manageability' of modern large-scale capital. This was especially the case when the liberalisation of trade and capital movements embodied in the Community Treaties undermined the very controls of trade and capital which, at a national level, had been essential to the relative success of the early plans in an economy such as France.

The first Community experiment in planning was interesting in as much as its Medium-Term Economic Policy Committee was set up without a specific remit from the Rome Treaty, and on lines which bypassed the obsession of the founding fathers with supranationalism and a 'vanguard role' for the Commission. It was an *ad hoc* body, with no majority-voting formula, composed of leading officials of member states at permanent under-secretary or top civil servant level, and was chaired by a national rather than a Commission official. It had been set up in 1964 by Robert Marjolin, then a Vice-President of the Commission, and formerly Secretary-General of OEEC and a senior official in the first French Plan.[32] Marjolin, in the OEEC from 1948, had tried to co-ordinate the 'plans' for the expenditure of Marshall Aid within a more general OEEC indicative plan. In practice, the recipient countries failed to plan, and mainly presented shopping lists of the main sectors in which they intended to spend the aid concerned. In addition, the West German authorities were opposed to planning in principle, not only as a reaction to Nazi economic management (which had run two full-term four-year plans), but also because 'planning' savoured too strongly of what was going on across the border within the East German government. The Nazi experience was too recent and the Communist model was too near.

West German opposition to either planning or the more innocuous 'programming' was still strong in 1957, when the Rome Treaty was signed, and partly explains why the 'positive' and interventionist philosophy of the Spaak Report was not embodied in the Rome Treaty itself. A significant factor, of course, was the predominance at that date of the Christian Democrats within the Federal Republic, and the personal sway of Adenauer. But by 1964 the hold of the Christian Democratic Party was weakening, besides which the Federal government found itself increasingly obliged to intervene in the management of the economy, partly as a result of the relative shortage of labour caused by the building of the Berlin wall and the ending of labour migration from the DDR.

In general the Medium-Term Economic Policy Committee gave Marjolin the chance to try out in the EEC what had not been possible in the early days of OEEC– a systematic comparison of nationally formulated medium-term programmes. Some critics have claimed that the forecasts of the committee were inadequate because insufficiently disaggregated, and that it did not amount to a planning mechanism because the Community lacked any instruments to 'enforce' the committee's targets on member states.[33] But this mistakes the nature of the committee in the first place. For one thing, the national governments which drew up their own medium-term plans in conjunction with those of the committee did so on the basis of data disaggregated both by sector and by region. Second, it was the national governments' officials rather than the Commission which drew up the Medium-Term Economic Programme itself. The question of Commission 'enforcement' did not arise because the member states themselves 'pre-agreed' the programme and its targets before these went to the Council for formal adoption.

In some respects, the approach of this committee and its first report represented a reaffirmation of the interventionist philosophy of the Spaak Report, and a departure from the straitjacket of the Rome Treaty. For instance, like the Spaak Report, it admitted that both the structural and spatial distribution of resources could be aggravated through economic integration. As it put it,

> the free working of the market is not in a position to assure a reduction of differences in regional prosperity, and the responsible authorities must initiate an active policy permitting the essential conditions for regional development, and eliminating those distortions which favour region disequilibrium. The creation of a unified economic area and the growth of trade with third countries intensifies competition between firms, with the result that various adaption problems, inevitable in any event, are posed more quickly than otherwise would have been the case in certain regions and sectors.[34]

The Committee stressed not only the problems posed by declining sectors for industrially undeveloped or depressed regions, but also the inadequacy of the free working of the market to assure the development of modern and advanced technology industries under European control. It emphasised the justification of pursuing policies of intervention on social and political rather than purely economic grounds, especially in those areas where the difficulty of measuring social costs and benefits meant that there was no strictly quantifiable justification for such policies.

The first report of the Medium-Term Economic Policy Committee thus showed an explicit endorsement of the need for intervention in the market to assure those ends which the market alone could not assure, or even aggravated. In this sense, it represented a 'positive' approach to integration. This was not a wholesale conversion of the Commission from one viewpoint to another. Like any international agency (or any government), the Commission reflected different views which were not necessarily complementary or consistent. The Medium-Term Economic Policy Committee showed Community countries asserting the need for an upgrading of the criteria and policy instruments of nation-states rather than a purely negative integration policy. On the other hand, the main member states were not prepared to hand over sovereignty in the industrial or regional field to the Commission, any more than they were prepared to allow the Commission to set their own medium-term macro-economic targets or the instruments by which they should be implemented. In general they were prepared to pool their sovereignty in areas in which they found their effective freedom of action already limited, and to do so in order to make it more effective through extension and co-operation.

What this meant was a cautious, international approach to the framing of joint policies on industrial and regional policy. But it was only an approach, and a method, rather than the forging of an economic union. Also, it remained essentially indicative rather than imperative. Yet this occurred at a time when national planners themselves were becoming increasingly aware of the need for imperative planning powers.

One reason was the limited use of indicative planning in the face of rising multinational capital. French planning in its post-war heyday had employed macro-planning with a combination of micro-economic incentives and constraints. While few business backs were broken under the early plans, French enterprise was well aware, nevertheless, that tariffs, tax and public purchasing could be employed as penalties for non-co-operation as well as incentives to fulfil targets in the Plan. But with the opening of the EEC, tarrif changes were pre-empted by the customs union. Also, French industry abroad and foreign industry in France were both less susceptible to the combination of sticks and carrots typical of the early postwar plans. Such business was bigger than the small enterprise of the classic micro-model, while its macro-horizons ranged wider than France itself.

Another reason, at national level, for moving beyond indicative planning, was the evidence that the super-growth of key West European economies, by the mid 1960s, was faltering. Overall growth rates stayed positive, and in some countries such as Belgium actually increased. But the high, smooth and sustained growth of the 1950s, stressed by Shonfield and Postan, had been interrupted.[35] In this situation, and virtually from the time that the first report of the Medium-Term Economic Policy Committee was published in March 1966, leading planners in France and Italy came to admit that Keynesian economics and indicative planning at industry level were too indirect to ensure that the power centres of the economy were harnessed to public objectives. Increasingly, they identified such centres in big business itself, rather than individual sectors, and realised that more direct state intervention would be necessary for effective planning. This included new forms of public ownership and contracts or agreements between governments between governments and leading firms.

Thus the Commission had joined the *indicative* planning bandwagon, just before national governments changed vehicles and tunes. Following suit was difficult precisely because the new policies demanded real state power and specific leverage on big business rather than the general instruments in the Keynesian macro-economic armoury. The Medium-Term Economic Policy Committe (MTEPC) became a talk-shop for macro-economic forcasting and a statement of good intentions in structural and regional policy. This was reflected in a macro-economic emphasis and lesser detail on industrial and regional policy in the Second and Third Reports from the Committee.[36] Lip-service was paid to the need to ensure that monetary union in the Community be matched by policies for economic union, shaped in part by the Committee. But in practice the MTEPC became subject to much the same constraints which Marjolin had witnessed in his earlier attempt to achieve an 'integrated' form of Western European planning in the 1940s.

By the mid-1970s, the very concept of indicative planning had been thrown into disarray throughout Western Europe by commodity and oil price rises, and the deflationary policies pursued by member governments without reference to Brussels. Keynesianism as the dominant ideology of capitalist planning gave way almost overnight to monetarism and reduced commitment to direct intervention in the economy. Such a collapse had already been anticipated by difficulties in new forms of capitalist planning — focused on big business — in countries such as Belgium, France and Italy since 1968. In each country it was found that *voluntary* contractual agreements with capital were one-sided and relatively ineffective in assuring a coincidence of public and private interests. Belgium, in particular, had by this time evolved some half-dozen forms of contractual arrangements of 'programme contracts' with big business.[37] But senior policymakers in the national planning office admitted that, without at least reserve powers of compulsion to *oblige* enterprise to change their behaviour, such contracts had become mainly public relations exercises sanctioning what big business had decided to do in the first place. In effect, even without the specific forms of crisis in the 1970s, the relations between big business and the state had moved into a critical imbalance in favour of capital.

In some respects the Fourth, and most recent, report of the Medium-Term Economic Policy Committee, published in 1976, was interesting not only in terms of its delay — granted that the Second Report had been published in 1968 and the Third in 1970 — but also because it was chaired by the Head of the Belgium Plan and chairman of the Commission's study group on structural factors in inflation of the same year: the author of the so-called Maldague Report.[38] The report, to which this author contributed, is perhaps interesting not so much because of its contents *per se*, but to the extent that the Commission has virtually suppressed it from public knowledge, failing to give a press conference on its recommendations, and giving only a gelded short version, devoid of its radical content, to members of the European Parliament.

The reason was simple enough, in as much as the Maldague Report argued that under conditions of new monopoly power, big business now is able to compensate for forgone sales during recession by raising prices to offset lost cash-flow, thereby contributing to the 'stagflation' phenomenon which has become so familiar in the 1970s. It therefore maintained that macro-economic policies of *re*flation would be necessary to reduce the unit costs of firms with major spare capacity, and that new planning policies should be endorsed by the Commission and implemented on a joint national basis by member governments to ensure that prices were reduced in line with recovered output. The report also claimed that effective planning for a new, social bill of goods would need to be jointly negotiated by governments with management and trades unions.

Not surprisingly, granted Robert Maldague's chairmanship of the study group on inflation and of the Medium-Term Economic Policy Committee, the Fourth Report from the committee showed elements of the analysis of the disputed report on inflation itself.[39] In this he was partly backed by the Economic and Social Committee, or at least by its trades union members, since the report on inflation apparently polarised that body for the first time in years on straight lines between employers' and trade representatives. None the less, the ideological challenge embodied in the Maldague Report lacked sufficient backing to ensure the embodiment of key recommendations on joint and planned reflation in the text of the Fourth Report of the MTEPC itself.

Economic Crisis

In principle, one of the key recommendations of the Maldague Report — the greater accountability of multinational big business — could be implemented by joint international action between governments at the Community level. In this respect, it might appear only rational for governments to grasp the importance of coming together to shape common policies towards big business. As importantly, Europe has moved into a beggar-my-neighbour round of deflation, with individual governments restraining imports — through general restraint of demand — while hoping to increase export performance and thus compensate for the higher cost of oil.

The perverse consequence of such deflations is considerably greater than any virtuous effects from internal tariff abolition and the establishment of a common external tariff on which the Commission prided itself through the decade up to 1968. The welfare loss through forgone income and employment under conditions of zero or minimal growth involves cuts in tax revenue, public expenditure and crucial services such as housing, transport and education.[40] This is against marginal earlier gains — so small as to be difficult to measure with accuracy and unequally distributed between firms, industries and countries — from greater efficiency through larger markets in a nominally integrated Community.[41]

In other words, the nominally 'successful' battle for tariff abolition between the initial Six and the subsequent Nine has been set back through failure to tackle the problem of recession and deflation. Massive subsidies have been given by member governments to their own enterprises, in the false hope that reducing their costs — through lowered effective taxation — will increase their readiness to go out and sell. One of Keynes's most basic lessons, that firms are influenced predominantly by demand and sales rather than supply and costs, has been swamped by application of the principles of 'home economics' and orderly housekeeping to the national and international economy. The key short-term need of enterprise is to cover spare capacity and fixed costs through higher sales. Without reflation of demand, and under conditions of monopoly in industry and services, it is hardly surprising that big business both takes public subsidy of its distributed profits and raises prices to compensate for forgone sales. Thus deflation actually contributes to the new inflation triggered by the OPEC and commodity price rises. Under such conditions, personal tax cuts in the main serve only to offset the loss of real purchasing power which those employed have suffered through inflation, and those unemployed suffer on the dole.

Besides which, there is a major crisis of structural unemployment in the Community today, which had already become evident from the mid-1960s. Technical progress under a capitalist mode of production gives rise to technological unemployment, unless the labour displaced by it can be absorbed either by a dynamic expansion of employment overall, or new industries and services which take in the unemployed. The dramatic nature of the crisis since the mid-1970s has helped disguise the extent to which there already was an underlying crisis of employment in industry in key Community countries and a crisis in financing public sector services. In the key manufacturing sector the capital widening and deepening which had characterised the 1950s (with both more capital per worker and more jobs overall) had given way from the mid-1960s to a trend to net contraction in manufacturing employment in industrialised Western Europe as a whole.[42]

Under new conditions, the combination of under-consumption with a trend to technological unemployment gave a new twist to the long-standing Marxist theories of crisis. In principle, social democratic policies of sustained public expenditure should have been able to create jobs in unproductive or less productive sectors of the economy, on Keynesian lines. But Keynesian policy assumed some kind of effective taxation, at least over the medium to long-term, whereby the new public spending could be financed through public receipts. It was such a principle which was being thrown into crisis through the failure to tax productive manufacturing industry effectively, especially since the investment hesitation dating from the early to mid-1960s, when rebates and tax allowances to enterprise were stepped up as an incentive to investment.[43]

EMU or Ostrich?

The main Community draft documents for economic and monetary union — the Barre Plans and the Werner Report — were shaped during the halcyon days before such fiscal crisis of the state and structural unemployment hit the Community.[44] Both were expressed in terms of the prevailing liberal capitalist ideology dominant in the Community, arguing essentially that the project for European integration begun in the 1950s, needed to be 'completed', rather than transformed through economic and monetary union. Yet in maintaining that 'the Community cannot stop at the point [of a customs union] which it has reached today', the first Barre Plan at least maintained that this was due to evidence of new divergence between member states, and to the fact that the developed economies of the Community 'are in practice strongly influenced and shaped by the economic policies of nation states *and the behaviour of big businesses* which develop their own strategies' adding that 'the incompatibility of these policies and these strategies risks throwing the customs union into question'.[45]

Both the Barre Plans (of February 1969 and March 1970) and the Werner Report (of October 1970) none the less stressed the co-ordination of the policies of big business via a Community authority. The Second Barre Plan even declared that 'it is established that the inter-penetration of economies necessarily entails a weakening and even the disappearance of instruments of national control' without relating the need for control to the 'strategies of big business' which the First Plan had stressed to be as big a problem as national policies themselves. Unconsciously, it appears, Raymond Barre and his colleagues were thereby advocating the co-ordination of already weakened national policies while assuming that 'the play of specialisation' in the integrated market would largely ensure a coincidence between private and public interest in the big-business field.[46]

In fact the Werner Report and Barre plans pay some attention to the question of structural and regional problems and policies to offset them. But the attention is minimal: significantly less than in either the Spaak Report or the First Report of the Medium-Term Economic Policy Committee. Moreover, the prescriptions for such problems in the Werner

Report show no awareness of the extent to which the problems themselves arise through the working of an unequal market system, whose uncommon advantages in favour of the central and strong thereby disadvantage the peripheral and the weak. Rather, the principles for EMU as recommended by progressive stages are almost exclusively *monetary* rather than economic: convertibility, leading to a common monetary unit; a centralised credit policy; a common external monetary policy; a unified policy on capital markets; common decision-making on the volume, scale, mode of finance and use of public budgets and budgetary policy, etc. Regional and structural policy get only a one-sentence recommendation, that they should be 'no longer the exclusive resort of member countries'.[47]

The 1976 Tindemans report on economic and monetary union asserted the need for Community progress to a federal structure with a single currency, yet met with an almost universal rebuff outside Bonn.[48] This was partly through lack of realistic admission of the economic crisis then patently afflicting the Community, and the bland nature of its assumptions that the free working of the market would assure the best for all – in the long run – in a single currency area. The Marjolin report of 1975 was more realistic in its premises: i.e. in admitting the scale of the economic crisis then gripping the Nine. But, in line with the conventional wisdom of some neo-Keynesians who seem to have forgotten Keynes's own emphasis on the need for effective demand – rather than lowered costs – to resolve underconsumption, the Marjolin Report combined a false analysis in the sense of wanting both aspects of the old economic order: lower wages and public spending to reduce costs, with higher demand to promote recovery.[49]

The Marjolin Report represented the cul-de-sac of Keynesian-neoclassical analysis in the face of real crisis.[50] Having wedded the micro-economics of the perfect competition model to the macro-economics of Keynesian demand management, the analysis had veered increasingly towards wage policy as a solution to asymmetry and imbalance in the economy. There was little to distinguish it in this respect from the older-style pre-Keynesian orthodoxies which are still sacrosanct in financial sepulchres such as the US Federal Reserve Bank, the Bundesbank, the Bank of England and the IMF. It was hardly surprising that these latter institutions welcomed the initiative launched in the summer of 1978 by Roy Jenkins – by then President of the Commission – for a European Monetary System.

The EMS proposal was similar in essentials to the previous experiment with a 'snake' of aligned currencies: i.e. an upper and lower limit for exchange-rate changes within which currencies could fluctuate. The French had twice entered and left the previous system, which hardly augured well for the new proposal. Yet with the change from Pompidou to Giscard D'Estaing as President in France, the attitude of the French government had changed in key respects. The neo-Gaullism of Pompidou had given way to a qualified but enthusiastic support for the Community from the more technocratic and more liberal Giscard, who backed EMS partly to reinforce his 'summit' role and partly to impose more discipline on French trades unions and their wage demands.

Also, between the Barre and Werner reports on economic and monetary union, the economic climate had changed. Keynesianism had bitten the dust in Washington, London, Paris and Bonn. Most crucially, West German economic policy was not only in the hands of committed monetarists in government, but was also substantially determined by the even more monetarist Bundesbank, which was independent by its terms of the constitution from the government itself. Thus, although sizable sums were mentioned, without much commital, in the run-up to the introduction of EMS itself, there was a real fear in the Labour Party and the Italian Socialist Party that the terms imposed on Britain or Italy for loans in the event of drifting to the lower limit of the permitted exchange 'band' would be monetarist and deflationary.

In the event the attitude of the British Labour movement, following a major setback for the Government in the rejection of its 5 per cent wages policy at and following the TUC and Labour Party conference in 1978, appears to have had some impact on the Labour Government (combined partly with a Keynesian rearguard action inside the British Treasury). Britain did not join the European Monetary System when it was launched in March 1979. In Italy, where the Christian Democrats were concerned at all costs to avoid real dependence on the Communist Party, the attitude of the Socialists also appeared to register a temporary certain success. But it was temporary. After initially declaring that it would not join, it fell into line – partly through fear of dependence of the lire on a weak dollar in the event of staying out.

For the foregoing reasons, it is highly arguable that monetary integration is irrelevant to the real needs of Western Europe now. Only a fundamental change in the mode of development of the Western European economies will be able to ensure that the productivity gains from technical progress are combined with social spending and relatively full employment.[51] However, this outcome, transforming technical progress from bane to a boon in society, will itself depend on the feasibility of transforming both the dominant criteria in resource allocation and the nature of the central relationships between capital, labour and the state in Western societies. In practice, such change would amount to a transformation of modern or state capitalism as we know it, involving new mechanisms of planning, public enterprise and social control. They would also involve a major change in the role of trades unions, with a negotiation of equalised employment hours or weeks, and a climate of greater social justice through an equalisation of income and wealth. If effective, such change could be revolutionary, though by democratic rather than violent means, and through consent rather than force.

At the turn of the century there were several nominally social democratic parties which conceived of similar change within the parameters of their own time. Key social democrats today, however, reject such fundamental change and transformation of crisis in favour of monetarism of the Friedman kind, or orthodoxies from a related intellectual stable in the form of monetary union. Thus Roy Jenkins, as President of the EEC Commission, argued in 1978 that the European Community is in crisis through the lack of confidence represented by different national currencies and exchange rates. In his view, only a single currency will create the common market worthy of its name, overcoming the investment hesitation and employment crisis of the current period. Nominally, in the Jenkins' analysis, as elsewhere, monetary integration depends on economic union for its effectiveness. But on either the record of the Community to date, or the crisis today, economic and monetary union has its head in the sand relative to the real problems of the European economy and society. It is the ostrich of the Commission's policy aviary.

NOTES

1. Agence Presse (Europe Agence Internationale d'Information pour la Presse): 12 Apr., 1 and 8 May, and 2 June 1965. See also *Le Monde*, 1 and 11 May and 2 June 1965.
2. Agence Presse, 29 June 1965, and *Le Monde*, 2 July 1965 and 18 January 1966. For a further, though different, account of the crisis see also John Newhouse, *Collision in Brussels* (Faber, 1968).
3. In an interview with the author in January 1966 Jean Saingeour, then Head of Planning at the Ministry of Finance, foresaw just such tensions two and a half years before the events of May 1968.
4. Agence Presse, 25 Feb. and 27 Mar. 1965.
5. Ibid.
6. Agence Presse: 5 and 28 Apr., 20 May and 1 June 1965. See also *Le Monde* 5 and 10 June 1965; *Financial Times*, 11 and 17 June 1965, and *New York Times*, 17 June 1965.
7. Agence Presse, 23, 28 and 29 Dec. 1965.
8. Agence Presse, 30 and 31 Oct. 1970. The British TUC also later criticised the merger promotion element in the proposed Company Statute on the grounds that rationalisation would threaten job security. See, further, *The Times*, 6 June 1972.
9. In the same month as the Continental Can decision in March 1971, *The Times* reported 'stalemate' on the whole area of a European Company Statute (29 Mar. 1971).
10. See, further, Alan Dashwood, 'Towards a System of Merger Control in the EEC', *New Law Journal*, 19 Sept. 1974.
11. See, further, *The Times* 9 Feb. 1970 and the *Guardian* 18 Feb. 1970.
12. *The Times*, 23 Mar. 1970.
13. *The Times*, 9 February 1971; *Financial Times*, 15 Apr. 1971 and the *Guardian*, 12 Nov. 1971.
14. *Financial Times*, 31 July 1972.

15. Andrea Boltho, *Japan: An Economic Survey*, (Oxford University Press, 1975).

16. EEC Commission, *Report of the Study Group on Problems of Inflation*, mimeo (Brussels: 3 Mar. 1976), henceforth referred to as *Maldague Report*.

17. The moves towards a Community managed steel cartel were sufficiently extensive to involve the suspension of the main provisions concerning competition in the Paris Treaty.

18. Mendès France, in a speech to the French National Assembly in Jan. 1957, combined this case for free trade versus a common market with criticism of the majority voting procedures anticipated in the Council of Ministers.

19. Michael Butterwick and Edmund Rolfe, *Food, Farming and the Common Market* (OUP, 1968).

20. 30 Jours de l'Europe, *Le problème des excédents et les vagues de vin*, Oct. 1975.

21. In 1974 average food prices in the EEC increased by 10.4 per cent against 14.6 per cent in the US and 29 per cent in Japan: EEC Commission, *Bilan de la politique agricole commune* (Brussels: Feb. 1975).

22. François Houllier, 'Annotations sur le plan Mansholt', *Etudes* (Mar. 1969).

23. Claude Baillet, 'L'exploitation agricole et son avenir dans la Communauté economiqué européenne, *Revue de la Société Française d'Economie Rurale*, no. 89 (July–September 1971).

24. See further Michel Pilipponeau, 'Politique agricole et problèmes régionaux', *l'Europe en Formation*, no. 122 (May 1970).

25. S. H. Franklin, *The European Peasantry* (Methuen, 1969).

26. EEC Commission, *Rapport sur la situation de l'agriculture et des marchés agricoles*, [Mansholt Report] (Brussels: 1968).

27. EEC Commission, *Rapport 1975 sur la situation de l'agriculture dans la Communauté* (Brussels, Dec. 1975).

28. Ministère de l'Agriculture, *Perspective à long terme de l'agriculture francaise 1968–1985*, and 30 Jours d'Europe, *Les exploitants agricoles face au plan Mansholt* (Feb. 1971).

29. Baillet, op. cit.

30. See, further, Claude Baudin, 'Crises monétaires et politique agricole commune', *Revue du Marché Commun*, no. 167 (Aug.–Sept. 1973).

31. EEC Press and Information, *Farm Reform: New Balance for the CAP* (Brussels, May 1972). It should be noted that a major criticism of the farm aid proposals lay in the fact that few self-employed family units would be likely to formulate 'development plans' of the sophistication necessary to gain the scheduled aid.

32. Marjolin stressed to the author in an interview after leaving the Commission that he had had to 'look around' the Rome Treaty for an article on which to pin what he wanted to do with the Medium-Term Policy Committee.

33. For instance, Geoffrey Denton, in his pamphlet *Planning in the EEC: the Medium Term Economic Policy Programme of the European Economic Community*. Chatham House — Political and Economic Planning, European Series no. 5 (1967).

34. EEC Commission, *Avant Projet de Premier Programme de Politique Economique à Moyen Terme* (Brussels, 25 Mar. 1966).
35. Andrew Shonfield, *Modern Capitalism* (RIIA-OUP, 1965); and M. M. Postan, *An Economic History of Western Europe* (1967).
36. EEC Commission, *Projet de Second Programme de Politque Economique a Moyen Terme* (Brussels, March 1968); and *Projet de Troisième Programme etc* (Brussels: (Oct. 1970).
37. See, *inter alia*, Ministère des Affaires Economiques, *Les Lignes de Force – Plan 1971–1975*, and *Textes Légaux et Réglementaires*, Document 1 (1973).
38. EEC Commission, *Report of the Study Group on Problems of Inflation*.
39. EEC Commission, *Projet de Quatrième Programme de Politque Economique à Moyen Terme* (Brussels: 1976).
40. In the case of the UK it has been estimated that the decline in public spending on goods and services as a proportion of GDP amounted to some £8000 million or the equivalent of a year's total spending on the National Health Service. See, further, Stuart Holland and Paul Ormerod, 'Why We Must Increase Public Spending', *New Society* (25 Jan. 1979).
41. See, further, the contribution of John Williamson to Stuart Holland (ed.), *The Price of Europe: A Re-Assessment* (Longmans and SGS Associates, 1971).
42. INSEE, *Economie et Statistique*, no. 97 (Feb. 1978).
43. For British evidence on 'non-taxation' of the corporate sector see, further, John Kay and Mervyn King, *The British Tax System* (Oxford University Press, 1978); for French evident see Jacques Delors, in Stuart Holland (ed.), *Beyond Capitalist Planning* (Blackwell, 1978) ch. 1.
44. EEC Commission, *Mémorandum de la Commission au Conseil sur la coordination des politiques économiques et la coopération monétaire au sein de la Communauté* [First Barre Plan] (12 February 1969); EEC Commission, *Communication de la Commission au Conseil au sujet de l'élaboration d'un plan par étapes vers une union économique et monétaire* [Second Barre Plan] (4 March 1970); *Rapport au Conseil et à la Commission concernant la réalisation par étapes de l'union économique et monétaire dans la Communauté* [Werner Report] (8 Oct. 1970).
45. First Barre Plan, (my emphasis).
46. Second Barre Plan.
47. Werner Report.
48. EEC Commission, 'European Union' Report by Mr Leo Tindemans, *Bulletin of the European Communities* (Brussels: Jan. 1976).
49. EEC Commission, *Report of the Study Group on 'Economic and Monetary Union 1980* (Brussels: Mar. 1975).
50. In this respect it not only represented a step back from Marjolin's own work a decade earlier, but sadly illustrated Leijonhufvud's legitimate distinction between Keynesian economics and Keynes's economics. See further Axel Leijonhufvud, *On Keynesian Economics and the Economics of Keynes* (Oxford University Press, 1968).
51. See Holland (ed.), *Beyond Capitalist Planning*, Chapters 9 and 10. These two chapters amount in essence to the recommendations of the *Maldague Report*.

Part Two
Capital and Integration

3 International Integration

The conventional theory of economic integration is striking for its failure to see the integration process itself as capitalist. The theory of customs unions and common markets was spawned in a backwater of international trade theory which neglected both capitalism itself as a mode of production, and changes within capitalism as a consequence of its international development. For the most part, such theory implicitly assumes a framework of harmonious relations between capital and labour and thereby abstracts from class relations in integration. Its economic models imply a harmony of interests between capital and labour in the integration process, and focus on imperfections in the 'adjustments' which should occur in trade, labour and capital movements through integration. It also neglects the extent to which the process of so-called integration in fact disintegrates economic structures and social relations. Nonetheless, to gain an understanding of the way in which the actors in Community policy-making tend to perceive and justify their own actions, as well as to grasp why their policies are so often frustrated in reality, it is important to analyse the scope and limits of conventional integration theory.

Stages of Integration
Economists differ about the definition of integration itself. But, more importantly, they differ about the ends which integration might achieve, and the means by which it should achieve them. One of the most useful ways of broaching the theory is to bear in mind the difference between integration as a *process*, and *stages* of that process – in other words to distinguish how you go about integration as well as how far you go.

In this text five main stages of integration are defined which correspond broadly with the main usage in the literature on integration theory and policy. At one end of the scale there is the independent national economy. At the other end is the economy which has become so completely integrated that it amounts in practice to a region in another wider economy.

Between these extremes are *five main stages* of integration including (i) a *free trade area*, in which internal tariffs are abolished but countries' previous tariffs *vis-à-vis* other countries are maintained; (ii) a *customs union*, where a common external tariff on products is established in addition to internal tariff abolition; (iii) a *common market*, in which restrictions to the movement of labour and capital between member countries are abolished; (iv) an *economic union*, in which some national policies are harmonised in spheres other than tariffs or labour and capital movements, but remain administered by the constituent member states; and (v) *economic federalism*, in which certain key policies are administered by a central federal authority rather than the member states and in which the previously independent national currencies are merged in a single common currency (or, on a weaker definition, bound in rigid and nominally invariable exchange ratios).[1]

As already indicated, the main disagreements between economists arise not so much from definitions as from wider-reaching questions concerning ends and means. For instance, some economists legitimately raise the question whether the ends which integration is supposed to achieve might not be more effectively reached by means other than the integration of national economies. They ask whether the integration process itself will not result in certain forms of national disintegration, such as an aggravation of regional economic problem and the intensification of regional separatist movements. Alternatively, one could propose that the main objective of economic policy should be the social integration of classes within nation-states, and maintain that such a process would be hindered rather than helped by a preoccupation with the problems of international adjustment which international economic integration could entail.

Even if they agree that international integration is desirable for specific political and economic ends, economists may differ on the means by which integration should be pursued to secure those ends. The choice of means entails judgements about particular economic policies. It also influences the choice of the stage of integration considered necessary to secure given ends such as international competitiveness, higher and more equitably distributed incomes, better regional balance, etc. Such choices cannot be made simply in terms of a self-contained branch of economics called 'integration theory', but relate to wider assumptions about the appropriate role of government in a market economy, the role of planning and intervention relative to allowing a free rein to the working of the competitive process, etc.

The Limits of 'Negative' Integration

The main approach to international integration was first labelled 'negative' by Tinbergen and has since been developed by John Pinder.[2] This really amounts to the limitation for some countries of the general case for international liberalisation of trade and factor movements (labour and capital flows). It basically assumes that the process of liberalisation will result in an optimal allocation of resources between labour and capital, firms and industries, and regions and countries. This would happen as the result of several mutually reinforcing effects, including (i) the stimulation of competition; (ii) greater specialisation in production; (iii) increased scale economies; (iv) higher productivity and faster growth of output; and (v) strengthened competitiveness in the markets of non-member countries. Stimulation of competition would result from the exposure of previously protected high-cost producers in some economies to lower-cost producers in others, causing them either to reduce their costs and prices or reallocate production to other lines. Such specialisation would mean greater scale economies in those lines in that they had a comparative advantage. These economies would mean higher productivity and faster growth, with labour and capital employed in those activities which secured the highest rate of return. In general these factors would increase the competitiveness of the member countries of the integrated area in the markets of non-member countries.

The liberal capitalist or 'negative' approach assumes that more integration is better than less. For instance, to take the five main stages of integration previously outlined, it assumes that the higher the stage of integration, the greater the gains sucured. A free trade area would improve the previous situation in which trade was impeded by tariffs, but the continuation of different tariffs with third countries would lead to 'origin and destination' problems. That is to say that a country with a relatively low tariff *vis-à-vis* third countries but no tariffs *vis-à-vis* member countries could constitute a 'back door' for the import of goods, thus 'distorting' trade patterns between members of the free trade area. Therefore a customs union would be preferable. But by the same token, 'distortions' would remain within the customs union unless it also proceeded to the stage of a common market for labour and capital, harmonised further policies in an economic union, and finally integrated national currencies in a federal system.

This approach to integration has met with substantial criticism from economists who reject the harmony assumptions of the theory on which it is based. But even its exponents allow that government policies will have to be maintained in the integrated area to ensure that the freer working of the market mechanism does result in welfare benefits. For one thing, they admit that collusive and monopolistic practices may prevent increased competition following the abolition of tariffs between member states. For another, they maintain that member governments will have to harmonise those of their national policies which affect mutual trade and factor movements. And this means a range of policies including company taxation, regional aids, social security, transport, state intervention for industrial restructuring, and the wider reaching policy instruments employed to influence the national macro-economic level of activity.

In other words, the liberal or 'negative' approach to integration does not mean the absence of government policies. It means that the policies pursued are intended to facilitate a freer working of the market mechanisms rather than to ensure that welfare ends met are by other means such as planning, which supplement or supplant the working of the market mechanism itself. A clear example is given by the Commission's 1972 statement on industrial policy, which declared:

> government aids to industry and other forms of state intervention in
> the economy could hardly be avoided altogether. But these must remain
> exceptions, rather than as a means to an end. The transformation of
> industry should be the spontaneous consequence of the creation of the
> Common Market rather than as a process requiring planning.[3]

The theory of economic and social harmony implicit in such negative
integration theory was challenged virtually from the start. For instance,
one of the pioneers of the theory of economic integration, Jacob Viner,
pointed out that the establishment of a common external tariff could
result in welfare losses rather than gains. This would arise when a country
had to raise its tariffs to the common level of the integrated area, thereby
cutting itself off from lower-cost external producers. In some cases, it was
possible that the abolition of internal tariffs in the area would mean
cheaper sources of supply. But Viner claimed that the smaller the union,
the higher the probability that the costs of the most efficient internal
producers were higher than those which could previously have been secured
from external suppliers. Trade *diverted* from member countries by the
establishment of the common external tariff therefore might exceed that
trade *created* through the members' access to lower cost and price internal
producers[4]

Questions on Size and Scale
The trade creation and diversion problem is a real one, and assumes especial
relevance in the context of British membership of the EEC, where the
adoption of the EEC tariff on agricultural products means the exclusion
of imports from lower-cost Commonwealth food producers. But many of
the economists concerned with integration have focused on trade creation
and diversion in terms which have been artifical and misleading. For one
thing, their analysis has been static rather than dynamic, comparing the
situation before and after the creation of a common external tariff in terms
of a 'once-off' contrast with the previous period. For another, the theory
assumes an absence of any scale economies to internal producers, i.e.
gains through lower costs in large-scale production after the creation of the
customs union. But, in practice, the creation of the EEC customs union
took took ten years for its initial members, and in the case of UK membership the transition period was five years. For industrial products, this
covers the five-to ten-year period in which firms will invest in new plant
and equipment of a scale and productivity-increasing type to meet the
competitive challenge to their domestic market share opened by internal
tariff abolition. Most of the conclusions based an absence of scale economies will therefore tend to be inaccurate, fortuitously accurate or incom-
plete as a prediction of the trade effects of customs union formation.

For one thing, not all member countries within a customs union will benefit equally from any stimulus to investment and scale economies from internal tariff abolition. This means that the theory, which neglects such scale and stimulus effects, fails to start realistic analysis of the results of customs únions. And since much of integration theory has stayed at the level of customs union theory, this has meant that it has stopped where the important issues begin.[5] Besides which, there is a clear contradiction between the neglect of scale economies and stimulus effects in the main literature on economic integration, and the key role which they play in the main statement of the liberal case for integration. The liberal or 'negative' integration case is ill-served by its main theoretical advocates.

This is illustrated by the very problem of monopolistic pricing to which scale economies or gains from size can give rise. Thus, according to the competitive model, as illustrated in Fig. 3.1 the firm which in a pre-integration stage I was producing at an average cost level A would be earning a 'normal' profit of the difference between A and p^1. After integration, at stage II, after a round of new investment following specialisation, it should reduce its price to p^2 to gain a 'normal' profit, following the reduction of its average costs to level B. But in practice the very increase in size which specialisation and greater scale entails may put it in a position to maintain price, i.e. establish it at level p^3 rather than p^2. Granted the findings of the Commission's own studies that there is a correlation between concentration of industry and inflationary pricing, elaborated in Chapter 4, there is every reason to maintain that such a perverse non-competitive effect has followed EEC integration.

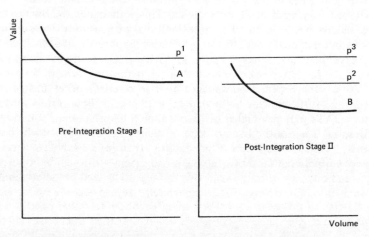

FIG. 3.1 *Scale economies and monopoly pricing*

Scepticism about liberal capitalist integration has been well expressed by Paul Streeten, who has claimed that some of its most important premises amount to 'fallacies of addition' i.e., whatever their independent merit, they are mutually inconsistent. For instance, the theory of comparative advantage assumes either constant or increasing costs, but these are incompatible with the decreased costs entailed in the scale economies which are supposed to be derived from larger 'integrated' markets. Similarly, although one of the main gains assumed to follow from the increased liberalisation approach is increased competition, the increased scale economies available to existing big business in a wider market may result in accelerated concentration and a reduction in competition.[6] The large internal market of the United States has certainly contributed to the growth of the largest and most dominant companies in the Western world.

But apart from any fallacies of addition, the independent merit of the main arguments in the liberal or 'negative' integration case can be challenged. For instance, it is implicit in the case for greater scale economies through international economic integration that the limits to any such economies have been reached in the national markets of the countries concerned. But there is considerable difference of opinion in terms of income per head about the minimum market-size necessary to secure production scale economies.[7] It has been argued that for medium-sized mature economies, such as Britain, France and West Germany, a large enough domestic market already exists for economies of scale in the production of all except a few advanced technology products and aerospace in which case the scale benefits from integration might be met by either bilateral or miltilateral joint ventures between public or private companies.[8]

It also has to be borne in mind that some of the largest and most successful companies in the world — for instance, Unilever and Nestlé — were developed from small economies such as The Netherlands and Switzerland. This success has been based on multinational expansion of investment as well as international trade. But in both cases it appears that a small domestic market may have acted as a stimulus rather than a restraint on company growth. In the latter case the crucial factor permitting dynamic expansion was not whether Switzerland was part of an *integrated* market, but whether Nestlé had sufficient access to foreign markets. In these terms, subscription to GATT may pay higher dividends than joining a common market.

Besides, it is less the issue of size of *plant* than size of *firm* which now counts; less scale economies of production, than scale and size in access to finance on preferential terms, hold over suppliers — through bulk purchasing — and buyers — through your own retail outlets, and brand attachment through mass advertising. Not least, overall size has become important as the barrier to takeover by others, and the boom to lower on those you want to take. Financial reserves — through the stock price one can command, or the credit one can raise — are crucial to survival. Small firms are not safe against elimination or takeover by virtue of their operation in big markets. Their best hope of moving into the medium or big league may well be dual markets or, alternatively, public ownership, rather than a common market.

Such problems were to perplex and plague the Community in the mid-1960s. Having assumed that the competitive process would ensure a balanced economic structure, it overreacted to the evidence on the penetration of modern industry in the EÉC by American multinational capital. While the operations of United States subsidiaries in Western Europe were not always large, they were backed by companies whose financial muscle, production backbone and cerebral know-how dwarfed that of many European competitors. Faced already with an apparent contradiction between the bias against size in the Rome Treaty, on the one hand, and the alleged gain from the common market of economies of scale, the Commission found itself posed with a basic dilemma: whether to support the accelerated concentration of European capital to strengthen it *vis-à-vis* thirdworld American penetration and, if so, how to preserve at the same time a predominantly competitive market framework. As stressed earlier, in analysis of the failure to achieve a Common Industrial Policy complementing the Common Agricultural Policy of the CAP, it was a dilemma which it failed to resolve.[9]

Structural and Regional Inequality
There is an argument behind both liberal capitalist intergration and the general case for free trade which amounts to Darwin revisited: i.e. survival of the fittest. In other words, it is claimed that relatively inefficient producers are a drain on national resources, and that their capital and labour would be better employed in other lines of production. But this implies either that those who are less efficient in an existing product somehow will summon the skills and resources to break into new markets, demanding disproportionately greater survival capacity in the transition, or that they will be taken over by others with greater entrepreneurial capacity and flair. According to the argument, what goes for firms should also go for economic structures in general. According to the theory there will always be some line of production, at some wage, where member countries will have a comparative advantage.

Lord Kahn, writing in the context of the 1950s proposals for a free trade area including both the EEC Six and the EFTA Seven, commented that 'trial by ordeal, which is what free trade will mean if businessmen allow it to operate seriously, is a poor and brutal way of deciding how the principle of comparative advantage is ultimately to operate.[10] The ordeal can be considerable, as a country such as Britain has experienced since joining the EEC. The United Kingdom commercial or visible trade deficit with other EEC countries deteriorated dramatically from 1971 to 1975, reaching a maximum of two-thirds of a £1 billion in the latter year, or the equivalent of the peak deficit reached in the 1970s with the OPEC countries. There may be grounds for saying that Continental European enterprises in the EEC focused their sales and exporting effort on Britain better than the British on them, but an 'EEC effect' seems evident granted that Britain's visible trade with other Western European countries remained more or less in balance during the same period.[11]

The simple imbalance of such figures needs some qualification. For one thing, Britain's capital was more multinational in structure than that of EEC countries. In fact, whereas an economy such as West Germany is structured towards the export of goods, Britain's economy since the war has been structured very much to the export of enterprise. The value of foreign production by British business abroad in the early 1970s was more than double total visible export trade, against a ratio of only one-fifth for West German foreign production relative to exports.[12] Moreover, there are grounds for questioning the principles of comparative advantage itself in trade which now is substantially multinational rather than international, i.e. involving trade between subsidiaries of the same companies in different countries rather than different companies in different countries.

None the less, the French with some reason have referred to internal tariff abolition of the free trade area or common market variety as 'tariff disarmament'. The free working of the market on 'negative' integration principles in no sense guarantees that relatively inefficient resources will be scooped up and reinvested more profitably within the same country. Successful import penetration may benefit foreign exporters by more all the time, or certainly over a long run in which the original producers or productive industries have died. Such long-run structural benefits have been evident for West German and Japanese exports to Britain during the 1960s and 1970s, and show no apparent trend towards reversal, despite wage levels which are considerably lower in the United Kingdom than in those two countries. Similarly, the decline in the value of sterling — at one stage in the 1970s no less than two-thirds down on the 1971 level *vis-à-vis* the Deutschmark — has not stemmed German imports or started a United Kingdom export-led recovery.

The Commission's difficulties in devising a common industrial policy as already described in Chapter 2, stemmed in part from its implicit assumptions — reflected in 'negative' integration theory — that the free working of the market would assure a balanced industrial structure.[13]

In regional policy, the experience of the Italians over a century of economic integration of the North and South of the country prompted some realisation that all was not for the best through liberalisation alone. This prompted the Italian signatories to insist on attachment of a special protocol to the Rome Treaty allowing them exceptional State aids in favour of the chronically less-developed Mezzogiorno.

However, as in industrial structure, there has been a basic dilemma or contradiction in the Commission's regional policy, which in part stems from and is reflected by the one-sidedness of the 'negative', liberal capitalist case for integration. Such a case assumes that trade, capital flows and labour migration between countries and regions will be self-adjusting and result in a general welfare increase. But in practice interregional flows of capital and labour tend to be one-way and cumulative in their effects. For instance, it is recognised that savings are channelled to the most profitable further investment which stockbrokers or banks can find for them. This tends to be in companies in more developed areas. Savings therefore tend to flow to investment in these areas rather than less developed areas. But it is also commonplace that companies in developed countries prefer to expand their plant and capacity either on or as near as possible to existing locations. Apart from anything else this is easier in the short-run than organising an entirely new plant elsewhere. For these reasons, the one-way flow of savings from less to more devleoped regions is not offset by a counter-balancing reverse flow of investment from the more to the less developed.[14]

In practice, the problems of structural and spatial inequality through the free working of the market are clearly linked. Both work through the process of concentration and centralisation. This has been well shown in an analysis of industrial and financial capital in the EEC by Roger Lee and, again, follows the analysis made by Marx in Volume I of *Capital*.[15] Of course, both the structural and spatial centralisation have major implications for the social distribution of product and income. In terms of GDP *per capita*, the disparities in 1975 ranged from 3 to 1 in favour of Paris *versus* Central Italy, and with extremes as high as 9 to 1 in favour of Hamburg and against the least-developed Italian region – Calabria. Moreover, such disparities have been increasing through the 1970s.[16]

To date, the perception of regional problems has mainly been focused on sub-regions of member states of the Community. But with higher stages of integration, and within the continued centralisation of capital, spatial inequality is becoming increasingly characteristic of nation states *as* problem regions in the EEC. In other words, through capitalist integration, an initially slow-growing nation-state such as Britain can become a backword problem region in Community Europe, such as Northern Ireland now is in the United Kingdom. In practice, gains from initially higher growth to leading firms in more developed regions of countries tend to be reinforced. To a major extent, unequal innovation and modernisation have ensured that faster firms develop and then dominate new markets. Under liberalised trade in an integrated area this tends to mean that lagging firms in slower-growing regions and countries cannot fully compete in their own markets with firms from outside the region. Aggravated by the multinational reach of big business, which gives it access to labour in less developed countries at a quarter to one tenth the cost of labour in Europe's problem regions, this unequal scope and structure of competition can permanently disadvantage a less-developed region. Such disadvantage is in no significant sense countered by incentives and subsidies of the kind operated through the EEC's Regional Fund.[17]

Migrant Labour and Uneven Development

Apart from this, the flow of labour in a common market does not tend to offset the inequality and uneven development arising from the spatial centralisation of capital. In fact, in contrast to 'negative' integration theory, it aggravates it even when the more developed areas are able to achieve relative full employment. For instance, if capital freely chose for a period of time to expand in more developed regions in an integrated area, but found itself running out of labour in a period of expansion, it might choose to locate new plant on a significant scale in less-developed areas. But the very provision for free movement of labour in the Rome Treaty which one might welcome on liberal political grounds, thereby undermines such a self-adjustment mechanism. Put simply, by staying where it is, or near its initial location, capital can attract labour from less-developed regions and countries with lower wages and higher unemployment. The more developed area thereby avoids the cost-inflationary penalties of over-full employment, and in effect raises its 'full employment ceiling' through immigration of labour rather than out-migration of capital.[18]

This process, which amounts in essentials to what Marx called the role of the reserve army of labour in capital accumulation, was certainly at work in the 'supergrowth' of West Germany and North Italy during the 1950s, and was a considerable factor in permitting the expansion of the Paris region versus the rest of France.[19] But, ironically, it worked most decisively during the period before and just after the opening of the EEC, at least for Common Market labour. The main flow of labour to West (from East) Germany, which dried up after the building of the Berlin Wall, had not been from a member EEC country in the first place. Emigration to other EEC countries from Italy in fact peaked at an annual rate of 180,000 persons a year in 1962 but fell to half that over the ensuing ten years. The bulk of the difference in foreign labour employed in West Germany came from non-EEC countries; Yugoslavia, Greece, Turkey in particular. Foreign immigration in France also came mainly from Algeria, Spain and Portugal.[20] Thus, again, the expectations of liberal integration that free movement of labour would be mainly *intra*-Community were falsified.

The social inequality of such migrant workers, of course, has been notorious. The *bidonvilles* in France and the virtual Apartheid of many workers' dormitories in West Germany have been well documented[21] The notable feature of such immigration has been the barriers to *social* integration of the labour involved, whether it came from inside or outside the Community. Essentially, it was not the logic of economic integration as such but accumulation of capital and its demand for labour which attracted migrants from less to more developed countries. Similarly, that capital repelled them — through unemployment — when they were no longer needed in the 'host' country. In the West German case, more than ⅔ million immigrant workers returned to their country of origin following the deflation imposed by the government after the commodity and oil price inflations of the early 1970s, which compounded structural with cyclical unemployment.[22]

In practice, therefore, the assumptions of negative integration theory, and the provisions reflecting it in the Rome Treaty, were contradicted by main dynamics of 'free' labour migration in the EEC in the twenty years following the signature of the Treaty itself. Immigrant labour came mainly from outside the Community, and mainly went home again when the Community itself failed to ensure maintenance of 'harmonised', balanced and sustained economic growth during the 1970s. The theory of common conditions of employment for migrant labour were falsified both by their uncommon conditions of work and living, and their unequitable repulsion from the host countries when they had served the purposes of local capital.

There is an implicit parallel between the relation of capital to State intervention — developed in the next section of this chapter — and its relation to migrant labour. Thus capital needs and will accept State intervention when it needs finance and aid for reconstruction and development. Similarly, it needs and employs migrant labour during periods of expansion. *But it rejects both State intervention and migrant labour when these needs have been served.* These key respects of the relation of capital to both labour and the State in economic integration have mainly been ignored by the advocates of 'positive' integration within the Community.

The Limits of 'Positive' Integration

It is important to stress that the difference between positive and negative integration is not the difference between integration policies on the one hand, and their absence on the other. Both positive and negative integration involve policies, in name and form if not in substance. But the former seek to implement change in the rate, structure and spread of resources, through modifying the market mechanism, while the latter seek to reinforce such mechanisms in the first place.

Broadly, the distinction can be seen as paralleling the difference between positive and negative intervention at the nation-state level; or, more simply, as the difference between 'thou shalt' (in the positive integration case) and 'thou shalt not' (in the negative). Thus the negative integration case is concerned to ensure that tariffs and other non-tariff barriers adopted by member states do not distort the free movement of goods, capital and labour. In the case of firms and enterprises, it tries to ensure no distortion of competition or abuse of the competitive process. These areas largely cover the first three stages of economic integration, as already identified: an internal free trade area, a customs union and a common market.

Positive integration in the sense of building up something new, rather

than breaking down something alrready there, is most clearly relevant
to the fourth stage of economic integration, i.e. economic union. The fifth
stage of monetary union through a single currency is mainly negative in
the sense of abolishing formerly independent currencies. In general,
positive integration is conceived by advocates such as Pinder as active
intervention to *modify* the effects of the free working of the market,
and to establish economic and social conditions which are not simply
the result of negating or abolishing previous policies. In this sense, it is
seen as covering the broad range of common industrial, regional, transport and agricultural policies. It is also relevant to common fiscal and
monetary policies.

However, it is important to stress that integrated policies for economic
union do not *in themselves* mean intervention to *modify* the working of the
market mechanism. It is conceivable that governments with a predominantly liberal capitalist ideology should try to establish economic union on
negative integration lines through a process of harmonisation of national
policies which downgrades their differences to a lowest common denominator. In this way it would maintain that member states should *not* undertake positive discrimination in favour of public *versus* private transport,
less developed *versus* more developed regions, declining *versus* growing
industries, and so on. At the fiscal and monetary level it would maintain
that member states should not operate discriminatory taxes in favour of
certain social or economic groups (e.g. lower value-added tax on food
versus higher tax on consumer durables) and that they should not operate
independent currencies with different exchange rates.

The dominance of such a liberal capitalist ideology reflects and accounts
for some of the major handicaps experienced in achieving planned policies
for positive integration in the European Communities to date. For instance,
in the 1950s, when the Rome Treaty was drafted and adopted, there was
general agreement between the signatory governments that the liberalisation of capital and free trade were a 'good thing'. This was partly due to
the hangover from the protection adopted by various countries before the
Second World War as a reaction to the depression, which was perceived in
terms of 'beggar my neighbour' policies, and a worsening of everyone's
chances of recovery. It also substantially reflected the interests of the
United States in securing a Western world economy open to American
goods, capital and influence. The downgrading of such liberal economic
principles to a common market entailed no major challenge to the dominant ideology in the Western economies under American influence. Social
democratic signatories such as Guy Mollet, for France, found little diffi-
cullty in putting their name to something so anodyne (or so secondary to
more important preoccupations such as the failed assault on Suez and the
war in Algeria).[23]

Moreover, as we have already seen in the attempt to shape a common
industrial policy, and the attempt to achieve common policies for medium-

term planning at the Community level, policies for positive integration are subject to basic limitations which reflect the power structures in not simply in integration *per se* but capitalist integration as such.

For instance, some of the pragmatists in the Commission, who had come from the various offices of French planning and were notable in the industrial policy directorate, may well have thought that the main issue was what they *thought*: i.e. that once the policy issue was decided at Commission level and endorsed by the Council of Ministers, action would follow. Certainly, in the earlier French plans in which they had participated, policy thoughts tended to be followed by action. Their problems, however, were not just in the divided opinions within the Commission itself, or in the Council, but in the fact that the structure of capital itself had been transformed since the war.

In other words, in the postwar period of reconstruction, capital in a country such as France was predominantly national, subject to controls over finance and foreign exchange, and looked to the State for a green light on the rate, scale and direction of its reconstruction. But by the mid-1950s, and decisively after the opening of the EEC, with its stress on liberalisation of both trade and payments, capital was no longer so circumscribed. The French planners themselves had sought to promote a in which 80 per cent of the activity in a sector was commanded by 20 per cent or less of enterprises. They had aided and abetted concentration and centralisation of capital's own structure. When such big business was by and large strong enough to go it alone without the help of the Ministry of Finance and its credit agencies, it did precisely that.[24]

Thus, during postwar French reconstruction French business by and large needed and welcomed positive State intervention. But once it had recovered and restructured itself with State aid, it did not. The institutions of such positive *intervention* either declined outright in importance, as in the case of the government-financed Economic and Social Development Fund, or were considerably undermined in effectiveness. A similar pattern emerged in the cryptic forms of public intervention in West Germany, where the Credit Institute for Reconstruction, set up by the government to channel Marshall Aid counterpart funds to industry, had by the 1960s lost its main domestic customers to the commercial banks, and was looking for lending outlets to Third World countries.[25] Countries such as Belgium and Italy, by the mid-1960s, were trying to devise new forms of positive intervention in the economy, but with limited success. Belgium's newly introduced five-year plans, like the new Italian planning, ran into difficulties because of the uncertain international impact on the domestic economy and the new power of big business. Belgium, France and Italy, from 1968, all tried to devise new direct forms of negotiation with big business through what they called Planning Contracts or Planning Agreements. But such agreements were bilateral, between government and management rather than also with the unions, and lacked real powers.

The multinationalisation of private capital during the period after the opening of the EEC certainly was critical to this undermining of new efforts at planned or positive intervention within capitalist economies. But, as will be elaborated in the following chapter, such a structural change from predominantly national to multinational capital also undermined the efforts to translate positive national *intervention* into positive international *integration*. By the time the EEC got round to devising policies which sought to translate the national formulae of intervention to the international or Community level, multinational capital not only did not need it, but actually did not want it.

The argument becomes important in terms of the inherent limits to positive integration, or policies of economic union. As will be elaborated in Chapter 6, different sections of capital had different interests as the structure of capital itself changed over time. Thus national governments found themselves increasingly called upon to support and aid national capital which found itself disadvantaged by liberalisation and multinational competition. They also tried, especially in Italy, Belgium and France, to build up 'national champions' against foreign multinational capital, through new forms of public enterprise.[26] But their support for policies of positive or planned integration, which could have advanced the EEC from a common market to an economic union, was frustrated by the combined forces of the prevailing liberal capitalist ideology, and its embodiment in the Rome Treaty, plus multinational capital and the class and interest groups which it represented.

Put simply, multinational capital has an interest in supporting policies for negative integration, i.e. the breaking down of State intervention through abolition of tariffs and restrictions on the free movement of labour and capital. But it has no interest in supporting policies of economic union which could restrict its freedom to allocate resources as, why and where it wants to. Similarly, such capital may support monetary union but not because it cannot cope to its own advantage from exchange rate changes, or because it lacks a single European money market. As argued later, it can offset exchange rate changes to its advantage, and already has access to a 'European' money market in the form of Eurodollars and Eurobonds. If it supports monetary union without economic union, it is because of a basically correct intuition that it would restrict the freedom of governments to pursue independent policies for positive intervention at the national level and to restrain big business freedom. Not least, especially in the mid- and later 1970s, it could well grasp that if monetary union was introduced under a prevailing climate of monetarism, it would tend to restrict the public versus the private sector.

Such multinational opposition to both positive national *intervention* and positive international *integration* substantially explains the frustration of Community hopes on effective common industrial and regional policies. Such integration policies, as already seen in the case of the Spaak Report, the First Report of the Medium-Term Economic Policy Committee, and other Community initiatives, have on key occasions been put forward in a positive interventionist context. They have aimed to reconcile social and private costs and benefits, or the public and private interest, in a planned framework. By contrast, negative integration policies such as a free trade area, a customs union, a common market or monetary union aim to free capital on the assumption that, broadly speaking, it will indirectly fulfil the public interests through efficient provision of jobs, goods and services in the integrated area. In practice, negative integration means the dominance of private interests and private criteria for resource allocation: i.e. a capitalist Community in which capital's interests are primary and paramount, while the public interest trails in a secondary and subservient fashion. Not least, negative integration itself negates State power, and aggravates the problems of structural, spatial and social inequality which positive integration is supposed to remedy.

NOTES

1. This parallels the distinctions used by Bela Balassa, in *The Theory of Economic Integration* (Allen & Unwin, 1962).
2. See, further, John Pinder, 'Problems of European Integration', in Geoffrey Denton (ed.), *Economic Integration in Europe* (Weidenfeld & Nicolson, 1969)
3. EEC Commission, *Industrial Policy and the European Community* (Brussels: Nov. 1972).
4. Jacob Viner, *The Customs Union Issue* (1950)
5. Even this did not take it very far. James Meade has commented that 'our main conclusion must be that it is impossible to pass judgement on customs unions in general', though this did not prevent him from stating, in his own words, 'with some general prejudice in favour of a customs union': J.E. Meade, *The Theory of Customs Unions* (1955) pp. 107—8.
6. Paul Streeten, *Economic Integration*, 2nd edition (1964) pp. 84—5.
7. See further C.D. Edwards, 'Size of Markets, Scale of Firms and the Character of Competition, in E.A.G. Robinson (ed.), *Economic Consequences of the Size of Nations* (1963).
8. Scitovsky makes the case that increased scale economies must be viewed in the dynamic context of *future* industries. But it is not clear that this meets either the joint venture argument, or the following points on stimulus and size of markets: Tibor Scitovsky, *Economic Theory and Western European Integration* (1958) p. 47.
9. The dilemma was highlighted by D. Swann and D.L. McLachlan in *Concentration or Competition: A European Dilemma* Chatham House-Political and Economic Planning, European Series no. 1 (January 1967). It was elaborated in their major study *Competition Policy in the European Community* (Oxford University Press, 1967).
10. R.F. Kahn, 'A Positive Contribution? in G.D.N. Worswick (ed.), *The Free Trade Area Proposals* (1960).

11. Source: *Monthly Digest of Trade Statistics*, various years. For a relatively independent view of the phenomenon, see Yves Barou, 'Contrainte extérieure et declin industriel au Royaume Uni', in *INSEE*, Economie et Statistique, no. 97 (Feb. 1978).

12. United Nations, *Multinational Corporations in World Development* (ratios for 1971) (1973).

13. EEC Commission, *Treaty of Rome: Protocol Concerning Italy* (Annex 2).

14. These arguments have been well established in regional theory at least since Gunnar Myrdal published his *Economic Theory and Under developed Regions* in 1957, the year of signature of the Rome Treaty.

15. Roger Lee, 'Integration, Spatial Structure and the Capitalist Mode of Production', in Roger Lee and P.E. Ogden (eds.), *Economy and Society in the EEC* (Saxon House, 1976).

16. EEC Commission, *Regional Statistics* (1976).

17. See further Stuart Holland, *The Regional Problem* ch. 4 (Macmillan, 1976).

18. See, further, Stuart Holland, *Capital versus the Regions*, ch. 3 (Macmillan, 1976).

19. Karl Marx, *Capital*, I, Chapter XXV. For similar arguments see Charles Kindleberger, *Europe's Postwar Growth: the Role of Labour Supply* (1967).

20. See further the authoritative account of Stephen Castles and Godula Kosack in *Immigrant Workers and Class Structure in Western Europe* (Oxford University Press, 1973).

21. Ibid., esp. ch. VII.

22. See Karl Georg Zinn, 'The "Social Market" in Crisis', in Stuart Holland (ed.), *Beyond Capitalist Planning*, ch 5. (Blackwell, 1978).

23. Mollet added in a personal meeting with the author that in any case no one expected the detailed articles of the Rome Treaty to represent a binding specific commitment on the member governments, since few other international treaties were binding in small print on their signatories.

24. See further Bela Balassa, 'Whither French Planning?', *Quarterly Journal of Economics* (November 1965); and Jean Bénard, 'Le Marché Commun et l'Avenir de la Planification Française', *Revue Economique* (Sept. 1964).

25. See, further, Stuart Holland, 'European Para-Governmental Agencies' in Sixth Report from the Expenditure Committee, *Public Money in the Private Sector*, (Minutes of Evidence) (1974).

26. See, *inter alia*, Stuart Holland, 'Europe's New Public Enterprises, in Raymond Vernon (ed.), *Big Business and the State* (Macmillan, 1974).

4 Multinational Integration

The multinational company has scarcely been integrated into the theory of economic integration. One reason is basically simple. Multinationals — defined as the *same* company operating in different countries — undermine some of the key premises of integration theory, based as the latter primarily is on the assumption of *different* companies in different countries. In short, they break up the theory.

There were further reasons. As already indicated in Chapter 3, conventional theory of economic integration was dominated by the application of international trade theory to the special case of customs unions. Inertia, plus the divorce of academic economics from politics and political economy, combined to leave the subject in a cul-de-sac long after the initial customs union of the Six was achieved (in 1968), or the Kennedy Round negotiations had reduced the Community's common external tariff to virtual insignificance — an average of 6 per cent for industrial products. In less developed countries which had attempted common markets, such as Latin America, a high proportion of theory and analysis was concerned with the multinational phenomenon.[1] But this was widely neglected in Europe because it was too far removed (either as a geographic region or as a discipline of development economics) from the preoccupations of juggling models of trade creation and trade diversion.

The framework of academic theory on economic and monetary union as developed from the later 1960s assumed that State power transposed to the Community level would be effective over the economic power of firms and enterprises. In large part it amounted to an assumption that the main instruments of the Keynesian armoury could be transferred to a Community level. The Keynesian camp is, however, partly divided. There are some who see monetary union as giving the Community a strong currency in world financial markets, thereby benefiting economies of countries such as Britain, which suffer through supporting a world reserve currency beyond its means. There are others who see the abolition of independent exchange rates as depriving member states of the key means of ensuring both domestic employment and some kind of balance of payments equilibrium, if not exported growth.

The differences between the Keynesians tends to reflect divisions between the neoclassical school (with its emphasis on self-balance and equilibrium through market forces) and the non-neoclassicals (with emphasis endorsement on the imbalance and disequilibrium forces in the market, as stressed among others by Gunnar Myrdal). But even within the latter group there has been a tendency to assume that *if* monetary integration were achieved with a genuine federal authority, the framework of fiscal policies of the modern Keynesian state could be transferred affectively to the supranational level and would prove effective in preventing imbalanced development in the Community. The special problems posed by multinational companies have scarcely figured in the debate.

The Multinational Phenomenon

The rise of multinational capital as a dominant feature of the Western European economy has been a relatively recent phenomenon, spanning mainly the years since the establishment of the EEC. Its impact has been uneven between regions and countries, firms and industries. There have also been qualitative changes within multinational activity, from the initial export of capital for the exploitation of raw materials in less-developed countries, to its rise as the predominant form of production in manufacturing, and services, in developed countries. It has both influenced and been influenced by different patterns of State intervention and State power.

None of this should be surprising. The very dynamics which underlie the growth of multinational capital have been based on inherent inequality and uneven development in the working of a dynamic capitalist system. The application of new techniques and processes by big business has been a complex interrelation between technical progress, demand patterns, supply structures, barriers to competition and State support. Specific changes in the incidence and penetration of multinational capital, with varying mechanisms of challenge and response, have occurred within the lifetime of the European Communities. Not least, the tariff reduction within the initial Six member states of the Community accelerated multinational capital, aggravating problems already caused for key member countries by the loss of tariffs as a means for controlling (or influencing) the balance of payments.[2]

Within this context, member States of the Community resorted to new forms of direct intervention in an effort to compensate for the loss of indirect control over resource allocation through tariffs. In part, as already indicated, this took the form of efforts to merge and promote national mergers to establish 'national champions' in the Community arena, and in part efforts to establish new State enterprise or extend the activities of State holding companies. Combined with their concern to protect the national base of accumulation against capital owned and controlled from abroad, this resulted in new forms of State capitalism and State nationalism contradicting the very principles of supranationalism which the Community was supposed to promote.[3]

In fact the problems caused for Community governments by the expansion of multinational capital were clearly enough stressed in a major report to the Commission in 1969. This concluded that multinational firms undermined government policy not only in advanced technology industry such as computers and nuclear power, but also in other major areas relevant to positive integration such as monetary and fiscal policy, industrial policy (including aids to industry), regional policy, policies for advanced technology industry, national economic planning and successful management of the balance of payments.[4]

However, this report, including detailed submissions by several independent specialists, was not published by the Commission. It was leaked in substance to the press, and reached several interested outside parties. Some of the reasons for refusing its publication are clear enough. For one thing, the scale of the problems posed by multinationals, and admitted in the report, underlined the limited, arbitrary and outdated assumptions of the model of competition embodied in the founding charter of the Community within virtually a decade of its being signed. Policies to deal with the problems would have meant moving beyond the 'thou shalt not' of negative integration to a new and more imperative 'thou shalt' of the positive integration kind. Such intervention was regarded by the West Germans as at best imperious, and at worst something done only 'over the border' in the other half of Germany. It implied four-letter words such as *plan*.

Also, of course, the Community was caught on the wrong foot by the tendency at this stage to identify the multinational phenomenon with American multinationals. It had been founded under the *aegis* of the United States to foster, if not the euphonious-sounding United States of Europe, then at least a reflection of the American model in Europe. What should the EEC do when its main problems in the multinational field allegedly were caused by US enterprise?

As shown later, there is reason to discount the cruder claims about an American takeover of European modern industry in the 1960s. None the less, some of the figures published at the time gave telling enough results. For instance, thoughout the first half of the twentieth century, Britain had been the European country most favoured by US companies for the location of direct investment. In 1950 the total value of such investment in the UK was one and a half times that of the initial Six members of the Community. By 1966 this ratio had been reversed, with the Six accounting for one and a half times as much US direct investment as the UK. Also, the switch from Britain to the EEC dated from 1958, i.e. the first year in which the new Community came into operation.

This change in focus was not unconnected with the relative growth rates of the Six and Britain. In fact the GNP growth of the British economy averaged some 2.5 per cent a year through the whole period, while Community growth averaged over 5 per cent in the decade and a half from 1950. In addition, the bulk of US direct investment went to the 'super growth' economy of West Germany over this period. A study cited in the unpublished Commission report on multinationals showed that 48 per cent of a wide sample of companies gave the opening of the EEC as the main reason for their locating new ventures in the Six rather than elsewhere in Europe. In other words, they were attracted by the Community's intention to proceed not only with a tariff-free internal market, such as was paralleled by EFTA, but also to introduce legislation to harmonise conditions in the markets of the member states.[5] Such an EEC 'pull effect' was corroborated by Bela Balassa in an article published in the mid-1960s.[6]

While US multinational companies were pulled to the EEC as a whole, and to West Germany in particular, national companies in the member states were initially slow to undertake joint ventures or mergers outside their own economies. The figures represent an indirect indictment — at least on its own terms — of the failure to achieve a Community common policy for mergers, as outlined in Chapter 3. Between 1961 and 1969 there were 257 mergers or takeovers between firms in different member countries, against 1861 mergers between firms in the same country. By contrast there were 820 mergers or takeovers between firms in member countires and non-member countries, especially US firms.[7] One result of EEC integration on company structure appeared to have been a reinforcing of defensive mergers between firms within member countries, and an offensive penetration of the Community economy by US firms which bought up or merged with member firms. Certainly the dynamism of US capital's penetration of the EEC during this period seemed marked and visible, with American firms frequently gaining preferential 'incentives' and premier sites in the more developed metropolitan regions of the Community.

The Non-American Challenge

Granted such phenomena, it may not appear surprising that Jean-Jacques Servan-Schreiber opened his book *The American Challenge* by claiming: 'fifteen years from now the world's third greatest industrial power, just after the United States and Russia, might not be Europe, but *American industry in Europe*. Already, in the ninth year of the Common Market, this European market is basically American in organisation'.[8] With a political journalist's panache, Servan-Schreiber also touched sensitive areas in claiming that nine-tenths of American investment was financed from European sources, and that innovation by US companies in Europe was frequently based on technical breakthrough by European laboratories.

However, while there is little doubt that direct US investment in the West Europe in the 1960s was encouraged by the opening of the EEC, it is strongly arguable that Servan-Schreiber fell for a statistical illusion in his claims on American multinational capital. In practice, statistics on the activity of US firms abroad were more readily available at the time than figures on European business and its own multinational spread.

The Servan-Schreiber thesis has been challenged on a comprehensive basis by Robert Rowthorn and Stephen Hymer, first in an article and later in a monograph.[9] Rowthorn and Hymer argued that the gap between

American and Continental European companies had not in fact changed much in recent years and that size alone, stressed by Servan-Schreiber, was not especially beneficial to growth. At least, between 1957 and 1963, or the six years following the signature of the Rome Treaty, Continental European firms grew much faster than American firms. They increased their share of *Fortune's* top 200 industrial companies from 30 to 41, while the number of Americans fell from 135 to 123. In 1969 there were 39 Continentals among the top 200 firms, against 128 Americans. But, as they comment, 'this slight improvement in the relative position of the Americans was nowhere near enough to compensate for their slow growth in the earlier period'.[10]

Rowthorn and Hymer did identify an 'American challenge' to European firms in some industries including electricals, and, to a lesser extent, engineering, during the period 1962–7. But they draw attention to the fact that in key 'modern' industries such as chemicals, oil and motor vehicles, there was no American lead in 1962–7, and in some cases there appeared to be a European lead. Also, when they looked at very large firms in the electrical industry the American superiority in growth was very much reduced. They stress that the key phenomenon of the 1960s was not so much the spread of US multinational capital, as the multinationalisation of capital in general. As they put it:

> international trade and investment have weakened the links binding firms to their national economies. Overseas sales, and to a lesser extent overseas production, now account for a substantial proportion of the total output of firms. This process of outward expansion has, however, been a two-way affair in which the firms of each industrial country have also lost part of their domestic economy to foreigners. The process has been one of inter-penetration.[11]

While the Rowthorn and Hymer study focused on the Continental European countries, a later analysis by Jacquemin and Lichtbuer paid more attention to the relative growth of British and Continental big business. They, too, were able to take their evidence into the 1970s. What they found was both a marked trend to monopoly power, and that Continental European firms were catching up with the initially more monopolistic British industry. Using data mainly from asset ratios, they observed,

> there is a convergence between the European evolution of overall concentration and industrial concentration. The growing weight of the giant firms in the manufacturing sector as a whole is confirmed by their growing importance in each particular industry.

In general they argued that while Britain showed a size supremacy in 1962 relative to every EEC country other than Germany, 'the evolution until 1971 makes clear that all the EEC countries are catching up on

Britain'. Comparing the survival of the leaders in Britain and other EEC member countries, they show that 'the stability of the largest British and continental firms is almost perfect: 94 per cent of the 1962 top 50 remain in the 1971 top hundred'. They also show that 'the relative position of the British and EEC groups is also very stable at the top 50 level: we find an identical survival ratio and the same proportion of firms in 1962 and 1971'. Their conclusion was 'that the largest European firms are already well established at the top of the industrial pyramid and that their national industrial as well as aggregate concentration is increasing'.[12]

Jacquemin and Lichtbuer found that British firms had a higher rate of profit than EEC firms, but observed that this could follow from their lower overall rate of growth. In other words, EEC firms could be maximising growth rather than declared profits, and retaining a higher proportion of income to finance future investment. But they also admitted that one possible reason was the already substantial expansion of British firms into the Continental EEC markets through direct investment (multinational operation). What they did not consider was the additional possibility that British firms were able to charge higher prices and declare higher profits because of their more monopolistic hold on the UK market. In fact, by 1977, the EEC Commission was reporting that more than half of the fifty most profitable firms in the Community were British.[13]

Certainly British firms had not been standing still during the interval. An analysis by S.J. Prais shows that the top 100 British manufacturing companies increased their share of net output from around one-fifth to nearly half over the period 1950 to 1970.[14] Derek Channon has also shown that this increase was paralleled by a multinationalisation of British capital during the same period, with the number of the top 100 companies operating six or more subsidiaries abroad increasing from a one-fifth to a half over the same twenty years.[15] British figures also show that by 1970 the top 100 companies represented about half of manufacturing employment.[16] Also, of course, by implication, such companies determined half of the pricing in the munufacturing sector of the economy.

Further evidence that a multinational trend was loose in Europe during the period following the opening of the EEC is given by Lawrence Franko in a study which further challenges the Servan-Schreiber thesis.[17] Franko observes that since only a handful of enterprise in the 1960s were undertaking transnational *mergers*, 'it was sometimes thought that enterprises on the continent were becoming increasingly *national*', not least, he might have added, by an under-informed and mis-guided EEC Commission. By contrast, he argued, a closer examination of the record shows that 'multinationality has never been an exclusive characteristic of American and British enterprise'. Interwar cartelisation across frontiers was more marked than postwar mergers. But the majority of European firms went 'multinational' on a major scale after the Second World War, and especially from the mid-1950s: 'The EEC was created in 1958, and the difficult road towards abolition of intra-EEC industrial tariffs was begun . . . pro-liferation of international operations occurred during a time when the walls of the negotiable environment were crumbling'.[18]

Such a statement strikingly corroborates the French claim of 'tariff disarmament', and tends to support the previous claim that negative *integration* negates State *intervention*. But Franko's main argument is quantitative. Bearing in mind that he excludes both British and American firms, he found that in 1970 there were 85 manufacturing enterprises in Western Europe whose sales of goods exceeded S400 million. Eighty of these firms were included on *Fortune's* list of the largest 200 non-American industrial companies, while the other 5 were family enterprises or financial holdings not listed by *Fortune*. Of these firms, 29 were head-quartered in West Germany, 21 in France, 9 in Sweden, 7 in Italy, 7 in Switzerland, 6 in Belgium, 5 in the Netherlands and 1 in Luxembourg. Thus, at least, it is clear that the structure and distribution of multinational capital in West Europe at the time was not exclusively Anglo-Dutch or American.[19]

Micro-Meso-Macro Implications

It has already been shown that one of the main cases for economic integration in the EEC is the alleged reduction of monopoly power by international competition. In other words free trade in a common market is supposed to reduce the power of a national monopoly through the buyers' freedom to purchase abroad. At a minimum, such integration is supposed to change the status of a monopoly in one economy into an oligopoly in the integrated area. By the same token, it is supposed to transform national oligopolies into firms which – in the larger integrated market conform more closely to the textbook small firms of the competitive model.

But, in practice, the defence of the competitive model through international integration is not so simple. First, European big business did not wait for governments to sanction international integration before embarking on multinational operations. Second, market-sharing agreements transcend international barriers (including common external tariffs) wherever the dictates of size, technology and profits command more attention than tariff levels. Third, and most importantly, big business in Community Europe is now big enough to dominate macro-economic activity.

One could be forgiven for not grasping this big business dominance from the Commission's own published figures. For one thing, even twenty years after the foundation of the EEC, the Competition Directorate of the Commission had not established a standardised and comprehensive accounting system for concentration of economic power on a Community basis. The best it managed to undertake was the sponsoring of several partial studies, excluding particular industries and services, made by various private or para-governmental groups at the national level.[20] This gave rise to an implicit understatement of the real level of concentration in the Community, since it frequently meant counting the same multinational company, operating in different countries, as if it were a number of separate firms.

An important analysis by Gareth Locksley of the Polytechnic of Central London, has begun to put the record straight. Instead of working with a fragmented mosaic of national concentration levels, Locksley has worked from overall data for the Community. As he shows, the top 100 EEC manufacturing firms accounted for nearly three-tenths (29 per cent) of employment in the sector in 1976, while the top 100 EEC industrial firms – on a conservative estimate – represented one-third of industrial sales in the Community in the same year.[21]

These are new commanding heights in the EEC economy. For one thing, when literally a few dozen companies represent so large a share of output, they both dominate direct pricing in the area of the market which they control, and indirectly act as price leaders for other smaller companies (as will be elaborated later). For another, manufacturing firms represent the main regionally mobile enterprise within any economy, since mining is geologically tied down to specific areas, and since transport, water and power distribution – like personal services – are geographically specific. Also, while no concentration study has yet analysed the share of total EEC trade commanded by a given number of firms, national studies indicate that this is much higher than output concentration. For instance, in the UK, while 100 companies in the early 1970s represented about half of net output, only 31 firms represented 40 per cent of visible export trade.[22]

It is in such a context that the new overall figures on industrial concentration are of the first importance for both theory and policy in international integration. In practice, while literally hundreds of thousands of small firms in the EEC conform with some of the main features of the competitive micro-economic model, a few dozen giant companies now dominate macro-economic performance in the Community. This economic structure of monopolistic, multinational enterprise can meaningfully be conceived as different in power and performance from the classic model of small-scale national enterprise on which conventional integration theory and the Community competition policy is still based. It constitutes a new *meso*-economic sector (Greek: *mesos* = intermediate) in between the micro-economic enterprise of the conventional models (Greek: *micros* = small) and the macro-economic level of aggregate economic performace and overall government policies (Greek: *macros* = large).

In essential respects, the dynamics of the trend of the new meso-economic power corroborate elements in Marx's analysis of the trend to monopoly in Volume I of *Capital*. This certainly includes the theory of unequal competition between big and small firms, and the extent to which large-scale production reduces the costs of big firms relative to those of small ones. On the other hand, Marx underestimated the extent to which the development of entirely new industries and services could – for long periods – prevent a fall in aggregate demand in capitalist systems. He also wrote well before the modern capitalist state became a big-time spender in its own right, with the power to influence aggregate demand levels. By and large, despite protests to the contrary, big business in the meso-economic sector was the main beneficiary of this rise in public spending. In literal terms, it had the lion's market share, and gained the dominant share of public spending.

With the economic crisis of the 1970s, aggravated when governments slammed on the brakes in overreaction to the OPEC oil price rises, big business has defended itself by claiming a profits crisis, while in fact raising prices to compensate for its fallen demand through sales, thus defending their own cash flow. The European Community endorsed governments which pulled labour, rather than capital into line, with a combination of incomes policies and deflation. They sought to recover by cutting costs, as if their national economies were just big companies, rather than to reflate demand and ensure price reduction through a combination of lowered unit costs and price controls.

There is a striking contrast between this new meso-economic phenomenon with the prewar situation when most business conformed to the competitive micro-economic model. In the 1930s, falling demand was associated with falling prices, in absolute terms. Now, faced with a new stagflation, we are suffering the reverse. If, in reality, the new meso-economic power meant competition between big firms to serve the consumer through lower prices, much would remain of the competitive model. By the same token, much would remain of the competitive assumptions of liberal capitalist theory on economic integration.

Price competition is crucial to the competitive model of capitalist integration in key respects. For instance, according to the conventional theory of micro-economics, firms are supposed to be price takers rather than price makers. In other words, while a monopolist with a total control of an industry is in a position to raise prices indefinitely, or make prices irrespective of the consumer's interests. By contrast, the small firms of the competitive model – crucial to trade and tariff theory – are supposed to *take* the prices determined by the free choice of a consumer between competing enterprises.

Monopoly Power and Inflation

The new trend towards bigger business has broken down this assumption that consumers are sovereign and producers their servants. In practice the larger enterprises tend to act collectively like a single monopolist. In testbook terms they are oligopolists rather than monopolists. In other words, like oligarchs, they share power between a few firms rather than concentrating it in the hands of a monopolist. Oligopoly comes in different forms and sizes. Some oligopolistic industries are highly concentrated, while the market share of others is more dispersed. In pricing terms, oligopolistic competition also shows varying degrees of stability or instability. Sometimes an ambitious enterprise will break the cosiness of shared monopoly and reduce prices. But in general, such leadership in reducing prices is an exception to the rule of upwards price leadership. The reasons are simple enough. Price competition is unstable. Once it has started there is no way of saying where it may end. The leading firms may end up with price levels which make them all losers relative to the initial price position.

In highly concentrated industries, a few firms may control so large a share of the market that they compete relatively little to introduce new products or processes at the kind of rate which would fully transfer the gains from new technology to the consumer. But in less-concentrated industries the degree of competition in such non-price areas can be real enough. The irony lies in the fact that, in order to finance it, the consumer pays in the long run through an average rate of price increase which both lowers real purchasing power and acts as a deterrent to purchase itself. Thus the rate of price inflation which benefits leading firms in the short-run, acts over the longer-run in such a way as to reduce their volume of sales and profits, and also national output. Estimates of the costs of forgone output and consumer welfare in the United States by Scherer and Shepherd have put the national cost as high as 6 per cent of GNP.[23]

There are further reasons for a long-term trend to monopoly to be associated with a trend to inflation. For one thing, big firms have to live with small firms so long as the nation state or international agencies pursue vigorous competition policies. Big firms tend to have lower costs then small firms, through either or both larger scale production and greater bargaining power with suppliers of goods and finance. If the firms passed on these cost savings in the form of lower prices they would cause havoc for the thousands of small firms which are crowding into the lower part of national markets. They would squeeze their profits and throw them into crisis independently of any profits squeeze which may be caused for the smaller companies through union bargaining. As a result, big firms tend to set prices at a constantly increasing level. This both suits their own profit performance (higher than average), and by and large keeps small firms quiet.[24] Small firms can turn over with lower or more normal profits in line with those they have traditionally earned, and therefore tend not to press anti-monopoly evidence into the hands of the competition agencies, whether in London, Washington or Brussels.

In addition, big firms are price leaders because of their relative market power. They set the pace for shared monopoly among a few firms by virtue of their size and market dominance. This means that if a major firm in an industry sets the pace with a new and higher price level, a smaller firm will oppose it at its own peril if it keeps prices at the previous level in an attempt to increase its market share. Such competitive behaviour can prompt counter-action by the price leader, who can set prices below the initial level for a temporary period in such a way as to squeeze the challenger's profits, or even eliminate him from the market.[25]

Strikingly, the EEC Commission has underplayed both the monopoly trend in the Community and the major implications which it represents for the role of the price mechanism in resource allocation. This emerges from the opaqueness with which it presents the results of its own studies on concentration.

But it also emerges from the failure to properly translate a key admission of the inflationary power of monopoly enterprise into the German edition of the *Fifth Report on Competition Policy* (April 1976). In the introduction to the report the Commission admits that 'inflation is particularly rife in concentrated industries in Member States'. This is, however, virtually a throwaway remark in the second to last paragraph of the introduction to the English edition.

Further, on the point of translation. The above statement in the English (and French) texts,[26] which admit — however briefly — the inflationary impact of big business, disappears in the German version, which reads: 'the significance of these studies will be reinforced by the inflationary tendencies in the Member States'.

It would be charitable to imagine that this was a simple mistranslation. But on internal Commission evidence it appears that it was not. As already indicated in Chapter 2, a similar disingenuousness was to meet the 1976 report of a Study Group on Structural Problems of Inflation, which argued a similar case to that developed in this chapter. Despite the fact that it was chaired by Robert Maldague, the Head of the Belgian National Plan, and also Chairman of the Medium-Term Economic Policy Committee of the Community, its recommendations — like the analysis of the 1968 report on multinational companies — were ignored by the Commission, and steps were taken to restrict its circulation both inside and outside the Commission.[27] According to the Commission, it seems we should have a directly elected European Assembly, but not one armed with sufficient ammunition to challenge the rules of the game established by an out-dated and backward-looking Rome Treaty. After all, with such ammunition, truth might out, and orthodox defences fall.

If fact, of course, the analysis of inflation is crucial to the whole strategy of Western European governments, based as it is at present on the assumption *not* that monopoly power is the key to the current inflation, but that wages and public spending are the main inflationary factors. By implication, if monopoly power is statistically identifiable as associated with inflation, industry by industry, then the whole force of Community policy should be thrown into restraining monopoly price increases and making monopoly power accountable to the public authorities and society.

Superficially, it might be thought that the evidence on the monopoly and multinational trend in the Community would encourage the Commission to advocate a joint international response to the problems posed by the new power-structures of big business. After all, in political discussion, one of the strongest arguments made by advocates of Community action is that multinational capital has already eroded or undermined national sovereignty.

Certainly, the argument itself is strong. There are a variety of ways in which multinational capital – or the international dimension of big business power – can and does erode the power of the conventional national armoury in economic affairs. However, as already indicated in the previous chapter, the dominant factors in Community policies are negative in character, enlarging the sphere and scope of private enterprise rather than restraining it. Moreover, while the Commission, following the Rome Treaty, admits the possibility of problems from abuse of competition and 'dominant' market positions, it has already been shown that it has rarely tamed the pretensions of a multinational company. It is worth identifying the new range of these problems, and their implications for the uncommonly biased policies of the Community to date with regard to big business, not least since the problems which they pose – for economic integration – were in part identified by the unpublished report on multinationals which the Commission itself sponsored more than ten years ago.[28]

Trade, Transfers and Exchange

First, as admitted by EEC Commission officials in the Competition Directorate – but scarcely highlighted in official Commission policy – multinational companies can charge themselves high import prices from subsidiaries abroad in excess of the price which would be charged under competitive international trade. In other words, while the import price in international trade might amount to £x, of x francs, or whatever currency, the multinational will charge itself x plus y per cent from a foreign subsidiary. This practice (i) reduces the declared profits of the national branch of the multinational while raising the profits of the foreign branch, with the transaction frequently passing through a holding company in a foreign tax haven; (ii) it thereby reduces the tax paid by the multinational and erodes the tax resources for social expenditure available to the government; (iii) it artificially raises the value of imports over and above the price which would have been paid under competitive international trade conditions.

It is important to stress that this triple-effect in no way depends on the existence of separate national currencies. Nor, therefore, would it be abolished by the establishment of a single European currency. It partly depends on the existence of the same company in different countries, i.e. the multinational phenomenon, and the ability of such companies to determine – at present – virtually what prices they please on trade between subsidiaries in different countries. But it is also operated by big business in internal trade between subsidiaries in the same country or currency area, i.e. the big multi-divisional, multi-company and multi-plant companies which now constitute the meso-economic sector. Multinational transfer pricing is the flagrant international dimension of the problem. As Ugo Piccione pointed out in the unpublished report on multinationals submitted to the Commission, it also involves tax havens which the present EEC clearly does not attempt to 'integrate' under its competition policies, for instance Switzerland.[29]

Furthermore, multinational companies not only can damage the domestic balance of payments through inflating imports in order to transfer profits abroad, but also tend to erode the effectiveness of devaluation or a downwards floating of the currency as an instrument of increasing the foreign price competitiveness of exports. The reasons here are simpler but still important. Multinational companies frequently produce and sell substituable products in different countries. Market security is important inasmuch as it enables them to plan the large-scale investments which are involved in a given product range over several years. They therefore tend to reduce international competition between their own subsidiaries to peripheral areas of the market. Car firms operating in several countries will allow imports from their subsidiaries abroad, but frequently at higher cost than their domestic substitutes. When a national currency is devalued, they will not normally reflect the full decrease in the foreign price of exports in their sales abroad for fear of undermining their production and sales in that country.[30]

One of the current EEC Commissioners, Christopher Tugendhat, in the halcyon days of his journalistic freedom, stressed just such a qualification of exchange rates changes. In a series of company studies of multinationals through Western Europe, he illustrated that many firms determined prices in trade on the basis, not of exchange rates, but of sheer capacity utilisation. He instances the Swedish ball-bearing and machinery firm SKF, which fully realises that cost and feasible profit depend very much on the extent to which investment capacity is used in the individual plant. If it altered the volume of production in one country in response to an exchange rate change, it would thereby underutilise capacity in another country. By and large, therefore, it ignores actual exchange rate changes — except to some extent for trends over the very long term — and relies mainly on the criterion of plant and capacity utilisation in its international resource allocation.[31]

Christopher Tugendhat's realism is in striking contrast with the illusory pursuit of monetary union as the answer to Europe's economic problem, as instanced by the other — and senior — British Commissioner at the time of writing: Roy Jenkins. Mr Jenkins seems to think that Europe is in an economic crisis of stagnant investment and several million unemployed because of monetary instability and constantly changing exchange rates. In his view, it seems, such exchange rate changes are the straw which broke the back of overburdened managers. Thus, apparently, they gave up unequal struggle and stopped investing or creating jobs. In reality, however, the plain fact is that management will lose its prerogative to manage if it invests for markets which do not exist. The problem of Europe's current economic crisis is not exchange rates, which scarcely affect big business except to the extent to which they can gain from them through appropriate leading and lagging of payments, or pure speculation. The problem is lack of effective demand, partly though consumer saturation, partly through overinvestment, and substantially through public expenditure cuts undertaken by Community governments in overreaction to the OPEC oil price rises since 1973.

Relation to Regional Policy
In addition, multinational companies undermine the effectiveness of both sticks and carrots in regional policies, whether these are pursued by national governments or by the European Community. For instance, the biggest stick in European regional policy is the British policy of Industrial Development Certificates. Nominally, this is a policy which requires any company undertaking a factory expansion above x square feet to apply for a development certificate. In principle, such certificates are not granted to those firms which, in the opinion of government officials, could locate new plant in the more backward regions and areas of the national economy. Therefore, in principle again, the firms which cannot get a certificate to expand in the more developed regions will locate the expansion in the less developed ones.

In practice, multinational companies can prevent this sanction largely at choice through threatening that they will go abroad if not allowed a certificate to expand in the area of their choice. For example, IBM wanted to expand at Havant, which is one of the more developed areas in the highly developed South of England. When told by the government that an industrial development certificate for such expansion would not be forthcoming, it replied that if one was not granted it would locate the expansion outside Britain altogether. The government therefore gave it an IDC to expand at Havant despite the fact that this undermined the policy of state control over the regional location of big firms.[32]

In effect, because they can locate multinationally, big firms can refuse to go multi-regional. But this is only part of the story. Going multinational in relatively labour-intensive industry, of the kind most suitable for creating jobs in problem regions and areas, gives big business in the meso-economic sector gains of such a size as to dwarf even massive regional incentives in developed countries. As the Burroughs Company submitted in evidence to the Expenditure Committee of the House of Commons, 'along with all other companies, [it was] increasingly locating in Taiwan, Brazil, Mexico, The Philippines and Hong Kong, where the cost of labour is very low'. When asked how low, the financial director of Burroughs replied that such foreign labour costs were about a quarter of those in Britain, and agreed with a member of the committee that a regional wage incentive (employment premium) 'would have to be very substantial' to locate in Britain.[33]

Indeed it would, since the government — or the European Community —

would have to subsidise up to 75 per cent of wages simply to equalise the difference in labour costs. And this does not take account of the massive gains which multinational companies can secure through transfer-pricing, or their gains on the capital account from going multinational outside Europe rather than multi-regional within Europe. These can easily total several times the percentage capital gain from state grants and preferential loans on investment in problem regions and areas. Under such conditions, perversely enough, leading companies in the meso-economic sector actually cannot afford to accept national or Community subsidy on location in problem regions and areas because they are so much lower than the gains from going multinational into the Third World tax and union havens.[34]

The implications for Community regional policy are clear enough. The multinational phenomenon, spanning not only countries but continents, undermines the effectiveness of a Regional Fund based on the assumption of location within only a Western European area. The phenomenon basically explains why the bulk of grants and assistance from the EEC's Regional Fund to date has gone to infrastructure and fixed investment projects rather than regionally mobile manufacturing industry. The leading companies in the meso-economic sector, whose location pattern dominates the fortunes of Community regional policy, are not subject to the pull effect of its incentives, and are pulled abroad by the imperative of taking advantage of lower labour costs in un-unionised and basically un-free countries. Donning their seven league boots, they bypass Europe's problem regions.[35]

Big Business and Monetary Union

As indicated earlier, one reason for claiming that monetary union is irrelevant lies in the fact that such integration has already been substantially achieved, by big business in the Community, in those areas where it needs it most: capital markets. In this respect the rise of the Eurodollar and Eurobond markets has achieved through the market mechanism what the Commission and Community institutions have failed to establish on target through common policies.[36]

Yet such integrated capital markets, aflow with funds through the 1970s, have not managed to overcome either the cyclical or the structural aspects of the current crisis precisely because enterprise lacks certainty of either short- or longer-term demand sufficient to cover new investment capacity. There is also, of course, the further question of public accountability and control of the finance capital markets of the Eurodollar and Eurobond type. But neither the problems nor prospects of such control are necessarily linked with the monetary integration of national currencies.[37]

On the currency side, the desirability of monetary union is open to serious question on other grounds. One is whether the private corporate sector actually needs it for its own operating efficiency and confidence *as such*, rather than wants it because such a single currency area in a federal framework would tend to lock the economies of Western Europe into a predominantly capitalist bloc, posing an additional obstacle to parties of the Left with radical programmes in individual Community countries.

Hitherto, there have also been conventional Keynesian arguments against a single-currency area, associated in Britain in particular with Nicholas Kaldor, which have run largely as follows.[38] Independent currencies give nation-states the capacity through exchange rate changes to define terms of trade which can make their exports competitive abroad, thus making possible a potential expansion of export trade and a protection of the domestic employment level. This argument looks relatively unconvincing after more than a decade of attempts to achieve 'export-led' growth in the UK economy, but its principles themselves have been qualified over the last twenty years through the dramatic multinationalisation of capital in both Britain and the rest of the European Community. As already stressed, big business is now increasingly its own competitor in other European countries, in the sense of operating subsidiaries in more than one country. Therefore, if it followed through a devaluation with lowered export prices to a market where it was already producing and selling, it would be undercutting its own prices abroad, with a net loss in cash flow and a likely retaliation from other big league companies.

In principle smaller-scale national enterprise could follow through a devaluation with lower foreign prices and thereby gain in export markets in other European countries. But the trend to unequal structures on the supply side of industry through the Community has now resulted in a dualism between big-league multinationals and small-league national capital. Few smaller firms at the national level are so rash as to engage in price competition with multinational leaders, through following through devaluation, when the leaders can retaliate by setting prices at a level which would effectively eliminate them from the market, or subject them to takeover offers on terms which they 'cannot afford to refuse'.

Such a counter-argument is consistent with the evidence from two major studies of the export pricing of British business since the 1967 devaluation. Both show that very few firms — big or small — follow through devaluation in the manner anticipated by textbook models of international trade and pricing.[39] Superficially, this could be taken to mean that the case against monetary union is weakened on Keynesian grounds. Partially, this would be correct enough, but in other respects on Keynesian grounds, the case still holds within the context in which monetary union is being proposed in the Community to date: i.e. deflationary monetarism and the denial of the primacy of public rather than private allocation of resources. For the reasons already given, the European economy cannot recover the old postwar model of growth simply by establishing measure to recreate business confidence. As Keynes himself stressed incentives to such confidence on the supply side are futile unless matched by intervention and mangement of an expanding aggregate demand.[40] And even Keynes anticipated that such a match of public macro demand management and private control of micro supply would not suffice to overcome an investment slump within twenty to twenty-five years.

A key case for maintaining independent currencies is not the capacity to devalue under uncontrolled *private* decision-making, but the capacity to establish *public* control over such strategic variables as pricing in domestic and international trade, investment allocation, job distribution, etc.

The British experience in this sense is relevant in a wider European context. If the Labour Government in Britain had taken its own seriously its own Party's programme for the 1970s, it would have introduced tripartite Planning Agreements in the big-business sector which dominates export

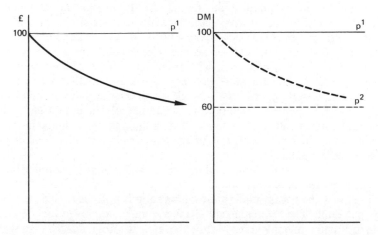

Fig. 4.1 *Multinational undermining of international exchange rate changes*

As illustrated in Fig. 4.1 if a multinational producing in both Britain and Germany reduces export prices to the German market by 40 per cent following an effective devaluation of that magnitude, it would cause price competition with itself abroad (p^1 to p^2). Thus if General Motors reduced export prices on Vauxhalls to Germany, it would cause a similar price reduction on competitive Opels in Germany. Thus price stays at p^1. A 40 per cent devaluation would mean the same sterling receipts for GM (UK) per car exported to Germany, but undermine the cash flow and profits of Opels and GM (Germany). Therefore either the multinational does not export at all (as is the case for virtual non-exports of Vauxhalls) or does not respond through reduced prices to devaluation. Perversely, partly through product differences, GM in fact exports Opels to Britain despite revaluation of the DM (thus contradicting the rationale of the old style devaluation argument).

trade. Such controls could have pressured the 31 meso-economic enterprises which account for two-fifths of visible exports, or the 75 firms
representing half such trade, to follow through devaluation with lowered
prices in key export markets.[41] Similarly, public policies backing smaller
firms in foreign markets where they experienced retaliatory 'elimination'
pricing by established and dominant companies could have been pursued
both at the national level and even − conceivably − through the use of the
Community's own Treaty provisions on the abuse of competition.

A related more general case for maintaining independent currencies, at
least in countries within the Community which approach a meaningful
'optimum currency area' in Mundell's sense,[42] is both ideological and political. Monetary union undertaken in the context of *monetarism*, com-
bining an attack on wages, public spending and public enterprise on
Friedman lines[43] would not only inhibit sustained medium-term reflation
of demand in the Community, but would also deprive individual member
countries and societies of the chance readily to change their model of
development, and elect governments in a position to pursue an independent
social and economic strategy for change. Conceivably, of course, such a
government in such a country could disengage from the single common
currency, and do so in a more meaningful sense than Eire *vis-à-vis* the
British pound sterling. But the struggle to disengage, even in countries
bigger than Eire (which certainly does not approach the conditions of an
'optimum currency area'), would be difficult enough in itself, and more so
for a government whose independent currency could be under pressure because of radical policies.

Above all, monetary union, like money itself, is not neutral. Under
capitalism its mechanisms would reinforce the strong and disadvantage the
weak. This is the background to the Community's policies for a Social and
Regional Fund. The former largely retrains some unemployed for the prospects of further unemployment, while the latter has not managed to prevent
a widening of the disparities between the rich and poor regions of Western
Europe during the decade of the 1970s in which it was introduced. If the
Community is to transcend such a situation, even on its own terms, it will
need more than the fig leaf of a common money to disguise the nakedness
of its policies for economic union.

NOTES

1. See *inter alia* Constantine Vaitsos, *Intercountry Income Distribution
and Transnational Enterprises* (Oxford University Press, 1974) and John
Dunning (ed.), *The Multinational Enterprise* (Allen & Unwin, 1975).
2. See further Wayland Kennet, Larry Whitty and Stuart Holland, *Sovereignty and Multinational Companies* (Fabian Society, 1971).
3. See further Raymond Vernon, *Big Business and the State*, op. cit.,
chs 1 and 2.

4. EEC Commission, *Les causes du développment récent des investisse-ments en provenance des pays tiers en Europe*, (cyclostyle) (Brussels: Dec. 1969).

5. EEC Commission, ibid.

6. Bela Balassa, 'American Direct Investment in the Common Market', *Banca Nazionale del Lavoro Quarterly Review* (June 1966).

7. EEC Commission, *Industrial Policy in the Community*, (Memorandum to the Council) (1970) p. 92.

8. Jean-Jacques Servan-Schreiber, *The American Challenge*, Harmonds-worth: (Penguin, 1969) first published as *Le Défie Americain* (Editions

9. Robert Rowthorn and Stephen Hymer, *The Multinational Corporation: the Non-American Challenge*, in C. P. Kindleberger (ed.), *The International Corporation* (Harvard University Press, 1970) and *International Big Business 1957–67*, Department of Applied Economics Occasional Paper no. 24 (Cambridge University Press, 1971).

10. Rowthorn and Hymer, *International Big Business*, ibid., p. 2.

11. Rowthorn and Hymer, ibid., pp. 84–5.

12. A. Jacquemin and M. Cardon de Lichtbuer, 'Size, Structure, Stability and Performance of the Largest British and EEC Firms', *European Economic Review*, December 1973.

13. Jacquemin and Cardon de Lichtbuer, ibid, and EEC Commission, *Sixth Report on Competition Policy* (Brussels: 1977) p. 164.

14. S. J. Praise, *The Evolution of Giant Firms in Britain*, (National Institute of Economic and Social Research and Cambridge University Press, 1976).

15. Derek Channon, *The Strategy and Structure of British Enterprise* (Macmillan, 1973).

16. *Department of Employment Gazette*, (HMSO, Feb. 1976).

17. Lawrence Franko, *The European Multinatonals* (Harper & Row, 1976).

18. Ibid., ch. 1 and p. 98.

19. Ibid., p. 3 and chart 1.1.

20. See European Communities, Commission, *Fifth and Sixth Reports on Competition Policy*, 1976 and 1977, part 3.

21. Gareth Locksley, 'Big Business in the EEC', *Cambridge Journal of Economics* (1979).

22. Department of Trade and Industry, *Export Concentration*, (HMSO, Apr. 1974).

23. Cf. F. M. Scherer, *Industrial Market Structures and Economic Performance* (1970) and W. Shepherd, *Market Power and Economic Welfare (1970)*.

24. Cf. Edith Penrose, *The Theory of the Growth of the Firm* (1959).

25. Paolo Sylos Labini, *Oligopoly and Technical Progress* (1962); second revised edition 1969).

26. French translation: 'L'intéret de ces recherches est accentué par la tendence inflationiste . . . dans les secteurs concentrés des pays membres.'

27. EEC Commission, *Structural Problems of Inflation*, mimeo (1976). The analysis and recommendations of the *Maldague Report* have already appeared in much of the Continental European press, and have been published by the Agenor group as a special paper. Its essentials have also

appeared, in different form, in the final two chapters to Stuart Holland (ed.), *Crisis in Capitalist Planning*, (Blackwell, 1978).

28. EEC Commission, *Les causes du développement récent des investissements en provenance des pay tiers, etc.*

29. Such transfer-pricing has been notorious in the pharmaceutical industry, as illustrated by the Hoffman-La Roche overpricing on Librium and Valium, discovered virtually by accident — rather than as the result of systematic policies obliging big business to reveal the structure of prices on inter-subsidiary trade on a systematic basis. But pharmaceuticals are only one example of a technique which now ranges through meso-economic enterprise in modern industry. See, further, Stuart Holland, *The Socialist Challenge* (Quartet, 1975), Chapter 3; Ugo Piccione, 'Strategic operationelle des investissements américains à l'étranger', Annex 7 to EEC Commission, *Les causes du dévelopment récent des investissements, etc.*, and Vaitsos, op. cit., especially ch. 4 and 6.

30. The companies in this sense become at best their 'own competitors' abroad, internalising trade within one company in different countries which previously would have been between different firms in different countries.

31. Christopher Tugendhat, *The Multinationals* (Eyre and Spottiswoode, 1971).

32. See Stuart Holland, 'Multinational Companies and a Selective Regional Policy, in *Second Report from the Expenditure Committee: Regional Development Incentives*, Minutes of Evidence (HMSO, Jan. 1974).

33. Ibid.

34. Ibid.

35. In some sectors of manufacturing, there already are indications of a return flow of investment from South-East Asia. In particular cases this reflects the political instability of the area in the 1970s. But in others, it represents the impact of technical progress, especially in some branches of electrical and electronics production. The rising technical composition of capital has now proceeded to such a stage that little labour is needed, not only in the Third World, but also in 'developed' Europe.

36. See, further, Michel Lelart, 'Comment les banques européennes creent des Eurodollars', *Le Monde*, 14 June 1977.

37. This is already admitted implicitly in much of the *Europa* currency debate, as in Giovanni Magnifico, *European Monetary Integration* (Macmillan 1978).

38. Nicholas Kaldor, 'The Dynamic Effects of the Commont Market', in Douglas Evans (ed.), *Destiny or Delusion*? (Gollancz, 1971).

39. D. C. Hague, E. Oakshott and A. Strain, *Devaluation and Pricing Decisions* (Allen & Unwin, 1974); and Peter Holmes, *Industrial Pricing Behaviour and Devaluation* (Macmillan, 1978).

40. J. M. Keynes, *The General Theory of Employment, Interest and Money*, ch. 12 (Macmillan, 1st edition 1936).

41. See *Labour's Programmes* 1973 and 1976 and the Labour Party, *International Big Business* (Transport House, 1977).

42. R. A. Mundell, 'A Theory of Optimum Currency Areas', *American Economic Review* (Nov. 1961).

43. See, *inter alia*, Milton Friedman, *From Galbraith to Economic Freedom*, IEA Institute of Economic Affairs Occasional Paper no. 49 (London, 1977).

Part Three
Class and Integration

5 Class and Elites

The conventional theory of economic integration largely neglects issues of social and economic class. In part such neglect is understandable in terms of the role of much economic theory in mystifying or obscuring the real power relations in capitalist society. This is not necessarily a conscious conspiracy by professional intellectuals. But concentration on economic techniques of analysis in social and political vacuum itself helps to obscure theoretical insight into social class and political power.

The superficial defence of such economism lies in the claim that questions of social class and political power lie in other areas of the social sciences than economics. An underlying reason may well be the process of specialisation, the division of intellectual labour, in higher education itself, which frequently alienates specialists in economics from those in politics or sociology, much as it frequently alienates teachers from the taught. In such a sense higher education still represents elements of a guild system in which a ritual apprenticeship in craft skills can act as a defence of a particular class structure.

Of course there are other reasons. Class analysis has Marxist connotations which raise issues of exploitation and power which are inconveniently disturbing to many of the élites engaged in intergration itself. Lifting the lid on class relations opens a Pandora's box of the kind which key exponents and advocates of international integration have been trying to close and bury for some time. This is closely linked with the support for the 'end of ideology' thesis in the 1950s, with its stress on social harmony rather than social conflict. The intellectual division of labour in the so-called social sciences can be more clearly understood in this context. In other words, like the conventional theory of economic integration, it assumed that separate 'sciences' themselves (economics, politics and sociology) were complementary in an objective, 'value-free' context which had transcended issues of class analysis.

The political support for European integration by social democrats, also, can be seen in the same wider perspective. Social democracy was a Marxist, class-based, international movement before the First World War. Its split from the strategy of violent revolution of the Leninist kind, and its rejection of the dictatorship of the proletariat under Stalinist horrors led to an identification of Marxist class politics with Soviet Communism, and in due course led to the rejection of class analysis itself. Internationalism remained as an ideal, and received impetus during the 1950s by the dual role of the European Communities as apparently both internationalist and democratic (in opposition to the Soviet bloc). The question whether supranationalism of the kind projected by the founding fathers of a United States of Europe was *inter*national or *supra*national remained unclear, as did the question whether the new institutional forms envisaged in EEC integration were an extension or reduction of effective democracy. But, as importantly, the rejection of class analysis restricted effective analysis of the process of European integration itself, especially in respect of the role of the nation-State and State power.

Elites versus Class

The ideologues of the politics of international integration none the less chose to stress the role played by élites and pressure groups. Ironically, as shown in this chapter, both the terms of their analysis and much of their methodology compare rather than contrast with Marxist analysis of class and power. Yet they ultimately suffer from failure to relate the role of élites to a given class structure, and to follow through or parallel the link in Marxist analysis between political superstructure and economic base. This shows in the extent to which the function of the élites is isolated at a political level, and assumes a relatively homogeneous economic substructure which is harmoniously 'integrated' via the political process. The analysis is 'dynamic' and 'functional', but in an artificial sense in which it is assumed that policies for economic integration, promoted by élites, will in turn promote integration at the superstructural level of common political institutions and policies.

A crucial *difference* between the 'functionlist' theory of political integration and Marxist analysis lies in the underlying premise of functionalism that society is basically pluralistic. Instead of a dichotomous class division between the interests of capital and labour, it is assumed that modern industrial society now is composed of a wide plurality of different interest groups, whose otherwise conflicting interests can be harmonised and served by international integration. The process is not, in itself, democratic, whatever the form of democratic institutions which may follow from it. This has been well illustrated by Haas:

> the initiation of a deliberate scheme of political unification, to be accepted by the key groups that make up a pluralistic society, does not require absolute majority support, nor need it rest on identical aims on the part of all participants. The European Coal and Steel Community was initially accepted because it offered a multitude of different advantages to different groups.[1]

In other words, it was claimed that uncommon interests could be reconciled by a common market. Behind the optimism lay the assumption that no one group was powerful enough to exact a disproportionate gain from integration, or to impose disproportionate loss on other groups.

Beneath this lay the further assumption that the nation-states concerned were 'already fragmented ideologically and socially'.[2] It is this assumed fragmentation which gives scope for élites to promote the integration of nation-states in a higher political structure. But, as Lindberg stresses, 'economic integration will lead to political integration only if it involves matters of significant concern to significant élites'.[3] It also is important, as Harrison has commented on the thesis, that 'governmental élites would be involved in the central decision-making process and increasingly identify with it'.[4] In other words, there is not so much a lack of State power, as a focus for conflict resolution in the nation-state, which is induced by élite initiatives to integrate internationally. Also, there are limits to the areas which such élites can exploit for integration. Military and defence questions are taken by Haas and Etzioni — paradoxically granted the range of integrated military alliances such as NATO — to represent low integration potential.[5]

Not surprisingly, the main potential area identified by the 'pluralists' for integration, proves to be economic. And it is here that the advocates of élite roles in integration stress links between political and economic factors, but express them in terms of 'feedback' and 'spillover' rather than political superstructure and economic base. They also argue in terms of groups such as 'business interests' rather than capital or class power. Thus Lindberg comments on the May 1960 agreement in the EEC to accelerate internal tariff abolition:

> Business circles, after initial reaction ranging from cautious support to outright hostility, had accepted the Common Market as a *fait accompli* and jumped in with almost breathtaking speed to form a network of agreements within the Six. An acceleration of the realisation of the Common Market, far from exceeding the pace desired by business groups, would only catch up with the pace they had already set . . . it was from business circles that much of the political pressure for acceleration originated.[6]

Granted the 'breathtaking speed' with which 'business interests' pressured for further integration, in contrast with the lack of pressure for integration from trades unions — most of whom stayed sceptical or hostile — it might well have been thought likely that the pluralists could have questioned just how 'fragmented ideologically and socially' the main pressure groups in integration proved to be. The facts which Lindberg chooses to cite suggest a dichotomous structure of organised capital and relatively disorganised labour. This point remains valid irrespective of fractionalisation within an individual class, as will be analysed in the next chapter. Similarly, when Haas comments on expansive integration as a process in which there is interaction between 'public and private élites pursuing similar goals' it might well have been concluded that he would follow through the analysis in more explicit terms which showed the combination of governmental élites and the self-electing élites of private capital, bound on a common venture in fulfilment of a common ideology.[7] In other words, the logical inference from the evidence suggests a mutually self-reinforcing relationship between the State superstructure and the dominant factor — capital — in the economic base or substructure of the system.

Pluralist Determinism and Dialectics

Even the best critics of pluralistic integration theory, such as Harrison, castigate Marxist analysis for its determinism. As he puts it, 'political man has defeated, historically, the Marxian prophecies based on the assumption of economic determinism'.[8] Yet, ironically, the very theories of political integration based on pluralist theory, and rejecting class analysis, are rigidly deterministic. As Haas himself has admitted, 'the determinism in the picture is almost absolute'.[9] Also, while eschewing Maxist dialectics, its method is in fact explicitly dialectical — as illustrated by Etzioni's use of the term in his title *The Dialectics of Supranational Unification.*[10]

Both the determinism and the dialectical method emerge in the concept of 'spillover', or the assumption that advances in economic integration will result in pressures for further political integration. Lindberg defines spillover in a way in which Engels himself could have approved, i.e. as a dialectical triad of thesis, antithesis and synthesis. As he puts it: 'a given action, related to a specific goal, creates a situation in which the original goal can be assured only by taking further actions, which in turn create a further condition and a need for more action, and so forth'. Haas writes of spillover effects occurring because 'policies made pursuant to an initial task and grant of power can be made real only if the task itself is expanded'. Such spillover theory graces the intuition of Jean Monnet and the founding fathers of the Community institutions that some integration will lead to more, by provoking new situations demanding a new political response.

The determinism shows in Haas's view that limited sectoral integration of the Coal and Steel Community type 'begets its own impetus towards extension to the entire economy even in the absence of specific group demands and their attendant ideologies'.[11] But it is also indirectly illustrated by the extent to which the pluralist theorists have sought recourse to economic growth analysis, fearlessly treading on ground which many economists themselves have abandoned as unsound.

Thus Deutsch, Haas and Etzioni have employed the term 'take-off', pioneered by Rostow, to describe the point at which limited initiatives in integration will achieve breakthrough to self-sustaining and self-reinforcing expansion.[12] Etzioni defines 'take-off' as taking place when 'a process has accumulated enough momentum to continue on its own: that is, without the support of non-member external units'. Deutsch and Haas define 'take-off' without reference to the support of external actors, such as the United States (as supporter of European integration in its early stages), or the rise of the super-powers as a stimulus to postwar European nation-states to combine and form their own super-power. But they stress that 'take-off' will occur at that point where the initial provocative impulse of a few enthusiasts (such as Monnet or Schumann) gives way to an integration 'which has acquired a momentum of its own'.[13]

The economism of these pluralist statements was striking. But, as markedly, it was unrelated to real factors in either the 'expansion' of the system to which Haas drew attention, or to the real dialectics involved in economic integration itself. The pluralist theory of a political dynamics of integration was developed without serious questioning of the premises of pluralist liberal economics on which it drew. Had there been such a questioning, Deutsch, Haas and Etzioni would possibly have realised that the Rostow 'take-off' theory on which they placed such reliance was heavily criticised for its assumption that economic growth was linear, smooth and homogeneous, rather than staggered, uneven, highly diverse and differentiated between firms and industries, regions and countries, and social groups and classes.[14] In key cases, where Rostow expected 'take-off' into sustained consumer-led expansion, the economies he identified 'crashed' into economic and political crisis, including the Indian sub-continent.

In short, in adopting 'take-off' theory, the pluralists made the mistake of the entrepreneur who saw only the upswing of the trade cycle and was taken for a ride. The political 'take-off' of European integration was identified as the period between the signing of the Paris and Rome Treaties. But this was followed by economic strains of adjustment in key member countries which ran into major balance of payments deficits (Italy and France). It also suffered strains of adjustment to a Common Agricultural Policy which had represented a least efficient, lowest common denominator solution dominated by a classic trade-off between France and other countries. More importantly, it never achieved the breakthrough to common industrial policies of the kind which 'spill-over' theory suggested. Proposals for economic and monetary union came off the runway, but ran into the mud of ten years' compromise on the CAP rather than 'taking-off' into the stratosphere of supranationalism.

Harrison rightly commented that 'it must be conceded, in the light of European experience, that the expectations of expansion based on spill-over were exaggerated'. As importantly, he has pointed out that initial success in achieving the Common Agricultural Policy

obscured, for the Commission at least, a clear vision of the new realities. It made proposals for supranational development, in a mood of unwarranted optimism, and so precipitated the crisis of 1965, with France boycotting all meetings of the Community until January 1966 when the French position was largely conceded at Luxembourg.[15]

In retrospect Deutsch saw the European integration movement as having

lost momentum since 1957–8, i.e. from the very years in which the Rome
Treaty was signed and the EEC established. Lindberg later concluded that
the success of a particular step in integration (such as conclusion of the
CAP) could act as a source of stress among a group of states and raise
barriers to integration.[16] In other words, one of the key theorists of the
pluralist school of integration could not fit his theory to the facts for the
main Community institution – the EEC – while another more frankly
admitted that the theory had got it wrong.

The Limits of Functionalism

The limits of pluralist élite theories of integration lie very much in the extent to which their 'functionalist' method operates in a class vacuum. They
seek to trace functional relationships by dialectical method, identifying
initiatives and response, action, reaction and interaction. But in their concern to avoid or surpass the mainstream Marxist tradition of dialectics,
they built models composed almost entirely of superstructural variables –
élites and states. They assumed that the relationships between these
political factors and the economic base were self-evident, and in particular
that states exercised effective economic power. The state became the
focus of their analysis, because pluralist theory assumed that the state was
the effective mediator of competing group interests.

Such limits of pluralist theory in the integration context reflect its
wider limits as a whole. Pluralism as a postwar orthodoxy was based substantially on the argument that the binary or dichotomous two-class
distinction of conventional Marxist theory had been superseded by a
plurality of social groups whose status and economic function was no
longer linked to a division between capital and labour.

More explicitly, commentators such as Raymond Aron and Seymour
Lipset argued that class polarisation on Marxist lines had not occurred.[17]
As a result of sustained industrial development, they claimed, the benefits of economic growth had become widely dispersed in favour of the
working class, rather than concentrated in the hands of the owners of
capital. Consequently, working people had been able to achieve increasingly middle-class standards of living, and, with them, middle-class status.
It was maintained that the rise of joint stock companies and the divorce
of ownership from control of capital had furthered the distribution of
shareholding and thereby the dilution of Marxist class theory. Social distinctions still persisted, but they amounted to *strata* rather than classes. The
theory of class division was challenged by theories of social stratification.
With the assumed transcendence of the class basis of former capitalist
society, it was argued that this society itself could no longer be meaningfully described as capitalist, rather than 'industrial' or 'post-industrial'.

In one sense it is easy enough to see why the new pluralist theories
were developed. Vulgar Marxist theories of class polarisation had not been
clearly corroborated in European practice. Crude economic determinism,

sanctioned by some mass parties of the Communist Left, had not been able to account adequately for the rise of the modern capitalist State as spender, planner, entrepreneur or social guardian. It had been challenged by rising State intervention in modern capitalism.

This is not the appropriate context for a detailed questioning whether such deterministic Marxism was in succession to Marx's own analysis, or a perversion of it. It may partly suffice to point out that Marx himself had admitted the extent to which even the limited joint stock companies of his day had qualified the basic polarised class structure of previous capitalism, and that both he and particularly Engels admitted that advances in the political strength of organised labour could yield the ends of socialism through non-violent means in some countries such as Britain.[18]

The main point is that pluralist theory substantially under estimated the scope of interrelation between economic base and social and political super-structure in Marxist analysis. By challenging the crude determinist thesis that society and politics were only the effect of basic economic relations, they overstated the power of the State – pressured by élite groups – to manage an economy which remained essentially capitalist in terms of who decided how to allocate what capital resources, where, in what proportions, employing whose labour, for whichever markets. In short, quite apart from the question whether the dispersion of share ownership actually had transformed the capital *owning* class, pluralist theory neglected the continuing reality of capitalist management's *control* over production, distribution and exchange.

Further, the determinism of pluralist integration theorists assumed that political pluralism between competing interest groups was matched by economic pluralism between competing economic groups, whether firms and industries or national economies. As in political analysis, this economic pluralism assumed that no individual group was sufficiently powerful, or likely to become so through integration, to dominate the others. Drawing, with little question, on the theory of comparative advantage and 'harmony of interests' through competition, the pluralists neglected the imbalance and disharmony characteristic of the unequal competition and uneven development stressed in Marxist economic analysis.[19]

Structures of Dominance
To evolve an analytical framework which actually aids understanding of the scope and limits of European integration, it is important to avoid determinism of both the cruder Marxist and the pluralist theories. Such a framework can be seen in terms of interrelation and interaction between five main factors in the overall power structure:

Politics, including both established parties and pressure groups.
The State, including government, the civil service, and the 'relations of force' of the state (judiciary, police and the military).

Ideology, in the sense of the power of collectively held concepts, values and ideas both shaping and shaped by reality.

Capital, in the sense of the power of management to determine what is produced, where, why, in what proportions, for whom, in what markets, at which price.

Labour, in the sense of the power of labour either through trades union organisation or spontaneously to influence the political and economic environment. (Labour's 'power' in this sense is different from the strictly economic definition of labour power in Marx's usage.)

Broadly speaking, factors 1 and 2 represent the political superstructure of the system, and factors 4 and 5 the economic sub-structure. Some Marxist analysis would place the third factor — ideology — in the super-structure, implying that ideas serve and reflect the interests of the capital which dominates the base. But, as argued here and elsewhere, ideology can more appropriately be conceived as fulfilling an intermediate role between the economic base and the political super-structure. It sometimes serves and sometimes hinders the effective representation of the interests of sections of capital and labour in the political process.

Thus the relation between politics and State power, in the super-structure, and capital and labour, in the sub-structure, tends to be mediated through the mechanisms of the prevailing ideology. In a simple sense, the former five main power factors within society can the be structured in the following way (see Fig. 5.1).

Naturally, such a representation is simple and, taken out of context, could well be subject to the scorn for base-superstructure models expressed, among others, by Edward Thompsom.[20] The base-superstructure approach has also been rejected by other theorists of the modern capitalist State

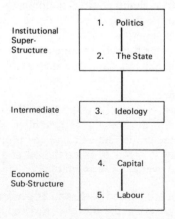

FIG. 5.1   *Base, super-structure and intermediate ideology*

such as Poulantzas. [21] However, it is arguable that , in their understandable concern to combat deterministic models, Thompson and Poulantzas have thrown out one of the most useful ways of conceiving and analysing power structures in capitalist society.

In particular, 'removing' ideology from the superstructure qualifies the deterministic assumption that the base directly dominates the superstructure: or, in other words, that economics dominates politics in a determinate sense. Not least, it provides a framework in which one can appreciate that ideology sometimes reflects, sometimes *refracts* and sometimes simply *distracts* (or mystifies) reality.

For instance, if the prevailing ideology of the European Community is liberal capitalist, assuming predominantly competitive national capital, when in reality the dominant economic substructure is composed of monopolistic and multinational capital, then ideology will refract reality and distract from those policies necessary for effective economic integration. This is very arguably the situation in the EEC today, with the conflict between negative and positive integration policies.

A simple, if provisional illustration can be gained by translating the main elements of Figure 5.1 to the Community level. Thus in Figure 5.2 one has a European Assembly, with virtually nil formal powers at the political level. At the level of State power, one has the relations between the Council of Ministers (representing nation States) and the Commission (assuming or claiming to assume State functions). At the intermediate level of ideology, there is a dominance of negative integration, reinforcing and serving the interests of the dominant section of capital (especially multinational enterprise). Meanwhile, labour remains predominantly national,

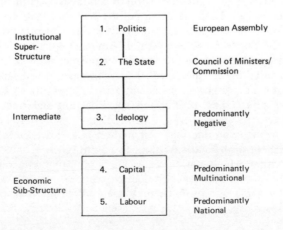

FIG. 5.2 *Base, super-structure and the EEC institutions*

calling on nation State intervention to oppose either policies of negative integration, or their negative effects in specific industries or regions (see Fig. 5.2).

Contradictions

If one is to get a better grasp of the role of élites and classes in both the political-economic process and the specific context of international integration, it is important to relate the analysis of structures, dominance and ideology in the above sense to that of 'contradiction'.

Again, if employed in a deterministic and ritual sense, the concept of contradiction can be abused. This is apart from the fact that it tends simply to confuse many of those raised in the empiricist tradition. But it can be an important explanatory factor in understanding, for instance, why a political-economic institution such as the EEC does not simply progress from one 'stage' of integration to another in a smooth and linear manner.

Clearly some of the pluralist-functionalist schools of integration analysis appreciate that such progression does not occur, and try to employ their own variant of dialectics to grasp why it does not. But their analysis is limited substantially because they assume away class factors in an élite-pressure group framework. Also, by stressing élite roles in the *control* of capital, they neglect the extent to which 'élite perceptions' on political issues such as European integration can be contradicted by the class role which the same élites need to pursue in preserving or extending their own section of capital. This can be reflected in contradictions between the posture of a particular nation-state in nominally supporting further integration, versus its actual role in preventing or frustrating it. In turn, it also relates to the concept of dominance.

For instance, if the dominant form of capital as a factor of production, distribution and exchange is monopolistic and multinational, with price-making power for big business and with capital investment substituting for trade, then meso-economic capital dominates micro capital in the area which is being integrated. But the predominant policies which nation-states may be undertaking to 'integrate' their economies have been liberal capitalist, assuming a pluralistic, price competitive structure of small national firms, who adjust their production specialisation and trade patterns to tariff changes. In effect, there is a contradiction between the nature of the dominant form of production, distribution and exchange in the area (or between the form of Factor 4 in our five-point schema) and the dominant ideology within which nation-states are attempting integration policies (i.e. Factors 3 and 2). The stimulus to monopoly trends in big business provided by tariff abolition thereby contradicts the aim of integration policies in as much as the latter was intended to increase pluralistic competition between firms in the integrated area.

There also is the extent to which competition with dominant multinational capital throws smaller national firms into a degree of crisis, since they cannot compete in productivity and costs with the bigger firms. This in turn prompts national governments to intervene and salvage smaller-scale enterprise (or larger firms in traditional industries, where these firms have failed to modernise and increase scale economies under private ownership). In this sense, even within the fourth of the five main factors – capital itself – contradictions emerge between big and small-scale, or meso- and micro-economic enterprise. These different forms of capital are unequally placed in relation to the integration process. Small-scale or traditional industry therefore stimulates a reaction from Factor 2 (State power), under pressure from international competition and through pressure groups such as industry federations and trade unions.

To respond to the problem, individual nation-states may increase intervention to support firms and industries over and above the level which they would have found necessary with the maintenance of tariffs, substituting *direct* intervention for the *indirect* intervention of tariff policy. At the same time they will be likely to show scepticism or hostility to Community attempts to reduce state aid and 'harmonise' competitive conditions in the integrated area. They also may oppose real measures for advance to higher stages of integration on 'harmonised' liberal capitalist premises, such as economic union. In such a way, related to the contradictions within the economic base, and within different sections of capital as a whole, a feedback from base to superstructure results in a brake on further integration.

The role of élites and classes can be better understood in such a framework than in the superstructural limbo of pluralist theory. For instance, the ideology of international or supranational integration, as formulated and advocated by the federalists in the 1950s, can be seen in one sense as a historically progressive force, seeking to transcend the nationalism of State power in the interwar period. But it also can be seen in a reverse or contradictory sense as a historical hangover from the past, or the best postwar method of avoiding the last war.

'Élite perceptions' of the case for European integration ignored the problems of conflicts between different sections of capital by assuming away the identity of capital as a power factor in the new consensus of 'industrial' rather than 'capitalist' society. While they may have been right enough in holding that overall conflict between capital and labour had been reduced, they did so by misreading the extent to which the consensus of the period of the postwar boom was dependent on the boom itself, and the reduction of the impact of uneven development (structural, social and spatial) to secondary importance so long as real income gains for most labour were sustained. Similarly, their 'surprise' at the speed with which capital welcomed the creation of the EEC (Lindberg's 'breathtaking' reaction of 'business interests'), neglected the fact that it was mainly the large scale capitalist groups which stood to benefit from such integration through a larger tariff free market, and who responded with such enthusiasm.

Smaller – scale capital tightened its claims on the nation-state for non-tariff protection via subsidy, public purchasing preferences and other forms of direct intervention.

Clearly, this indicates that a base-superstructure approach to the analysis of economic integration is complex rather than simple, with various potential or actual combinations between the main power factors as identified, i.e. politics and the state at the 'superstructural' level, the intermediate function of ideology, and the economic 'base' of capital and labour. There is no simple determinism in the interaction of these factors. The interactions are not simply between base and superstructure, but between them, within them and within their specific constituent factors.

What this means is a clear admission that the superstructural factors of politics and state power are not merely functions of the economic base of capital and labour and their relations of production. It means admitting that politics and state power *under certain specific conditions* may be able to determine economic and social outcomes, rather than be determined by them.[22] On the other hand, it indicates the scale and range of factors which the state, or supranational institutions, must be able to dominate, neutralise, or mobilise if successful policies are to be pursued.

The potential obstacles to such success are very considerable. For instance, if one capitalist party or coalition dominates political power, it may have the explicit support of capital in a general sense, relative to anti-capitalist parties, yet not be able to resolve the contradictory interests of different sections of capital. Impasse from such contradictions is particularly probable when several states combine at the political level in an attempt at economic integration. Further, the dominant ideology by which economic reality is perceived or misconceived may suit one section of capital, but not another. For instance, in this sense, the ethos of increasing competition pervading European integration is real enough for small-versus large-scale capital, but at the same time masks the latter's real dominance of the former. To the extent that the ideology influences the manner in which policies are framed, and the way in which their implementation is tried, the ideology – including that of liberal capitalist integration – may itself become an obstacle to the policies.

NOTES

1. E. B. Haas, *The Uniting of Europe* 2nd edn, (Stanford University Press, 1968) p. xxxiii.
2. Ibid., p. xxxiii.
3. Leon Lindberg, *The Political Dynamics of European Economic Integration* (Stanford University Press, 1963) p. 94.
4. R. J. Harrison, *Europe in Question* (Allen & Unwin, 1974) p. 80.
5. The 'feedback' analysis is developed by Karl Deutsch. See, further, his *The Nerves of Government* (Glencoe, 1963); E. B. Haas, 'International

Integration: The European and the Universal Process, and A. Etzioni, 'The Dialectics of Supranational Unification', in the Anthology, *International Political Communities* (1964).
6. Lindberg, op. cit., p. 170.
7. As Harrison comments on functionalist theories of integration in general: 'The motivation and power bases of political élites (traditional ruling classes or new ruling classes) are not examined', op. cit., p. 36.
8. Ibid., p. 185.
9. Haas, op. cit. Haas later rejects teleology in the sense of social demands emerging from an economic environment. As he puts it,

'in terms of a social process based on a rational human perceptions and motives, no mere concept 'calls for' or 'needs' anything: a discrete set of group motives . . . results in a certain pattern of policy . . . and later policies may well change the environment in a wholly unintended fashion'.

(See, further, E. Haas, *International Political Communities* (Anchor, 1966) pp. 93—110, reprinted in Michael Hodges (ed), *European Integration* (Penguin, 1972).
10. Etzioni, op. cit.
11. Harrison, op. cit., p. 83.
12. W. W. Rostow, *The Stages of Economic Growth* (Oxford University Press).
13. See, further, Harrison, op. cit., pp. 86 and 185. With typical perceptiveness, Harrison comments that 'neo-functionalism might, in the last analysis, be summed up as neo-Marxian in the very loose sense that it assumes economic imperatives will impose themselves on the political arrangements of society'.
14. In effect there was too little attention given to the disequlibrium and imbalance analysis of either Myrdal or Perroux, and too casual an imbibing of neoclassical economic theory. See further, *inter alia*, Gunner Myrdal, *Economic Theory and Underdeveloped Regions* and *Asian Drama* (3 vol. edn), Penguin, 1968); or Francois Perroux, *L'Economie du XXe Siècle* Presses Universitaires de France, 1964). The Perroux approach certainly had a major influence on key French officials, who backed De Gaulle's opposition to a supranational Community on the grounds that its economic liberalism would damage French industry.
15. Harrison, op. cit., p. 87.
16. Lindberg also admitted as much for the failure of the Community's transport policy, which has devised little to date save for 'forked tariffs' restricting the range within which allegedly competitive pricing can be spread, plus the terrorisation of many urban areas through monster lorries whose reduced unit freight costs are not transferred by tax or other adjustment to compensate those who suffer from them. See, further, for Lindberg's admission, Leon Lindberg and Stuart Scheingold, *Europe's Would-Be Policy* (Prentice Hall, 1970) pp. 163—81.
17. Raymond Aron, *La Lutte des Classes* (Gallimard, 1964); for a more recent work in the European context, see, further, his *Plaidoyer pour l'Europe Decadent* (Laffont, 1977); S. M. Lipset, *Political Man* (1959).
18. See, further, Lucio Colletti, *Ideologia e Societa* (Laterza, 1975) pp. 61—5.

19. For a penetrating analysis of the myopia of the 'harmony interests' approach, see Paul Streeten, *Economic Integration* 2nd edn, (Sytthoff, 1964).
20. See, further, E. P. Thompson, *The Poverty of Theory*, (Merlin Press, 1978) p. 193 ff, especially his satirical Plates I to IV.
21. Nicos Poulantzas, *State, Power, Socialism* (New Left Books, 1978) p. 16 ff.
22. In Althusser's term (which he admits he is not particularly 'taken by') superstructural factors can 'overdetermine' the substructure or base. But the substructure and the 'economic factor' − under capitalism − will remain determinant 'in the last instance': Louis Althusser, 'Contradiction and Overdetermination', in *For Marx* (Penguin, 1969) pp. 100−1.

6 Class Role and Control

For some of the European Left, it has been commonplace to claim that the European Community is capitalist, serving the interests of one class versus another, without facing the need to face or specify the complexity of class power and class relations in contemporary capitalist society.

Part of the problem lies in an over-concentration of the basic conflict between the interests of capital as a whole and labour as a whole, without admission of the conflicts within capital and within labour caused by integration. In other words, while class conflict is essentially dichotomous, specific differences can and do occur within the two main classes in society. Another problem lies in some over-simple identification of Community Europe with monopoly capital and state monopoly capital, without admitting the extent to which European integration has in part caused problems for national capital and nation-states which in turn have obstructed further integration.

Elements of both these tendencies are reflected in the assumption that the EEC, by directly serving the expanded reproduction of capital in a larger market, will therefore succeed in achieving a federal structure or super-state, upgrading the defence of national capital to a supranational level. Despite some sophistication, such arguments tend to reflect essentially simple assumptions about the relations between the economic base of integration and the political and institutional superstructure which allegedly will reflect, accompany and serve it.

Thus Ernest Mandel had claimed that

the increasing inter-penetration of capital within the EEC, the increasing number of banks and businesses which cease to belong to this or that national capital and become the property of capitalists in all the member states, constitute the process that creates the material infrastructure for genuinely supranational *state* organs in the Common Market.

The claim is dramatic, not least since Mandel rightly adds that 'so far this process has hardly begun', and later had to admit that the EEC retreated from economic and monetary union during the 'second slump' of the 1970s, rather than responded to it by further federalism.[1]

To challenge Mandel is not to say that Community Europe never could become a super-power, but rather to argue that the constellation of forces necessary for such a power structure to emerge are more complex, and more distant, than either its enthusiasts or detractors for the most part assume. The relationships between the different specific modes of capita-list production, different social classes and different forms of state power have implications for the respective strategies of the Left and Right in Community Europe. But the implications, like the relationships themselves, are very much dialectical rather than linear, and complex rather than simple.

For instance, in terms of a simple base super-structure model, a capitalist United States of Europe would only be probable if there were clear evi-dence of a specifically European capitalist class. Inversely, a socialist Com-munity would be probable only if there were a relatively homogenous European working class. But there is neither. Both capital and labour in Europe are divided between sub-groups or sections of the main class dis-tinctions. While the main conflict of interest remains between capital and labour overall, the specific interests of sections within the main classes are related to different functions served for them by national state power, supranational institutions and international integration.

The following argument considers different functional relationships between class power (or class weakness), ideology and the state. The key relationships are meaningful objectively, rather than subjectively. They concern the working of class, mode of production and state power in the integration process irrespective of the 'opinion poll' declarations of mem-bers of those classes who may be 'pro', 'anti' or 'neutral' on a particular view of Community Europe at a particular moment. This is *not* claimed in a determinist sense that subjective views are determined by objective factors alone. It is claimed as an effort to clarify why subjective statements of support for Community Europe (or intent to advance to higher stages of integration) run into conflict with objective factors of class interest and national power which may not be clearly perceived by individuals or élites themselves.

Fractions and Strata

Poulantzas has been foremost in promoting the concept of fractions of class in the context of class dominance. His use of the term is broadly similar to what we have called sections of a particular class. Despite a high level of abstraction, his argument is relevant to the main issues in hand.

Thus Poulantzas stresses that one cannot reason in terms of a homo-genous class such as the 'bourgeoisie' without taking account of different fractions of such a class: i.e. the grand bourgeoisie, the petty bourgeoisie and the 'new' petty bourgeoisie. Nor can one simply distinguish the grand and petty bourgeoisie as big and small producers. These are divided be-tween the classic craftsmen and small traders of the 'old' petty bour-geoisie and the non-productive wage earners of the 'new' petty middle class. While he does not give examples of the latter, which is typical of the level of abstraction, one might assume that he means those in the nominally non-productive, and broad, sector of petty officialdom.[2]

Challenging the élite theorists of the pluralist models, Poulantzas stresses that such distinctions of *fractions* of the same class are different from the concept of social *strata* 'since they coincide with important economic distinctions'. He argues that it is wrong to think of the non-productive 'new' petty bourgeoisie as a 'technocracy' rather than a fraction of capital. As he puts it, 'strata, fractions and categories of class . . . always belong to a class'. On the other hand, he distinguishes 'fractions of classes' — as a substratum of social forces which are capable of becoming autonomous — from 'social groups' (*couches sociales*) such as high levels of the State administration. The former have what he calls 'pertinent' effects and the latter only 'secondary' effects.[3]

Simplifying his case, Poulantzas distinguishes the primary role of classes and fractions of classes from the secondary role of social groups, including civil servants and bureaucrats. This relates to his distinction of class relations as *power*-relations, with a primary effect on the exercise of State power, and the secondary *influence* of social groups at high levels of the State administration (or at the level of EEC bureaucracy). Importantly, he argues that State intervention is specifically designed to resolve conflicts posed by unequal development between classes and *within* them (e.g. the conflict between the interests of a national small-scale or petty bourgeoisie and a large-scale grand bourgeoisie). The state's economic role therefore does not necessarily serve the interest of a particular fraction or class, but relates to its *political* role in maintaining and exercising the overall rule of the capitalist class as a whole.[4]

Poulantzas also argues that what matters is not élites and their conflicting aims (as we have seen stressed — in the context of economic integration — by the functionalist or pluralist school), but the differences and relations *between* fractions of the capitalist class: i.e. between industrial and finance capital, monopoly and non-monopoly capital, etc.[5] In his own terms, which are not purely Gramscian, the *hegemonic* class is that class fraction which leads within a dominant group of classes. In other words, the hegemonic or dominant class (for instance, monopoly capital) is not itself either the ruling or the reigning class. If it were, it would mean that those who operate the top-state apparatus would themselves constitute a reigning class rather than, in his terms, a social group. Thus he claims that the correspondence between the interests of big capital and the state apparatus depend not on purely personal or subjective ties — such as common social or educational background — but on an objective role or function.[6]

It is not necessary to share the whole range of Poulantzas's analysis or conclusions to see that his emphasis on fractions of class is important. Put in simpler terms, it illustrates the way in which much of the mediation of the modern capitalist state (or the European Community) can challenge or restrain the activities of one fraction of the capitalist class while remaining in essence the defender of a capitalist mode of production and capitalist class relations. He also has reason to argue that

> the State is not a mere tool or instrument of the dominant classes, to be manipulated at will . . . The State epitomizes the class contradictions of the social formation as a whole by sanctioning and legitimising the interests of the dominant class and fractions in the face of other classes in the formation.[7]

American and European Capital
However, Poulantzas's analysis of the nature and consequences of European integration is much influenced by the terms of reference of the so-called 'American challenge' thesis, which has already been questioned in Chapter 4. Thus he tends to see the activities of multinational *versus* national capital very much in terms of a classic US imperialism, over-stressing the role of US foreign investment in Western Europe. This weakness is related to his claims for an 'interior' bourgeoisie, which can be compared with Ernest Mandel's 'national' bourgeoisie, and the same concept as framed by the French Communist Party.

As Poulantzas puts it, 'the interior bourgeoisie possesses its own economic base and its own base of accumulation of capital, which distinguishes it from the bourgeoisies of the peripheral countries'. Consequently, he argues,

> important contradictions thus exist between it and American capital: they are without the power to lead [the nation state] forward to the adoption of positions of effective autonomy or independence in the face of this [American] capital, but they do have effects on the [national] state apparatuses . . . in their relations with the American state.[8]

In such a way, the analysis is framed in the context of the 'American challenge' rather than in the more general framework of national *versus* multinational capital, which Poulantzas rejects. His reasons for doing this are weak, both because of the more recent evidence that multinationalisation is not simply a phenomenon of American capital, and because of the extent to which he accepts that 'what poses the problem is the national State versus multinational firms'.[9]

After all, if there is reality behind the concept of an 'interior' bourgeoisie and its conflict with American multinational capital, why should it not also have a conflict of interests with multinational capital in general, including European multinationals? Also, if the 'interior' bourgeoisie can 'have effects on' the national state apparatus with respect to American capital, why can they not register similar effects in seeking to defend their national interests against those of other multinational capital?

Similarly, Mandel's analysis has been much dominated by the US-European capital distinction. Also, as elaborated later, Mandel's assumption that the 'national' bourgeoisie is constituted by the great monopolies of European capital is weak, since this understates the role of national small and medium-sized enterprises which are thrown into crisis by big business and its market dominance, whether national or multinational. Mandel argues that 'the frailest companies allow themselves to be bought up or taken over by American companies ... [and that] the wealthier, more dynamic European businesses generally have a wider choice and prefer to take the path of European co-operation and capital inter-penetration'.[10] If Poulantzas is wrong to assert that these claims 'are contradicted by the facts',[11] there remains the point that Mandel does not grasp the extent to which the national member states the EEC are called upon to defend the interests of smaller-scale national capital against unfavourable takeover terms, or the negative effects of unequal competition with the big business elsewhere in the EEC, thus restraining the extent to which the Community can proceed simply to represent the interests of the 'monopolies'.

It also is not evident that Poulantzas has reason to criticise Herzog when the latter maintains that 'we are careful not to characterise the new stage as a struggle between "national" and "transnational" or "multinational" capital', not least because he sometimes makes the same distinction himself.[12] Yet Herzog maintains that 'currently, the great national monopolies and foreign capitals have common interests and "resistance", like "competition" loses its "national" character. It is groups with partially linked interests, or groups about to become cosmopolitan, that confront each other'.[13] This leaves unanswered the question of just which national and multinational capital have common interests, and which are confronting one another.

Capital and Class
One attempt to sidestep the limits of the interior/exterior distinction has been made by Jaumont, Lenègre and Rocard.[14] In practice, they claim that there are three main categories, which they distinguish as follows.

First, a *nationalist* bourgoisie or middle class, which has difficulty in modernising its economic base to cope with the pressures of international competition, and which in general is fairly hostile to the Common Market. Second, an *international* bourgeoisie which either is the *porteparole* of multinational capital, or closely attached to it, and fully satisfied with the sphere of influence it has gained from the creation of the Common Market. Third, there is a *national* pro-European bourgeoisie, with West Germany the classic example, which favours the Community framework for the simple reason that it has done well from it and expects to do as well or better through an extension of its powers in future.

Jaumont, Lenègre and Rocard expected the first *nationalist* class to be short-lived, and condemned quite simply to disappear through incapacity to survive international competition. Logically, therefore, one could expect the institutions of the Community to have a viable future, granted that the other two main class categories – in their argument – appear either fully or provisionally satisfied with their gains from integration.

Yet, they comment that the Common Market 'carries within itself mechanisms which prevent the appearance of a political entity', i.e. a super-state or super-power. Their reasons lie in an either/or argument. Either, at the present stage of capitalist development in Europe, the enterprises which could serve as the base for a European superstructure 'are not of a European scale or only have specifically European interests in a provisional manner'. Or, on the other hand, the provisional support for Europe now will disappear as that small-scale capital merges and expands, so that 'the logic of capitalist growth will lead it to develop its influence outside Europe and acquire a multinational structure with consequent interests which will not any more coincide with those of Europe'.[15]

Thus, with the anticipation of the euthanasia of the *nationalist* middle class, Jaumont, Lenègre and Rocard anticipated also the transformation of the *national* bourgeoisie into an *international* class in its own right, rather than simply being the dependent of non-European multinational capital. In practice, they seem to have been unaware of the scale and speed of this process of internationalisation during the period in which they wrote and published. Like others at the time, they overestimated the character of the so-called American challenge and underestimated the multinationalisation of European capital.

In any case, their anticipation of the euthanasia of the nationalist bour-geoisie seems premature. Certainly, as illustrated in Chapter 4, the logic of concentration and centralisation of capital has proceeded apace in both industry and finance in the postwar period. But it has not yet gained the same vigour in many services, or in agriculture. Further, policies of inter-vention for which such a nationalist bourgeoisie has called – effectively – have frustrated the process of centralisation in at least two key cases. One has been the opposition to France supermarkets or *grandes surfaces* in cen-tral urban areas, fought by the small shopkeepers of the petty bourgeoisie. The other is the working of the Common Agricultural Policy within the EEC itself. By maintaining support prices at a level which allows the least efficient producers to survive, the CAP has certainly given monopoly rents to the large farmers in agri-business, but has also frustrated that centralisa-tion which otherwise would have occurred through the free working of the market.

The irony of the lobbies, protests and votes exercised in the context of the Common Agricultural Policy should be clear. First, in agriculture, not all of the farmers concerned are capitalists, in the sense of hiring and firing dependent labour, rather than self-employed family concerns or dependent tenants. Second, while in many cases nationalist in the sense, for instance, of opposing the extension of the Community to include Spain, Portugal and Greece and their competitive agricultural produce, some of the strongest support for the pro-EEC Socialist Party in a country such as France comes from farmers in agricultural areas. Third, and not least, the assertion of national, class or sectional interest in agriculture is undertaken within rather than against a Community framework. In other words, the pressure and protest are specific, not general opposition to the principle of the CAP itself.

Superficially, the strands of analysis may seem knotted on a Gordian scale. However, it is classic that Gordian knots are better cut than unravelled. A better understanding of the nature of class power and class conflict in the context of European capital and its integration may be gained by a *complementary* dimension to the main distinction of national and multinational capital. This is the difference between large- and small-scale, or meso- and micro-economic enterprise. In this sense there are at least *four* rather than *two* main dimensions to the structure of capital and the sectional class interest which it represents. I.e., instead of national versus multinational, or large- versus small-scale capital, there is a combination, in varying proportions, of all four.

It is in such a context that one can more clearly see how Mandel's analsis is weakened by the identification of a national bourgeoisie with large-scale monopolistic capital, neglecting small-scale national capital and its 'Poujadiste' pressure on nation-states.

Similarly, Poulantzas's analysis runs into difficulties when in conceives the nation-state as simply opposing foreign capital 'at home' and promoting its own capital 'abroad'. For instance, one of the main reasons for the contradictory nature of key EEC policies lies in the extent to which European nation-states look to the Community institutions and the integration framework to support the foreign expansion of their large-scale national capital, yet seek to prevent the big business of other member states from penetrating and dominating their national economic structures. We have already seen in Chapter 2 that De Gaulle sought to bypass this contradiction by establishing a framework in which national big business could expand within the Community on a joint venture basis. In other words, he sought an international solution based on the extension of sovereignty rather than the supranational control sought by the EEC Commission. This was illustrated the extent to which supranational EEC pretensions for the 'best' common denominator failed to meet the needs of a simply 'better' solution for the French nation-state.

In effect, while there is a qualitative difference between national and multinational capital, and between large meso-economic and small micro-economic enterprise, the two distinctions are not coincidental. Most big business is multinational, especially in manufacturing and banking, but not all is so (including not least much nationalised enterprise). Similarly, while much small business is national as well as *reactive* in defence of its interests, not all of the economic and social class which it represents is both nationalist and reactionary.

Ideology, Role and Control

Thus there are various permutations on four of the main economic categories which represent different sections of the capitalist class. Further, it is crucial to distinguish the *role* of particular representatives of a social class from class *control* within a particular economic and political formation. Also, it is important to grasp the concept of ideology not just in the limited sense of ideas alone, but also of assumptions, presumptions, preconceptions and plain prejudice of the kind which characterises the overall *Gestalt* or form with which individuals and social groups order (or disorder) their particular 'view of the world'.

In this context a distinction should be made between the allocators and controllers of capital, at the top level of such business, and the broader-based technical and supervisory staffs, or 'techno-structure'. One of the main limits of Galbraith's use of the latter term has been his failure to distinguish the 'input' *role* of the techno-structure in such a general sense from the 'output' role of the boards of major corporations – i.e. the secondary role of designers, technicians, lawyers, draughtsmen, scientists and other white-collar workers in the intermediate structures of big business from the primary role of top management as the decision-makers and allocators of resource use. The former may define or limit the range of choice on products, technologies, location, market potential, etc., of the top decision-makers, but the final and real decisions remain those of the latter alone. Such top managers do not own their enterprises outright. But they exercise the crucial class function of *control* of capital and thus resource allocation.[16]

Therefore within the large-scale multinational capital typical of the meso-economic sector, there is a difference between the *role* of those who essentially service capital (the techno-structure) and the function of those who *control* it (top management at board level). If there is a contradiction between the formal concern for the 'public interest' voiced by top multinational management and its actual disregard for it, this need not be faced by the broad category of white-collar staff and personnel in such business. Thus, while top management might occasionally feel mis-giving about the squaring of the circle of corporate and public interests (whether the interest is allegedly national or Community European), there is less or little difficulty for the techno-structure in doing so. An engineer, designer or accountant for multinational such as IBM, ITT or Ford, whose prime interests as companies range far wider than either single-nation states *or* Community Europe, may consider himself both a good national and a pro-European with impunity and a clear conscience.

Similarly, the group which Poulantzas characterizes as social rather than economic or political, i.e. the group of top officials in the state apparatus – or by extrapolation the EEC Commission – may think themselves good Europeans. They do not view themselves as simply reflecting or serving the interests of national or multinational capital. Yet in practice senior officials at national level will be called upon to defend the interests of national *versus* multinational capital in key cases such as computers, aerospace, nuclear power, steel or shipbuilding, while the latter tend to find that their general responsibility to promote the liberalisation of trade and capital movements does not enable them to discriminate between European and non-European capital within the Community.

Thus, in contrast with Poulantzas's assumptions, the role of such élites is not simply social, but also both economic and – by implication – political. Whatever their general subjective perception (or ideology), they exercise a specific and objective role which is crucial to the maintenance of a capitalist mode of production and capitalist class relations: i.e. precisely the class role which he otherwise recognises as important.

Moreover, while there are many perceptions and actions by capitalists which do not simply reflect their economic role within the capitalist mode of production as a whole, they share the aim of maintaining it, and thus perpetuate their own interest. Whatever the head sometimes thinks to the contrary – in terms either of the public or 'European' interest – the heart of even a soulful corporation pumps on profit. But in practice, some sections of the capitalist class depend primarily on national intervention of a specific kind, while others do not. Very little, at least until the evolution of Community-sponsored cartels in coal and steel in the mid-1970s, actually depended on the European Community.

This is one reason, whatever their subjective views or aspirations, why so few capitalists or groups of capitalists have sought to put the European Community before either the nation-state or wider international institutions such as GATT. In effect, the Community has fallen between two stools. It combatted nationalism during a period in which the dominant section of capital, in its own interests, supported international trade and promoted multinational expansion. It worked for 'Europe', while capital – playing from an adequate national base – gained a wider world.

In other chapters, it is stressed that a further reason for the non-achievement of the EEC to date lies in the extent to which state (or Community) intervention is not static over time, but changes in relation to the real needs of the dominant section of capital. Thus, national capital needed positive state *intervention* in postwar Europe to aid and abet its reconstruction, but big business also needed negative international *integration* (removing barriers to the movement of capital, labour and trade) once such reconstruction had been achieved, and limits to its extended reproduction had been reached in national markets. Such analysis contrasts with Mandel's assumption that the 'European monopolies' need a European

super-state to serve their interests, which would amount to positive or
binding common policies ranging beyond liberalisation.

Subjects and Objects

The previous argument amounts to saying that, subjectively, the representatives of a specific social class may see themselves as one thing, while what
they do objectively is another. This has been emphasised by Göran Therborn
in his significantly titled book, *What Does the Ruling Class Do When It
Rules?*[17] While superficially paradoxical, the difference is of considerable
importance in terms of the false hopes and frustrated common policies at
the Community level.

Put directly, individuals in a social class can vote for more European
integration, in the sense of supporting parties which endorse a federal or
confederal framework. They may wish to see a European Assembly with
real powers to cope with the problems of the time, such as employment,
inflation, public welfare or the quality of the environment. But what such
a social class actually *does,* in servicing capital, from nine to five, can
contradict what it *thinks* should be done at the political level. In thought,
opinion and vote it can be subjective. In daily action, function and role it
objectively may support capital which frustrates, sidesteps or simply obstructs its intentions.

Such contradictions between subjective ideology and objective role
occur for both national and multinational capital and big and small enterprises. None the less, there are differences of objective interest between
these four main categories of capital, which are reflected in different degrees of support or opposition for policies furthering European integration.
Such permutations between subjective ideology and objective interest can
and do range through the four main distinctions already made, including
both multinational and national capital, and big and small enterprises at
the national level.

The distinction made between the social status and economic role is important. Thus, as previously stressed, economic actors in the techno-
structure of enterprise may subjectively perceive themselves as part of the
management hierarchy within an enterprise, and part of a particular class.
But their social status and economic role may be active/passive, or primary/
secondary depending on whether they allocate and control, or service and
support capital itself.

Even at the level of the owner-entrepreneur, there is scope for inconsis-
tency between perceived political interest and actual economic interest.
Thus a small-scale entrepreneur in Bordeaux or Bologna may think that
European integration is a 'good thing' and worthy of active support in
elections, while none the less demanding and gaining the support of the
French or Italian government to prevent 'unfair' competition from companies of a similar kind in other Community countries, thereby frustrating his political aim.

Thus there is no necessary coincidence between the subjective ideology or political assumptions of small micro-economic capital at the national level and the objective interest of that capital *vis-à-vis* national government.

However, the scope for divorce between perceived interests and real interest appears greater at the level of large-scale capital, essentially because of the greater divorce — for a wider section of management — between the *active control* of capital by top management and the *passive role* of servicing and supporting it for intermediate techno-structures.

Essentially, large-scale multinational capital has an objective interest in supporting negative integration in the sense that such policies widen its freedom to do what it chooses, on its own terms. By contrast, it has a counter interest in opposing positive integration policies which might challenge its freedom to do what it wishes, when, where and as it wants. It is ready to accept national state intervention, but on a secondary rather than primary basis, and mainly on its own terms.

By contrast, large-scale national capital (mainly within the public sector) tends to have an objective interest in the state's capacity to deliver positive intervention in its favour, and to prevent or obstruct those effects of negative integration which hazard its dominance at home. Similarly medium- and smaller-scale micro-economic capital will tend to rely on the nation-state rather than the European Community to protect it against the consequences of increased liberalisation and competition.

Such analysis should indicate how votes for a United Europe do not necessarily deliver European unification. The objective interest of multinational big business, and its controllers at board level, lies in supporting negative integration. Therefore, *inter alia*, their contributions to the pro-Market campaign which accompanied the initial British accession to the Community, and the Labour referendum after Tory entry. The contradiction for advocates of positive integration lies in the extent to which policies intended to control and plan capital run against its essential concern to escape controls through European integration.

In this respect, the dominant section of capital, in big business, is aided and abetted by the prevailing ideology of liberalisation and *laisser-faire* embodied in the Community's own treaties, which themselves reflect the dominant ideology of the postwar era. Voters and politicians wishing to reverse the dominance of capital in this Community should be aware of the extent to which the complexity of subjective and objective factors in practice mystifies and distorts a basic desire by big business to escape public policy constraints. What captains of industry may say they want distracts from the Europe they need. The failure of economic union and positive integration, in this sense, is not merely an accident of botched institutions or failure of will in leadership élites. It reflects the basic dominance of economics over politics in a capitalist system, and the key interest of a capitalist class in maintaining its prerogatives over the rest of us.

Class and Disintegration

If not checked by the mobilisation of countervailing forces, the freedom of capital through its integration, on its terms, can *disin*tegrate systems which hitherto have been held indestructible save by physical force.

For instance, Osvaldo Sunkel has stressed the extent to which multinational capital can disintegrate national cohesion through its negative effects on social and economic structures.[18] It does so by partly *re*ducing and partly *se*ducing specific sections of both capital and labour. Thus multinationals draw with them, and integrate into their own form of production, local entrepreneurs (as sub-contractors), middle-class professionals (as intellectual workers) and part of the proletariat (as manual workers). A new social structure emerges which is integrated not in the sense of joining states and societies, but incorporating the more dynamic capital and the more skilled labour in particular systems. Thereby a new social structure emerges which separates such 'integrated' groups from others whose activities not only become segregated, but also backwashed by the dynamic force and dominance of the multinational sector.

Sunkel's analysis is mainly concerned with less developed countries, and in particular Latin America. But his argument is importantly relevant to the question of international economic integration between developed countries, and the division of interest between independent national capitalists and that part of the middle class which identifies its interests predominantly with multinational capital. Furtado has also stressed that as multinational companies

> progressively extended their control over the most dynamic sectors of industrial activity . . . the best talents that emerged from local industries were absorbed into the new managerial class . . . National independent entrepreneurship was, in the process, restricted to secondary activities or to pioneering ventures which, in the long run, simply open up new fields for the future expansion [of multinationals] .[19]

Sunkel adds that this process limits the scope not only of a national entrepreneurial class, but also that of the national middle class as a whole, including those intellectuals, scientists, technologists and other professionals who are blocked from and marginalised by the multinational sector. As he puts it:

> The effects of the disintegration of each social class has important consequences for social mobility. The marginalised entrepreneur will probably add to the ranks of small or artisan manufacture, or will abandon independent activity and become a middle class employee. The marginalised sectors of the middle class will probably form a group of frustrated lower middle class people trying to maintain middle class

appearance without much possibility of upwards social mobility and terrorised by the dangers of proletarianization.[20]

In Europe, nation-state power and national entrepreneurship is much stronger than in Latin America. The initial penetration of US multinational capital was concentrated in Britain, and proceeded for over half a century before the UK's Great Power status was decisively challenged in international affairs. Common ties of language and culture, plus the focus of US capital, in many cases, in entirely new industries, eased its establishment. Besides, the United Kingdom after the United States, was itself the second largest exporter of capital in the world, and its dominant ideology and institutions favoured multinational companies. In Germany, multinational capital was especially welcomed after the Second World War, as not only providing employment when capital was scarce, but also tying-in US interest in support of the Federal Republic during the Cold War. In France, the institutions of strong central state power had been established before Latin America was even colonised, and the *étatist* tradition of state intervention in the economy dated at least from Colbert, despite periods of liberalism, such as the reaction to the Napoleonic period (comparable with German postwar liberalism after the Third Reich). After the Second World War, the state apparatus was significantly strengthened both under direct Gaullist influence and through the development of national economic planning. In Italy, the rise of direct State capitalism – *inter alia* through state holding companies – presented a real obstacle to foreign multinational penetration, especially in the oil sector after the creation of the ENI in 1954, and through the IRI state holding company in the 1960s.

None the less, similar patterns of economic and social disintegration at national level in Europe are observable as a result of the rise of multinational capitalists in a social and economic class. The European Communinationals represent a force for international integration, on their own terms, they have caused new problems both for national governments and for national capitalists as a social and economic class. The European Communities have been useful to them in creating a tariff-free internal market of considerable size, but for the main part they anyway need to be inside national markets and established in the national productive or distribution structure. This is partly a consequence of product differentiation, with different local tastes and design characteristics in particular local markets, and partly a matter of gaining leverage on the national governments which still dispose of major real resources through public expenditure in a manner which the EEC does not.

The simple federalist response to such a phenomenon runs on the lines that it is only when Europe has a state structure, with its own budgets, projects and contractual power that it will be able to contervail multinational capital by a multinational state. But this overlooks the extent to which the process of Community integration itself has weakened State power at the national level (through tariff disarmament and pressure to reduce capital controls) and has actually caused a reinforcement of State intervention through the favouring of what Vernon has called 'national champions in its enterprise. [21] Again, much of the allegedly 'nationalist' reaction to both Community internationalisation on the liberal capitalist model (tariffs and trade) and to multinational capital (with its penetration of productive structures) has not been a failure of will, or accidental, but resulted from real forces which threaten national disintegration.

1. Ernest Mandel, *Europe versus America?* (New Left Books, 1970) p. 56: first published as *Die EWG und die Konkurrenz Europa-Amerika*, (Europäische Verlaganstalt, 1968): and *The Second Slump*, New Left Books, 1978): first published as *Ende der Krise oder Krise ohne Ende?* (Wagenbach Verlag, 1977).
2. Nicos Poulantzas, *New Left Review*, no. 78, p. 38.
3. Nicos Poulantzas, *Pouvoir politique et classes sociales*, (Paris: Maspero, 1972) vol. I, p. 85.
4. Nicos Poulantzas, 'Internationalisation of Capitalist Relations and the Nation State', *Economy and Society*, vol. 3, no. 2 (May 1974).
5. Nicos Poulantzas, 'The Problem of the Capitalist State', in Robin Blackburn (ed.), *Ideology in Social Science* (London: Fontana/Collins, 1972) p. 244.
6. Poulantzas, *New Left Review*, no. 78, pp. 44—6, and 'The Problem of the Capitalist State', p. 247.
7. Poulantzas, 'Internationalisation of Capitalist Relations', p. 171.
8. Ibid., pp. 166—7.
9. Ibid., pp. 168—9.
10. Mandel, op. cit., p. 56.
11. Poulantzas, 'Internationalisation of Capitalist Relations', p. 169.
12. Ibid., p. 170.
13. Philippe Herzog, 'Nouveaux développements de l'internationalisation du capital', *Economie et Politique* (1971).
14. Bernard Jaumont, Daniel Lenègre and Michel Rocard, *Le Marché Commun contre l'Europe* (Seuil, 1973).
15. Ibid., pp. 62—5.
16. For Galbraith's argument see, further his, *The New Industrial Estate* (Hamish Hamilton, 1972) p. 116.
17. Göran Therborn, *What Does the Ruling Class Do When It Rules?* (London: New Left Books, 1978).
18. Osvaldo Sunkel, *Transnational Capitalism and National Disintegration in Latin America*, Social and Economic Studies.
19. Celso Furtado, 'La concentracion del poder economico en los Estados Unidos y sus proyecciones en America Latina, *Estudios Internacionales* (Oct. 1967—Mar. 1968). cit Sunkel.
20. Sunkel, op. cit.
21. Raymond Vernon (ed.), *Big Business and the State*, op. cit., (chs 1 and 2).

Part Four
State-Power
and Integration

7 Politics and State Power

Faced in the 1960s with the so-called 'American Challenge', many European federalists echoed Servan-Schreiber in the argument that the only way not to be beaten by the size and scale of the United States was to imitate it. In other words, the case for economic and monetary union was conceived in terms of the European Community becoming a federal 'super-power'.

In the late 1970s, such an argument looks different. The United States, with a large internal common market, has not been able either to retain whole sections of industry in areas such as television, electronics, and electrical goods, which have 'run away' to South-East Asia.[1] Nor has it been able to defend the dollar from the previous fate of sterling, and what had been thought to be a specifically British disease, the symptom of an economy allegedly 'too small' to maintain a major world finance and trading role. Meanwhile, both West Germany and Japan, countries of a similar size to Britain, France or Italy in terms of population and *potential* domestic market, have managed to maintain economies whose exports and currencies are if anything over strong in world markets. In addition, in its international military role the United States has been defeated by the Vietnamese, partly as a result of being 'muscle-bound' by precisely the scale and power of its advanced technology, which was not suited to the people's war then, literally, in hand.

Such a situation, in itself, should cause one to question whether big government can be identified with strong government, including the basic power of politics to master the economy. If this is true of the international role of a capitalist 'super-power' such as the United States, it certainly has been true for a long time in domestic US politics. During the period of marked austerity in Europe and Japan immediately after the war, it may well have appeared that the US federal system had 'licked' the economic problem at home. But it certainly had not 'licked' it in the 1930s. In fact, America went to war with a vast reserve of labour backed by internal shifts in the working population, drawing both blacks and women into the labour force on a major scale for the first time. In essence, it was because of the contradiction between developed technology and capacity, on the one hand, and unemployed resources on the other, that the United States was by and large to add wartime production to her peacetime consumption levels. Armaments, rather than a federal structure and the New Deal, gave America high income and high employment.[2]

It has sometimes been argued that the *only* way for nation-states to control multinational big business is to combine in a federal union. Yet domestic federal government in the United States, however extensive in the sense of providing social and economic 'infrastructure' (transfers through social security benefits, road building and urban renewal programmes, the location of defence establishments in states and regions of relatively high unemployment, etc.), has remained classically weak in relation to the commanding heights of big-business power. In one sense this is indicated by the fact that no big business in the United States has been broken up through anti-trust action for over half a century. Standard Oil was the last main example of such an exercise of public power, and that company has not since been notable for conforming either to the public purpose or to the textbook competitive model.[3] In the New Deal period itself, Franklin Roosevelt and his supporters had to wage a major battle to promote even general public spending, despite the fact that this notably favoured the construction and automobile lobby (through road building) as much as the small farmer or entrepreneur. The main theme distinguishing the Republican and Democratic Parties in the post-New Deal period has remained the question of the extent to which the federal authorities should intervene in such public works and welfare benefit programmes. In essence, it has been a debate over the scope and scale of federal power.

Federalism as Weak Government
One underlying reason is the extent to which federalist structures have actually been *intended* to constrain or reduce central government power. Thus the founding fathers of US federalism, Hamilton and Madison, invoking the support of Montesquieu, found that 'among the numerous advantages promised by a well constructed union, none deserves to be more accurately developed than its tendency to break and control the violence of faction'. With remarkable frankness, they added that different states and different parties represented obstacles 'opposed to the concert and accomplishment of the secret wishes of an unjust and interested majority'.[4]

Harrison has drawn attention to the federal 'maximalist' Nigoul, who argued that the undemocratic and olingarchic elements in national party structures represented a case for the reduction of national powers. Nigoul argued in favour of regional devolution, which has its own echo not only in contemporary regionalist movements in Europe, but also in the case of European federalists such as John Pinder and Roy Pryce, who argue in favour of a three-tier Europe of the Community, member states and regions, with a dispersal of present national state power to the higher and lower levels.[5] Similarly, Bryce, in his evaluation of the American Commonwealth, argues that the federal system provides a barrier against the excessive exercise of state power through the countervailance of the federal authority by the member states of the federation. Harrison has also stressed that Proudhon, as a disillusioned revolutionary, posed the concept of multiple sovereignties as an answer to excessive centralisation of political power. Guy Heraud makes the same case. Federalism dilutes power and obstructs the dominance of single philosophies or ideologies: *'integrated* economic, social and cultural federalism especially dilutes power, dividing it between all groups and all people, and as a result proves *depoliticising'*.[6]

The implications for disenfranchisement, in the sense of reducing the effective realisation of majority political choice, could hardly be more clearly put, despite the fact that the federalists, virtually without exception, see themselves as protecting individual freedom through a reduction of central state power.

Summarising comparative federal studies, still dominated by American researchers, Harrison astutely comments that most of them in fact deliver *adverse* judgements against federalism: 'they confirm that a federal structure does tend to set limits, though not absolute limits, to central government action, entrenching local interests and *delaying any radical reallocation of values'*.[7] In other words, federalism tends to entrench conservatism.

Neutralisation of State Power

Such reduction of state power is now powerfully reinforced by the extent to which multinational capital is concerned to avoid a strong central political authority in the European Community. This case, mentioned in previous chapters, deserves elaboration.

In the immediate postwar period, European capital was mainly national in character, and anxious to secure state intervention to facilitate its postwar reconstruction. It therefore not only welcomed Marshall Aid, but also bid extensively with the state bureaucracies for its share of state assistance. The process was facilitated by the fact that, in most instances, governments previously unaccustomed to so close a relationship with business personnel established new institutions to pump and administer public money into the private sector — for instance, the Industrial Credit and Finance Corporation established by the postwar Labour Government, and the Kreditanstalt für Wiederaufbau in West Germany. Business also welcomed state underwriting of the costs of research and development, either directly or indirectly, in the form of government bodies established to undertake long-term research projects whose results would be disseminated to the private sector. Such research frequently represented the application of wartime technologies to civilian use.

However, by the end of the 1950s, the main phase of postwar reconstruction and the application of military to civilian technologies had substantially been achieved. With the expanded reproduction of capital, and its concentration among large-scale enterprise, big business transcended the frontiers of national markets, and with them the need for direct state assistance. The new leader firms became less dependent on a close relationship with the nation-states, and more concerned to avoid national restrictions on their multinational operations. They were glad to maintain the 'servicing' role for their continued expansion and accumulation represented by *passive* state intervention to provide their economic and social infrastructure (construction, power, transport, education and social services). They were also anxious to continue the assurance of public purchasing, which facilitated their capital expansion through guaranteeing that a certain share of costs and profits would be covered by state orders. But they did not want *active* state intervention in the form of capital controls (practised before the EEC in France), constraints on their location of activity (widely exercised in Britain), or other forms of intervention (such as the contractual planning with big business in the process of evolution in Belgium) where this limited their freedom to determine how capital should be allocated on a global scale.

In short, after the re-establishment of its respective national base, big business sought increasingly to avoid the incidence of state power and to neutralise its capacity to influence the allocation of capital. The form of this tendency differed between countries in a manner which could be expected with uneven development, with different gains and losses, in different countries.

In Italy, it took the shape of strong opposition from the big private capital groups to locational controls, i.e. the obligation on big business to place a certain proportion of investment in Southern Italy. Despite major parliamentary debate, involving the advocacy of such controls by members of the parties of the Right and Centre as well as the Left, such planning proposals, in the Giolitti draft plan of 1965, were abandoned in the 'sanitised' Pieraccini Plan for the period 1966–70.[8] One of the strongest arguments used by groups such as FIAT and Pirelli was that they might be able to adjust to EEC integration *or* locate new ventures in Southern Italy, but could not simultaneously undertake both.[9]

In France, where capital controls had played a key part in the first three national plans, via both the CDC (Caisse des Dépots et Consignations) and the FDES (Fonds de Développement Economique et Social), big business sought to trade-off the relaxation of price control for undertaking rationalisation and merger, which anyway was in their interest. To a significant extent they managed to neutralise such state intervention, undermining the government's attempted price 'Stability Contracts' of 1966, and largely using the subsequent 'Programme Contracts' of 1968 in their own interest. An important factor lay in the extent to which the very success of the bigger French business which the planners had sought to achieve in the earlier plans thereby raised their degree of self-financing and reduced their dependence on state funds for further expansion. In other words, their rise to meso-economic status increased their bargaining power with the state and tended to neutralise state power.

An indirect illustration of the tendency of European integration to neutralise state power is available also from analysis of the obstacles to positive integration policies as attempted so unsuccessfully in the EEC.

Positive integration may well be acceptable to those firms and industries, social classes or regions which are losers from uneven development and unequal integration, but not to the gainers from the integration process. Since the gainers by definition tend to be stronger than the losers, the gainers may refuse to agree to the kind of planning which would result in restrictions on their freedom to allocate capital where, why and as they choose (in the case of multinational capital), or their freedom to allocate income and incentives via taxation as suits their electorate (in the case of a strong economy such as West Germany). The positive integration efforts by some élites in the Commission, backed by some national governments with an interventionist tradition, such as France, may not prove able to overcome the 'negative' integration or liberal capitalist ideology which has proved dominant in other Community countries.

The difficulties of planned or positive integration become greater if one considers the scale of the problem posed by planning in modern economies when the process of capital accumulation itself is checked by internal factors such as over-investment, external factors such as major increases in oil and fuel prices and imports, or a combination of both. There are strong grounds for arguing that the pattern of most modern capitalist planning, in economies such as France, never was a primary factor in the growth of investment, employment and income, but rather, was a secondary factor which trimmed, modified and redirected a process of accumulation promoted by basic factors such as sustained profits and profit expectations for the managerial class.[10] The difficulties of the French planners since 1974 are an illustration of this, with the optimistic targets of the Sixth Plan undermined, and the projections for an expansionary Seventh Plan shelved in favour of the Barre austerity programmes.[11]

Crisis, Planning and Power

The question whether planning is primary or secondary is important to the general question whether political action and the exercise of state power can dominate economic outcomes, and to the specific fate of Community efforts at planning. In practice, as evidenced by its virtual abandonment during the current economic crisis, planning under capitalism tends to be secondary rather than primary. This has its own class implications. For instance, so long as European integration brings real income and employment gains to both labour and capital, unions may remain unconcerned that a higher share of the gains goes to management and the shareholding class than to labour itself. But when the accumulation of capital in the form of investment, orders and new jobs is checked, unions may organise (as in Italy during the later 1960s and early 1970s) in such a way as to press delayed wage claims high enough to compromise further capital expansion, reducing profit expectations on further investment.[12]

In such circumstances, European governments hesitate to intervene to oblige firms to change their investment and production. Stagnant investment, high unemployment and continually rising prices thereby tend to break down the consensus politics whereby organised labour is prepared to wait with depreciated real earnings for an improbable recovery of employment through 'super-growth'. In this context, the hesitation of political and state power to challenge capital's power of decision over why, when and where to locate new investment could result in a polarisation of class consciousness and class politics of a kind unknown during the sustained growth of the postwar period.

The question then posed would be whether a new radicalism in consciousness and ideology would result in a political polarisation in favour of the Left or the Right. To the extent that uneven development yields different gains and losses from integration, with different responses in terms of capital and labour, ideology and politics, the national polarisation of politics would itself be likely to prove uneven and different. It is in this context that the possible determination of economic and social outcomes by the political process becomes important. If the Left in Europe presents a coherent and plausible analysis of the underlying crisis factors in the system, and establishes sufficient political support to command socialist solutions, it could achieve a transformation of economic policy in particular Community countries.

But to prove successful, such an advance would need not only positive *intervention*, but also major advance towards a transformation of the dominant mode of production, distribution and exchange. In other words, it would need to assure advance towards a predominantly socialist mode of production, with sufficient publicly supported intervention to ensure the mobilisation of investment, jobs and incomes in a planning framework, rather than waiting for capital to expand. Such a transformation would demand changes in the terms on which investment was undertaken, for whose use, in which markets, with *social* criteria substituting for private criteria, and public benefit for private profit.

Federalist Community policies, based on the lowest common denominator principle, and representing the relative neutralisation of state power at EEC level, cannot implement such a transformation in anything like the foreseeable future. The combination of different ideologies, different political perspectives and different sanctions for the exercise of 'legitimate' state power would compromise any initial radical proposal for transformation of the dominant mode of production, distribution and exchange in the Community as a whole. Direct elections to a European parliament which was itself divorced from effective executive power would be likely to disenfranchise substantial political majorities who were in favour of Socialist policies at the national level so long as they were in a minority in the Community elections. In other words, the Socialist policies necessary for a planned recovery of investment, jobs and incomes for social use – and necessary to ensure an increase in Community imports from those economies remaining in a predominantly capitalist mode of production – would be frustrated by the neutralisation of state power in a federal structure dominated by capital and its interests.

Marginalised Political Power

The combined factors sufficient to neutralise state power at Community level certainly tend to neutralise and marginalise political power. The conditions and circumstances vary according to the specific combination of the main factors identified in social, economic and political power: politics, the state, ideology, capital and labour.

For instance, during a period of consensus politics, when ideological differences are at a low level, a sufficiently sustained accumulation of capital may ensure enough real gain in both profits and wages for labour and its political representatives to accept the prevailing system without challenge. This tended to be the case during the consensus period of the 1950s and early 1960s in most EEC countries. EEC integration was presented as a major political initiative, but was less threatening to national sovereignty or sectional interests than its two stillborn predecessors – the proposals for Political Union and a European Defence Community. In ideological terms, it represented both a pragmatic scaling-up of the Coal and Steel Community and a down-scaling of the dominant and largely unchallenged Western capitalist ideology of liberalisation and free trade, as already accepted in international agreements such as GATT. As apparently a bit more of the one and a bit less of the other, it seemed to pose no fundamental change, despite the ambitions of its authors.

At national level, a variety of further favourable circumstances facilitated both signature of the Rome Treaty and its political acceptance by majority parties. For the most part, parties of the moderate Centre of the Right were in office. Specifically Christian Democratic parties of the Centre-Right were in Government in West Germany and Italy. In France, the nominally socialist Guy Mollet signed the Rome Treaty, but did so in a climate in which he needed a respectable international initiative to offset his appalling crises of Suez and Algeria. De Gaulle was shortly to take power in France, but under conditions in which Mollet persuaded a number of nominally socialist deputies to vote for him rather than face the prospect of *'les paras'* raining from the skies on the Place de la Concorde. Britain stayed out, but in a climate of ongoing negotiations to determine an 'inner Six' and 'outer Seven' through the association of EFTA. The very character of these 'free trade area negotiations' gave many the impression that the new Community was starting pragmatically, and threatened no radical reappraisal of the framework for conventional postwar politics.

There were some dissenting voices from the Left and Centre. As already indicated in Chapter 2, Mèndes France powerfully opposed the Community on both ideological and political lines as a revival of nineteenth-century *laisser-faire* and a formula for the undermining of political sovereignty. The Communist parties in France and Italy at this time expressed views ranging from outright hostility to serious criticism. The British Labour Party was already preoccupied with criticism of the EEC, and Hugh Gaitskell was soon to launch his opposition with a reference to the ideology of national independence ('a thousand years of British history') and political sovereignty (of the British Parliament).

But in general, the dominant political interests of the time (Centre Right) were not in conflict with the dominant ideology of EEC integration (liberal capitalism) or the dominant mode of production in West Europe as a whole (capitalism itself). Specific historical factors reinforced this combination, including West Germany's desire to gain international respectability, plus the interest of the Benelux countries in avoiding a Europe dominated by major powers. The one wanted a political place in the sun, and the others wanted a place in the Council of Ministers.

None the less, whatever the specific reasons for a particular European Community some quarter-century ago, when heads of governments put pen to paper and signed the Rome Treaty, there are key reasons why politicians of a different generation, today, can and should dispute the marginalisation of political power implicit in Community integration and its institutions.

One of the most important relates to the argument on the irreversibility of much Community decision-making. The Community Treaties entail not only formal acceptance of majority *versus* unanimous voting, but also specific powers given to the Commission in the form of *directives* which are supposed to be binding on member states. Such directives range through the main Community policies enshrined in the Treaties, and specifically in coal and steel, transport and agriculture. In purely legal terms, they give precedence to the Treaties and the Commission's powers over any national legislation.

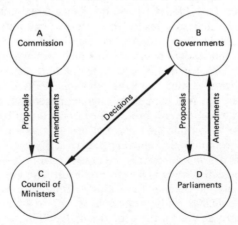

FIG. 7.1   *International decision-making*

The manner in which such directives marginalise the exercise of political power is illustrated in Figs 7.1 and 7.2. Fig. 7.1 indicates what would be the case in an international decision-making framework where political authority was still sovereign. In this context, the Commission would still have the right to forward proposals to the Council of Ministers, and decisions affecting Community Europe would still be dependent on joint agreement by the Council, with reference to and legitimation from national governments. But the agreements entered into by these governments would be subject to both ratification and amendment by national parliaments, which could reflect the needs and interests of those sections of society which were significantly disadvantaged by integration itself. Such an institutional structure, making governments and thus the Community in the final instance dependent on *specific* support, would ensure not only that the strong did not ride rough-shod over the weak but also, ironically, could increase support for closer co-operation between governments as the European level.

By contrast, Fig. 7.2 represents the pretension of the present Community and its institutions. According to its logic, initiative between the Commission and the Council lies with the former, and the Council has the right only to amend initiatives taken by the Commission. In addition, joint decisions by the Council should in principle be taken by majority vote, thereby relegating whole nation-states and major regions to minority status. Further, the Commission itself has the power to issue directives to governments, binding them to its own interpretation of the public interest in terms of the founding charters of the Treaties. For those parliaments in member states whose governments were in a minority in the Council of Ministers, such decision-making would negate the power to decide or

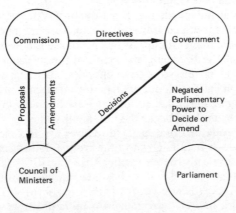

FIG. 7.2   *Supranational decision-making*

amend Community policy. In this sense, the political process would be marginalised and its power to reverse executive decisions eliminated.

The original reasons for incorporating such directives in the Treaties have already been indicated. In other words, the founding fathers were concerned to give teeth to Community institutions in order to avoid the unenforceable statements of good intentions which characterised most of the activities of the interwar League of Nations.

Also, it could well be argued that, at least to date, such directives have amounted to threads rather than ropes binding member states. In other words, many of them have gone by default through lack of the powers of enforcement available to the Commission (despite its nominal powers of reference of breach of directives to the European Court of Justice).

Put differently, a determined nation-state may be able to drive a horse and carriage through nominal Commission directives, and thus through Community supranationalism. The Gaullist period in France was an example of this. Yet De Gaulle's successful opposition to supranationalism depended on very specific factors, including a strong balance of payments and major gold reserves which gave substance to his claims for an independent France and even, at one stage, looked set to devalue the dollar before the 1970s.

Also, for a variety of reasons, De Gaulle managed to establish the dominance of his political authority and political power over the state apparatus in France. Thus, whatever the inclinations of senior officials in the state apparatus who, by personal disposition, might be 'pro' Community Europe, De Gaulle managed to ensure through a combination of personal authority, a 'presidential' constitution, and a *cabinet* system giving real influence within ministries to his own Ministers, that his 'line' on policy was reflected at departmental and thus governmental level. Under his leadership, there was no question of the civil service, rather than the government, running French policy towards the Community.

Effective national independence in a Community framework depends very much on such specific conditions. For weaker member states with economic difficulties, the feasibility of independence is not nearly so clear-cut. For instance, if the financing and credit of their balance of payments deficits is dependent on the stronger economies, and in practice on West Germany, then their independence relative to Community institutions and policies thereby is circumscribed so long as West Germany in combination with other surplus economies backs the Community line.

Besides, the threads of Community directives can in practice prove as binding as those which held Gulliver to the ground on his first beaching in Lilliput. Though physically much smaller than himself — as Commission officials might well appear relative to heads of national governments —the Lilliputians nevertheless managed to restrain the giant for some time.

Such binding of a national government is more probable where it lacks the kind of political authority which De Gaulle embodied. Governments with either small majorities, low consensus support, or no majorities at all, tend to be very much subject to the pressure of events. Nominally, in a democratic framework, such pressure should come from the people, through the vote. But in practice, it tends to come through the prevailing class and power structure, mediated by the prevailing ideology.

Historical Perspectives

To date, the power pretension of Community institutions has largely been held in check by nation-states and national power itself. For Euronatics this is reprehensible and retrograde sentiment. But one of the main reasons for the stubbornness of national power versus Community institutions to date has lain in the *need* for state power as a means for mediating the problems posed for different sections of capital and labour by the unequal and uneven development of capitalism. In other words, the reality of nation-states in Western Europe is not simply a matter of sentiment or culture, but reflects real roles necessary for social cohesion and the maintenance of a particular form or mode of society itself. The very emergence of nation-states through history has occurred as an objective process in which subjective factors such as political will and initiative have played only a part, and not the exclusive part.

For instance, in the broadest historical sense, Louis XIV as sun-king could not have completed the isolation of the aristocracy from political power – or the neutralisation of their political influence – without the heritage of a centralisation dating for centuries, back to the Capets. Similarly, only the most ardent Bonapartist would claim that Napoleon I would have created the First Empire without the French Revolution itself, which combined the centralisation of the *ancien régime* with the political and economic liberation of the bourgeois class during the Revolution. The forces to which he gave military leadership were created for him by those assiduous bourgeois Jacobins who organised all of France on a regionalised basis for the defence of the Revolution, and thereby created the first standing armies.

Ideologically, the Napoleonic Code was the expression of the dominant bougeois and anti-feudal ethic, and therefore powerful, rather than state legislation deriving its power from an exceptional individual. Even politically, Napoleon neutralised the peasantry and the *sans-culottes* of nascent urban proletariat by giving them a *role* rather than allowing them to contest the *rule* of the bourgeoisie under his aegis. By social mobility in promotion, made possible both by the Revolution and by its Jacobin ideology, he veiled the reality of new bourgeois power by the mystique of a marshal's baton in every soldier's knapsack. Besides, to the extent that his poor bloody infantry were both the vehicle and the instruments of new imperialist power, they constituted one of the first labour aristocracies, compensated through privilege when they survived abroad for what they lacked at home.

Again, in broad historical perspective, the rise of industrial capitalism, with its uneven initial development and unequal impact on different countries, took forms in which political leadership was severely constrained by objective factors. In some cases, as with Bismarck in Germany, the willingness of new social classes to accept a *role* rather than to challenge the *rule* of a particular class gave scope for an individual of genius to mediate between classes in such a way as to establish a relative autonomy for the state. But, again, as with Louis XIV or Napoleon, Bismarck's relative autonomy involved a neutralisation of political power for specific social and economic classes. Thus, during the period of establishing the Reich, before 1871, he drew on a nationalist ideology and the exaltation of the state in a succession of German philosophers from Hegel, thereby obscuring different class interests. In the subsequent period, he sided with the bourgeoisie against the rising German proletariat, with anti-socialist laws. But he had to take account of different sections of the bourgeoisie, allying the Junker aristocracy with the liberals and the urban trading middle classes through to the 1870s, and then switching his support rapidly to the industrial bourgeoisie with the introduction of protection against (mainly British) industrial goods in 1879.

The recognition of new social and economic classes, and political adjustment to their interests, underlay the classic neutralisation of the Reichstag which A. J. P. Taylor has brilliantly chronicled.[13] The neutralisation continued even after the repeal of the anti-socialist legislation, thanks to the false perceptions of German Social Democrats on the relation between State power and political power. The SPD — like the aging Engels, who shared their illusion — mistook the rising share of its vote in the country at large, and its increasing union and parliamentary membership, for real power. Preoccupied with the arithmetic of its impending parliamentary majority, it overlooked the fact that, in the Reichstag as shaped by Bismarck, the majority simply did not have the power to appoint the executive. Government remained in the hands of the Kaiser, and its Ministers at his discretion — even to the extent that Lord Grey could protest at the outset of the First World War that there was no one in Berlin with whom he could meaningfully negotiate, including the Foreign Secretary, without approach to Wilhelm II himself. The SPD votes in the Reichstag were sound and wind, signifying little so long as the Socialists failed to use the political process to challenge the basis on which an alliance of Junker and capitalist interests dominated real power in Germany. Bismarck's Reichstag neutralised the Socialists by granting them a neutered political institution.

A Neutered European Assembly?
The analogies with the unreal and nominal powers of the EEC Assembly will be apparent. The comparison is clear between the posture of those Social Democrats who count potential votes for a 'Left' majority in

Strasbourg, and the Social Democrats who counted heads in a rising parliamentary majority in the Reichstag. The genuineness and idealism of those involved, in both cases, is not in question. What remains in question is the extent to which the achievement of such a majority would actually result in a transformation of the power relations of the Community in favour of labour, or socialism, as some Social Democrats who support political union maintain. The idealism, as with the Rousseauite Jacobins in the revolutionary Convention, masks the extent to which economic, social and political power is a hybrid structure, itself representing basic class interests.

In effect, the extent to which purely political expression in a European Assembly can influence the distribution of power, in whose favour, will depend on a complex combination of other factors in the power structure, including state power, ideology, capital and labour. This is not to say that politics in the European Assembly can or will count for nothing. But intention and reality vary considerably.

This was well illustrated by the motion put in 1976 by the Labour member, John Prescott, in the European Assembly, when he proposed that the bribes admittedly paid by multinational oil companies to the Italian government were an abuse of competition under the rules of the Rome Treaty. The startled Commissioner for Competition Policy, M. Borschette, replied that no one imagined that the EEC Commission was a 'penal institution'. In other words, M. Borschette did not envisage that the Commission would adopt penalties towards monopolistic, multinational capital in the Community, rather than against member states.

Another illustration, in the same year, was represented by the Report on Inflation, sponsored by the Commission and undertaken by a group including the author, chaired by the Head of the Belgian Plan and Chairman of the Medium-Term Economic Policy Committee of the Community, Robert Maldague. As previously stressed, this explicitly endorsed the analysis of meso-economic capital and its transformation of competitive structures in the Community, advocating admission by the Commission of the extent to which this new power structure, with unequal competition between meso and micro-economic enterprise, demanded a response in terms of new policies, including the joint negotiation by governments, unions and management of the manner in which big business with a macro-economic impact employed its resources in relation to the interests of the Community as a whole. The report, which came under M. Borschette's jurisdiction, was effectively suppressed, with refusal to issue either a press release on its recommendations or to allow copies to be given to the press.

In practice, Prescott's initiative and the Maldague Inflation Report polarised opinion in both the EEC Assembly and the Economic and Social Committee. The persistent refusal of the Commission to publish the findings of the Maldague Report wider than the Community's own specialist committee resulted in the decision by its members to undertake independent publication in French, Italian and English.[14] It thereby became a point of reference for debate within sections of the Left in the Community.

It is too soon to analyse the implications of such a challenge to the capitalist ideology in the Commission, and to the deflationary policies of member governments. Probably it will constitute yet further writ on the wall, while Commissioners seek to run capitalism with a human face in the Community, stressing the interest of the consumer in what remains an uncommon capitalist market. The problem for such a Community lies in the fact that it will fail to perform the classic role of the state in mediating class interests in society. In the political shuffling which will ensue, the parties of the European Left may manage to identify the slow-step of political bankruptcy and demand that transformation of the Community necessary to achieve socialist objectives. And this means the dominance of a socialist mode of production, distribution and exchange, not simply socialist members of the Assembly. It also means a common ideology for the transformation of capitalism, reflected in common programmes, backed by organised labour as power concerned with political challenge to capital rather than with a mere defence of its own collective bargaining for better terms from capital.

According to the federalists, a directly elected European assembly will facilitate socialism. Yet there is no common ideology between the members of the so-called Socialist International, even excluding the question of the European Community. To a substantial extent, twenty years of Community institutions have shown many socialist members at Strasbourg more clearly in the role of abandoning demands for transition to socialism, since waiting for a supranational Community — for many of them — has replaced the more difficult task of working for socialism. Moreover, so long as they support liberal capitalist policies for bettering the consumers' interest while hesitating to involve themselves with the accumulation of socialised capital, they will leave the economic field dominated by private monopoly and multinational capital. To the extent that they advocate wage restraint and public expenditure cuts during a period of stagnant private investment and rising prices, they will preside over a massively unequal social distribution in favour of capital and against labour.

This is not to say that there should not be a common programme of the broad European Left at the Community level. But it does mean recognising the differences of the Left both between and within member countries of the Community. It also means taking account of the extent to which a new state capitalism in member countries arguably represents an advance on the left-wing capitalism of some governments such as British Labour in the 1970s, which seems determined to attempt the reconstruction of capital with a degree of non-intervention which would seem incredible to many French Gaullists or Italian Christian Democrats.

More importantly, it is critical to recognise the extent to which formal enfranchisement through a directly elected European Assembly may actually *dis*enfranchise people. This can be seen at one level through the simple mechanics of a majority at European *versus* national level. In practice, it would be perfectly possible that majorities in favour of socialism in two major Community countries could be outvoted at Community level and put into a minority. The permutations including more than two minor Community countries are considerable. Granted the extent to which the policies for weaker regions or countries of the Community not only are against the interests of the stronger ones, but also caused by them – via the dynamics of unequal development – the tendency towards a dual Community of the strong and weak would prove probable. Its probability is already illustrated by the call for an inner and outer Community by some notable German Social Democrats. Thus national majorities, relegated to minority Community status, would be effectively disenfranchised.

The political problems of permanent minorities has been illustrated graphically enough by the Ulster problem and the move towards nationalism in Scotland. But these dimensions of institutional minority are reinforced by the extent to which the neutralisation of State power by capital occurs on a major scale in the Community. The rise of the modern capitalist State accompanied the defence of the interests of national capital. The increasing involvement of governments in economic issues, and the increasingly incestuous relationship between big business and the state, have reduced political institutions to relative insignificance in key member countries. The Wilsonian platitude that 'governments must govern' veils the fact that they often are governing their parliamentary parties with more rigour than they are governing capital in the public interest. The divorce of executive

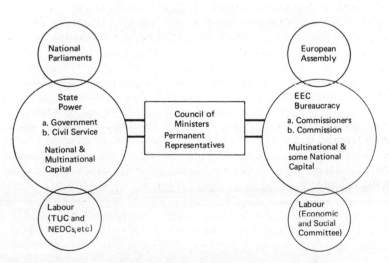

FIG. 7.3   *Central and peripheral power in the EEC*

from legislative power in the constitution of the United States, reflected in a similar divorce in the institutions of the EEC, represents merely the formalisation of a separation of powers which has already occurred in practice.

Add to this the specifically neutralising elements of the federalistic formula as conceived by its original advocates, taking power further away from national governments, and the prescription which results is for a yet more uncommon and unequal Community. Add again the sectionalisation of labour, defensively national during a period of aggressively multinational capital, and it is not hard to prescribe the role of national 'governments' as providing the framework for a social underwriting of economic costs imposed by unequal competition and unequal development. The nation state in a capitalist European federalism would provide the economic infrastructure for capital, while the political superstructure would be void. Positive intervention at the national level would become more difficult, while negative integration would reign at the federal level. In such circumstances, it is not surprising that Roy Jenkins has started his presidency of the European Commission by what amounts to a call for the consumer interest: as with much consumerism in America, it is the classic call against big business by those who cannot transform it. It is the politics of protest, not political power.

The limits and problems of direct elections to a European Assembly are illustrated by the diagrammatic representation of the distribution of power both within nation states and between them and the Community institutions. (Fig. 7.3).

The main power axis at present lies between the level of state institutions (government and civil service) and the Community institutions (Commissioners and Commission). Within the prevailing capitalist ideology throughout the Community, interests of national and multinational capital dominate the policy decisions of both national and Community institutions. It is their interest, their profit or loss schedules, their criteria for the allocation of resources which largely determine policy considerations at the nation-state and EEC level. The central institutions in the interface between national and Community institutions are the Council of Ministers and the Permanent Representatives (i.e. the officers of national civil services resident in Brussels).

The institutions of both politics and organised labour are marginalised in this power distribution. They are external to the main ambit of power relations between capital and the state. This is not to say that they have no role in the process of decision-making on resource allocation or the shaping of policies. But their role is secondary rather than primary, and for the most part reactive and negative in character, rather than initiative or positive. At the national level, parties do initiate policies – in opposition – but then tend to be reduced to a secondary form of opposition during periods of office, where their role is subordinated to rule by governments more concerned with trying to make the prevailing social and economic system work by its prevailing capitalist criteria than with transforming those criteria. This is, of course, especially true of the constituent parties in coalition governments.

Under capitalism, whether state capitalist or liberal capitalist, the prevailing mode of production and the dominant ideology tend to assure that parties of the Left are more marginalised in the exercise of state power than parties of the Centre or Right. This is, of course, especially true at the EEC level, and will remain so for as long as the Social Democratic parties remain opposed to working political alliances with the new 'Euro-Communist' parties. This position was echoed by Willy Brandt in an interview following the 1977 meeting of the Socialist International in The Netherlands. If it prevails, the Social Democratic parties of the EEC could only gain a nominal majority of votes in the European Assembly through *de facto* or formal coalitions with Centre parties.[15]

Such coalition-type voting in the European Assembly will not actually change Community decision-making significantly, for the reasons given earlier regarding the mere 'sounding board' character of the Assembly. But, for the argument just given – and elaborated elsewhere – even a formal change in the powers of the European Assembly would not be likely to change the fundamentally capitalist character of the EEC. In other words, even an extension of the powers of the Assembly, giving it a wider right to veto policy proposals of the Commission or the Council of Ministers, would not provide a framework for extension of the feasibility of socialist policies within member states without much wider ideological and political change between labour movements (both parties and trade unions) in the EEC, rather than within the institutional suprastructure of the Community (Assembly-Commission relations or relations between the Council and the Commission). Not least, further powers to the Assembly would tend to negate, neutralise and discredit parliaments at the more basic national level.

In effect, any feasibility of major advance for socialist policies within the Nine (or the Nine plus new members) will depend on a transformation of the present peripheral role for political parties and trades unions, or the role of politics and labour, relative to capital and state power. At a minimum, it would demand the realisation in practice of what at present remains a purely formalised myth in the liberal capitalist model of the state. It would mean establishing sovereignty for parliaments and the democratic process over the state apparatus (governments and civil services). Put differently, the democratisation of Community Europe will depend on the democratisation of relations between political parties and the state apparatus, and industrial and regional democracy in the economic and political substructure of European society. Such *primary* issues should be on the Left's priority agenda, rather than ballot-boxing for a European Assembly.

The Eclipse of Public Power?
Only fantasists and fatalists claim to foretell the shape of things to come. But if crystal balls are both speculative and fragile, how does the book look?

The Community clearly appears to have made major progress by agreeing to the holding of direct elections to the European Assembly. But, even with the candidacy of 'heavyweights' such as Willy Brandt and François Mitterand the political effectiveness of the Assembly will tend to be restricted by unCommon national interests and differing ideologies.

These conditions, stemming in part from the unequal nature of capitalist integration, and partly from different specific national circumstances, affect the Community Left more than they do the Right. But even the Right is not homogenous or unified in its attitude to common policies at the Community level. This is indicated not only by the record of uncommon differences on policies which by now should have been cornerstones of economic union – such as the ill-fated Industrial Company Statute – but also by the differences on the role of national *versus* Community power reflected in the division between, for instance, Jacques Chirac and Giscard d'Estaing.

The current trend can be indicated with reference to the main factors in the political economy of state Community versus State power, as illustrated in Fig. 7.4. This extends the base superstructure model introduced in Chapter 5, and distinguishes three main phases in the integration process.

Phase I amounts to the initial establishment of Community institutions, including the European Assembly, the Commission and the Council of Ministers. The dominant ideology of the Commission, as initiator of policies and guardian of the Treaties, is negative integration. Similarly, at a European level, that capital which transcends the national level is already multinational in character. Its main basic relation with labour is offensive. It takes the initiative on what is produced, why, where and in whose interest. The main reaction of labour is defensive and reactive, responding to the initiatives taken by capital. While strongly unionised in much of the multinational enterprise in countries of origin, or in cases where the initial growth of that capital accompanied the rise of the trades union movement earlier in the century, much of the labour employed by multinational capital is either non-union or weakly unionised. Even joint action by labour at an international level in response to multinational capital tends to be rare, temporary, and relatively ineffective. The Dunlop-Pirelli joint union action in Britain and Italy is noteworthy precisely because it has been exceptional.[16]

At such a phase, corresponding to the late 1950s, when the integration process in a meaningful sense either had not begun or was only beginning, national parliaments and governments were nominally subject to the principles of the Treaties, but were not yet subjected to them in practice. The dominant ideologies at national level – in the specific sense of that

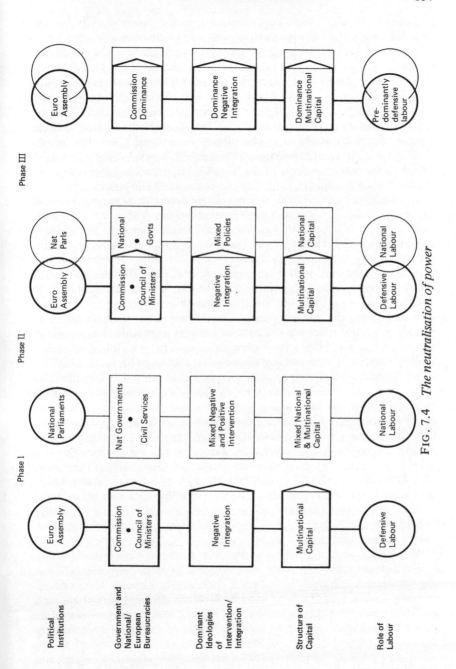

FIG. 7.4 *The neutralisation of power*

framework of values and ideas affecting state policies — ranged through various combinations of negative and positive *intervention*.

Phase II indicates the stage of international integration at which the Community and nation-states could meaningfully be said to have arrived by the end of the 1970s. It indicates the extent to which there is already an eclipse of national political sovereignty by the claims of the European Assembly, the Commission and the Council of Ministers. At the level of political institutions, the real power of the Assembly is limited. But its negative *implications* are real substantially because of the eclipse of increasing areas of decision-making by the range of powers already arrogated by the Commission in terms of the Treaties and common policies, such as those on trade and tariffs, agriculture, coal and steel and transport.

It should be stressed that this power to negate or neutralise national authority — whether of governments or parliaments — does not mean positive capacity to cope with key issues of common import. The bulk of Commission and Community policies are 'negative' in character. 'Legitimated' both by reference to the Treaties and — currently — by the prevailing ideology of monetarism, they amount very much to fulfilment of the distinction already made between the 'thou shalt not' of negative integration and the contrasting 'thou shalt' of either positive integration or intervention. In a real sense, the anti-intervention in the dominant ideology of Community integration, despite the contradiction of large-scale intervention in agricultural policy, helped to prepare the ground for the similar but wider-ranging negativism of monetarist ideology on a more global scale.

Similarly, multinational capital, with its vested interest in negative integration of a kind which widens its freedom for manoeuvre on its own terms, has over the last twenty years increased its share of output and employment in the Community. Its eclipse of national capital is evident from the figures given in Chapter 4, with an approach to half the output, pricing, employment and other macro aggregates of the Community as a whole commanded by giant meso-economic and multinational enterprise. This qualifies the effective economic sovereignty of those states which may wish to transform the main power relationships between big business and the state at national level, while the combination of negative ideology and policies at Community level impede an effective Community countervailance of such sovereignty loss.

Meanwhile, national labour, although formally 'integrated' within national power structures, with various forms of vertical representation at the superstructural level, is finding it increasingly difficult to ensure an effective defence of its own interests in terms of employment through historic union structures. During the current contraction of manufacturing employment, neither national governments nor unions are showing themselves capable of intervening to ensure the maintenance of investment and jobs in business which is already multinational in scope and operation.

Phase III, as represented diagrammatically, is not inevitable or neces-sarily irreversible. But it is probable unless there is a major change within the main power relationships, including the role of politics, ideology and the state at national or Community level. It is such change in the power relations between capital, labour and the state, rather than institutional change at the Community level, which can make possible a transformation of the welfare of Western Europe as a whole.

Meanwhile, multinational capital, which has grown, is growing and is set to grow bigger in future, is both marginalising national capital and thrusting national trades unions increasingly on the defensive. At the same time, negative *integration* as both the dominant ideology of the Community and the dominant characteristic of joint policies, is set to eclipse the mixture of negative and positive *intervention* still practised, in however contradic-tory a manner, by most national governments. In this respect, as already emphasised, the negative element in the Community Treaties and policies is currently being reinforced by the general negativism of the monetarist response to the economic crisis of the 1970s.

Thus the Commission may not come literally to dominate the Council of Ministers. But the implications of monetarism, with its attack on public spending, and its antagonism towards public intervention in general, is likely to result on present trends in a dominance of those Commission policies which reflect the non-interventionist ideology of the Rome Treaty. At the same time, partly because of other factors undermining national sovereignty on present trends, and not least because several major parties in Western Europe wish to see it gain enlarged powers, the European Assembly is set to increasingly negate the nominal sovereignty of national parliaments. Without positive policies for the defence of its interests at Community level, national labour would tend to find its national base eclipsed by negative policies without a corresponding integration of its interests at Community level. It should be stressed, again, that such an out-come is not inevitable. However, it is likely so long as Community integra-tion remains capitalist integration, which itself is probable so long as the Right remains in office and the Left remains divided on Community poli-cies.

NOTES

1. See, further, Richard J. Barnet and Ronald E. Müller, *Global Reach* (Cape, 1975) ch. 11.
2. Monnet himself seems to have noted the symptom rather than the cause of this American economic achievement during the war. See, further, J. Fourastié and J. P. Courthéoux, *La Planification Economique en France*, ch. 2 (Presses Universitaires, 1968).
3. See, further, Anthony Sampson, *The Seven Sisters*.
4. Clinton Rossiter (ed.), *Federalist Papers*, nos 9 and 10 (New American Library, 1961) pp. 77, 84; cit Harrison, op. cit., p. 56.

5. John Pinder and Roy Pryce, *Europe After De Gaulle* (Penguin, 1969).

6. Harrison, op. cit., pp. 46–52.

7. Ibid., p. 70 (my emphasis).

8. Cf., further, Stuart Holland, *Underdevelopment in a Developed Economy: The Italian Case*, Regional Studies (1971).

9. FIAT and Pirelli were later to modify their resistance under pressure of two factors which increased their 'political sensitivity' (or responsiveness to government pressure: first, the example of major state enterprise location in the South; and, second, trades union pressure to undertake such location). See, further, Sixth Report from the Expenditure Committee, *Public Money in the Private Sector* (HMSO, 1972) vol. III, Minutes of Evidence, appendix 24.

10. See, further, Jacques Delors, 'The Decline of French Planning', in Stuart Holland (ed.), *Beyond Capitalist Planning*, ch. 1 (Blackwell, 1978).

11. Cf., *inter alia*, M. Barre insiste sur la nécessité d'une remise en ordre de l'économie', *Le Monde*, 4 Jan. 1977.

12. Cf. D. Grisoni and H. Portelli, *Luttes ouvrières en Italie de 1960 à 1970* chs 2 and 3 (Aubier Montagne, 1976).

13. A. J. P. Taylor, *The Course of German History* (Hamish Hamilton, 1948.

14. The French text was widely reproduced in the Belgian and French press at the time. An Italian translation was produced by Sinistra Europea, and gave rise to a conference attended by PCI, PSI and foreign spokesmen in Rome in 1976. Agenor published the full text of the English version as pamphlet in 1977.

15. BBC Television, 'Tonight', 20 Apr. 1977. It should be noted that Brandt stressed that he was not against EuroCommunism as such, which he claimed might well provide a model for Third World – conveniently for the SPD – countries.

16. See, further, *The Times*, 10 June, 3 July and 27 Oct. 1972; *Financial Times*, 10 June and 21 Oct. 1972; *Corriere della Sera*, 7 June 1972, and *l'Unita*, 9 June 1972.

8 Super-Power or Supine Partner ?

Europe versus America

Without strong US support there probably never would have been much force behind the movement for a United States of Europe. This was not only because the concept had a pleasantly familiar ring to the US federalists, but also because it reflected real political awareness that Continental Western Europe was the first line of defence of US interests in the immediate postwar period, and especially during the period of what became know as the 'Cold War'.

In the immediate postwar period, when Germany was under direct rule by the 'big two' of the United States and the Soviet Union, and the 'small two' of Britain and France, US international attention was directed mainly at events elsewhere, and not least in China. Roosevelt had been more concerned with what happened to Chiang Kai-Shek than with what happened in Western Europe. In general, he was convinced of the irreversible decline of France, intended to ensure the continued reverse of Germany, and counted on a continuation of the 'special relationship' with Britain to order West European affairs.

The succession of Harry Truman, and the appointment of George Marshall as Secretary of State in January 1947, marked the change towards more active US interest in the shape of Western Europe. The settlement of the Second World War had avoided the reparations of Versailles. But Marshall realised, in addition, that victors and vanquished alike would need economic underpinning and political support if unemployment and impoverishment were not to give fuel to Communism in Western Europe. Leadership given to resistance against Fascism by the Communists had played an important part in their participation in postwar coalition Governments in France and Italy, and their placing themselves near to potential state power.

In other words, whatever its humanitarian motives, Marshall's offer of reconstruction aid in June 1947 to both the Western and Eastern European countries was a shrewd political move. Its rejection by the Soviet Union, the creation of the Cominform, major strikes in Italy and France in November and December that year, and interim emergency aid to these two countries to maintain necessary imports, was followed in February 1948 by the Communist *coup* in Prague and the partial blockade of Berlin in April. Under the circumstances, the US Congress voted the Marshall

Aid funds for Western European countries in a mood of animated self-interest. Marshall's aid seemed the best way of underpinning the front line of global capitalism, in Europe.

The victory of the Communists under Mao in China the same year reinforced this focus of US interest in Western Europe. For the time being, it appeared to be the decisive area of US international politics, and crucial if the United States was to avoid a repetition there of the collapse which had preceded Mao's success. In such a global context, they undertook, via Marshall Aid, to make available $4 billion a year for three years in reconstruction funds. Much of this, in any case, would take the form of demand for American exports, and would help sustain employment in the postwar US economy.

It was very much in this context that, in the decade following the war, the United States took a marked interest in the movement for European integration. This ranged from specific support for the Council of Europe in May 1948, for the Schuman Declaration of May 1950 (heralding the creation of the Coal and Steel Community), as well as interest in the abortive proposals for a European Political Community and a European Defence Community which would have graced the political and military legitimisation of the new West Germany.

The contest also gave particular scope for the political talents of the European federalists such as Jean Monnet and the determined band of idealistic federalists whom he sponsored. Monnet had been in the United States since 1940, operating at the highest level. He played a major part in the shaping of the 'Victory Programme', including its astronomic armaments targets, and had worked with Marshall (when the latter was chief of staff) to organise the allocation of production targets to the giant enterprises which had come to dominate US industry in the interwar period. Through Harry Hopkins, he had important access to Roosevelt, and through his pupils and disciples, such presidential influence was to hang over, in modified form, into the postwar era.[1]

There are strong grounds for claiming that these heady years left an indelible mark on the enthusiasts of the European movement. Individuals who had seen the isolationism of the United States between the wars, came to believe that a profound conversion had affected the American body politic. Idealists themselves, they felt that the power of ideas had been justified by Monnet's initiatives, and thereby exaggerated their power over more sordid but more basic state and corporate interests. The apparent effectiveness of subjective action by an élite gave the impression that enlightened élitism could transform recalcitrant reality. Subjective ideology, it appeared, could transform the political, state and economic interest of giants such as the United States.

It therefore came as an increasingly bitter disillusion to some of those idealists to realise that the momentum of ideas over reality appeared to be losing its sway when De Gaulle threw the spectre of his view of France on

Monnet's blueprints for a United States of Europe. In practice, however, something else had changed, leaving the European idealists stranded. Economically, the interests of large-scale US capital were already satisfied by the creation of the Common Market from 1958. Internationally, US political and state interests had already moved substantially elsewhere.

The shift of US primary interest away from Europe stemmed partly from the Korean War, which signalled increased concern with South-East Asia in general. It was accompanied by the arrival of John Foster Dulles, under Eisenhower's presidency, to the US State Department in 1953. But it was also underlain by the very success of Marshall Aid in underpinning an unprecedented success in the Western European economies. The economic security of capitalism in the Six ECSC countries appeared well assured some time before the EEC was created. Military security was already secured via NATO.

Dulles took advantage of this situation to occupy himself with attempted repeat performances elsewhere, aiming to sucure US hegemony on a global scale. He did so through a system of military, economic and political alliances with such countries as Iraq, Iran, Pakistan, Thailand, Formosa and, not least, the regime of Ngo Dinh Diem in South Vietnam. SEATO was meant to complement NATO. Elsewhere, in Africa, little pressure at all would be brought on South Africa to modify her racism. In black Africa, colonial ties were being loosened by Britain, if not France, while the Arab oil producers had not yet discovered OPEC and were in the hands of the multinational oil companies. In Latin America, the Monroe doctrine found ardent new application in the postwar period, ultimately including, in 1961, the euphemistically titled Alliance for Progress. Institutionally, the Latin American Free Trade Area would complement the European Common Market structure, in intention if not reality.

Besides, in Europe, the invasion of Hungary in 1956 had followed the remarkable Khrushchev 'destalinisation' speech to the Twentieth Congress. On the one hand, such events might be a preliminary to an undermining of the Soviet bloc in Eastern Europe. On the other, the recognised spheres-of-influence approach isolated the Hungarian crisis on the other side of the 'iron curtain'. The Berlin crisis of November 1958 had its echoes in further intimations of potential crisis through to the early 1960s. But the catalytic effect on the United States was virtually non-existent relative to the earthquake caused by the partial blockade and airlift in 1948. Berlin in the early 1960s was nothing in comparison to Cuba. And Cuba, as it proved, was the instance of direct US-Soviet confrontation on the global stage. Both super-powers had enough trouble on their hands elsewhere to encourage what later became know as *détente* – the Soviet Union with China, and the United States with Vietnam. In particular, the possibility of Sino-Soviet differences erupting into military conflict, and the Soviet concentration of troops near China, underlined the unlikelihood of a military invasion of Western Europe. During the period of the Vietnam war,

US interest in NATO became secondary. Interest in the active furthering of Common Market integration became virtually non-existent.

The globalisation of US interest away from Western Europe was reinforced by the globalisation of the means of conflict and the relations of force. In the immediate postwar period, when bomber power had not been superseded by intercontinental ballistic missiles, Western Europe was a crucial strategic base for the United States relative to the Soviet Union. But after the ICBMs, the US no longer needed Western European launching sites for missiles aimed at Moscow. With Atlas in 1960, the Titans in 1961 and the Minuteman in 1962, the United States had secured domestic launching sites for its nuclear armoury. Within only another year, the USA had dispersed them undersea in Polaris submarines, literally on a global scale. Even the NATO forces found themselves equipped with submarines, operating way beyond the Common Market. The coincidence between political, economic and military interest which prompted such acute US concern with Continental Western Europe in the decade after the war had been transformed in the next ten years.[2]

Besides, if the United States did not actually come to view the EEC as a Frankenstein rather than a favoured child, the emergence of a Community with a significant common external tariff against, in particular, US food exports, sombered the idealism of the early years of support for a United States of Europe. The paradox whereby the United States has maintained much of its balance of payments strength by agricultural rather than industrial exports has been commonplace for some time. It also took some time before it became a common factor in US pressure to eliminate EEC protection through first the Dillon then the Kennedy Rounds for tariff reduction on a global scale. One of the very first studies of the impact of the EEC, by Jacob Viner, as mentioned in Chapter 3, had stressed that the Common Market could well be trade-diverting rather than trade-creating, with disadvantages for non-member countries.

With supranational self-deception, the Commission of the EEC chose to see in the Kennedy Round a compliment to its own pretensions. Thus it stated in 1962 that

> it is a great event, recognising the considerable advance made by the Community in four years of existence, to see the United States allow that it now finds in Community Europe a partner of comparable scale with which it can treat equally in both reciprocal trading relations and tasks to be undertaken together on a world scale.[3]

Thus the Europeans agreed to a tariff reduction of 50 per cent with the United States, and opened themselves to increased competition with US food producers who, on average, employed one-fifteenth as many workers per unit of land and about a quarter the share of overall working population in agriculture as themselves.[4]

Thus, during the early 1960s, the US pulled its armaments back home while the EEC agreed to a major tariff disarmament towards US imports. The asymmetry of the operation has only in part been offset by the agreement in 1979 to base cruise missiles as a supplement to ICBMs in Western Europe. Ironically, but not typically, this period of virtual abolition of the common external tariff of the Community, which was to reduce protection on industrial goods an average of some 6 per cent, coincided with a spate of academically credited exercises in trade creation and trade diversion resulting from external tariffs, which were to be imposed on students of economic integration into the 1970s. Meanwhile US multinational capital bought out weaker European competitiors with dollars from the US payments deficit and exploited the Common Market on a scale which the Europeans could not parallel by reverse purchases in the US. In this respect, if few others, Servan-Schreiber was on the mark.[5]

Jack Kennedy did not live to see the completion of his Round. While it progressed through the 1960s, his successor was preoccupied with defoliating Vietnam. When Richard Nixon finally gained the White House, he found that the 'European' policy of the State Department was in the unreadiness which one might well expect of a country which had just won outright on both the trade and capital account in its unequal contest with the EEC. But Richard Nixon was a man concerned to double-check his advantage. He demanded a profit-and-loss account on the question of the impending enlargement of the European Communities.

The results revealed two opposing views in the State Department. There were those who continued in the context of support for a powerful European movement, and wished well to the Community in its enlargement programme. Their current or outdated realism was contrasted with those who saw a United Europe, potentially armed with a single currency, as a threat to a US monetary, economic and political hegemony on a global scale.[6] The then Special Adviser to the President, Henry Kissinger, voiced the case that, while some Americans had hoped that the European Community would be a first step towards liberalisation of trade, others had argued that it remained a protected area which could raise even more lasting and more dangerous tariff barriers against the United States.[7]

Atlantic Europe

As Secretary of State, Kissinger was to pursue the same line with his customary vigour, leading to the proposal of a New Atlantic Charter. Thus, in London, in April 1973, he argued that there was a real danger that the Atlantic Community, which had ensured peace in Europe since the war, would be eroded by the enlargement of the Community. He later made a major declaration in December 1973, at the time of the Copenhagen Summit, claiming that EEC enlargement should not be made at the cost of the wider Atlantic Community, that Europe clearly could have a wider world role and that this was welcomed by the United States, both politically and economically. But he wanted more stress on convergence and less on divergence between Europe and the United States, and in particular more consultation between Washington and Brussels before the European Community took its initiatives.[8]

It was clear that Kissinger may have been under a misapprehension about the speed or likelihood of higher stages of integration in the EEC. But the prospect of a formal commitment of the Heads of the Nine to Economic and Monetary Union by 1980, was more than the US could contemplate with equanimity, not least during a period in which defeat in Vietnam was causing an agonising reappraisal of America's global role, and when the dollar had been under pressure as a world currency, leading to its effective devaluation. The United States had originally supported the European Movement, but under different conditions. The original Six had then been weak, whereas now they were strong. Their currencies had then depended substantially on the dollar, whereas their strength had now in part helped destabilize it. From Washington, it may well have appeared that a single European currency could transform world monetary domination by the US; that it could challenge US financial hegemony, including that exercised through non-EEC institutions such as the World Bank and the IMF, and that it could equalise an Atlantic Partnership which the US hitherto had dominated with virtual equanimity.

One of the major aggravations in US-European relations through the 1960s had certainly been the failure of individual Community countries to respond with the alacrity expected by President Johnson to the request for (even token) military support in Vietnam. The Yom Kippur war helped to exacerbate relations, when the US found itself refused landing facilities to re-supply the Israelis. But it was the general shift in US global interest which underlay the new American concern. The change was well expressed by the former Gaullist Foreign Minister, Couve de Murville, who argued that 'having made its agreement with the Soviet Union [on the principle of *détente*], the US embarked on a policy to re-affirm its control over Europe and Japan'.[9] The normalisation of relations between East and West Germany, as achieved by the Brandt *Ostpolitik*, had removed yet a further plank of the old relations between the hitherto most dependent partner in the Western Alliance and the USA. The Nine might declare that they wanted an 'equal partnership' with the United States.[10] But it was leadership, not partnership, which the US wanted.[11]

De Gaulle, of course, was both aware of this reality behind US policy to Europe, and opposed to it. Instead of an Atlantic Europe, as already stressed in Chapter 3, he wanted a Europe *from* the Atlantic to the Urals. Instead of a supranational Europe he wanted a Europe of nation-states (to be dominated, not surprisingly, by France). But with the passing of the giant's mantle to Georges the banker Pompidou, the force of this anti-Atlanticism was blunted. With the succession of Giscard d'Estaing, French European strategy underwent a double reverse: it returned to the supranationalism of formal commitment to economic and monetary union, and to Atlanticism. By January 1977 Giscard was committing himself to a confederation of Europe, with an elected assembly for the Community.[12]

It would be facile to argue that Giscard represents the arrival in France of the technocratic élite who have abandoned transforming aims for Europeanism, on the lines admitted by some of the pluralist theorists.[13] Implicitly, both Pompidou and Giscard had moved from De Gaulle's support for national capital and the national capitalist class to support for multinational capital and that section of the capitalist class which it represented. It could be argued that Giscard saw the problem subjectively, in a simpler way. But it is clear enough that he had realised, through his experience as Minister for the Economy and Finance in the 1960s, that France could not 'go it alone' in a Gaullist manner without a major change in both her global and her domestic politics, on a scale which would transform politics itself in France.

What is clear is the extent to which Giscard, by the later 1970s was facing major difficulty in pursuing a policy of Atlantic Europeanism *vis-à-vis* the old guard of the Gaullists, and the new forces behind the Common Programme of the French Left. From the Right, his former Prime Minister Jacques Chirac was mobilising opinion against him through the Rassemblement pour la République. Chirac's populism was putting Giscard's presidential chances in jeopardy. While the President chose to talk of 'a sort of collective pessimism' in France since the onslaught of the economic crisis, Chirac was expressing nationalism as a visceral response to international disorder. He thereby illustrated forces which were arguably more real than the blueprint for European confederation backed by Giscard.[14]

But, behind the abstraction of nationalism alone Chirac was also expressing the interests of a *class*: that section of national capital threatened by the process of international and multinational integration backed by Pompidou and Giscard. While dressed with a romantic and apparently backward-looking rhetoric, Chirac in practice was representing the interests of a real power group in the social and economic structure, who saw their interests threatened if State power were neutralised either through integration with Europe or a subservient Atlanticism.

Super-Power Potential?
The claim that the European Community is a nascent super-power has included both Right and Left of the main political spectrum. But from either perspective, the prospect seems indefinitely remote. The reasons are both internal and external to the Community.

Jean Monnet, as godfather of the campaign for a United States of Europe, and like many of his spiritual godsons over thirty years, assumed that an internal economic dynamic in the Common Market would in due course provoke political union. Their determinism — assuming that political institutions would respond to and reflect economic integration — is in one sense real. The directly elected European Assembly is now a reality. But Monnet and company had expected real political powers for such an institution rather than a fig-leaf for Commission bureaucracy.

On the other hand, Johan Galtung's 'Marxist' thesis shares a good deal of both matter and method with the non-Marxists. His key argument is that in the EEC 'a new super-power is emerging'. Even his subtitle on this theme, *A Superpower in the Making*, compares directly with the title of the Hallstein testament *Europe in the Making*.[15]

Galtung admits that the start, stop, re-start syndrome in the Community may tend to disguise its super-power potential. But he sees the EEC in terms which many of the Euro-enthusiasts, explicitly or implicitly, would share, as an attempt 'to recreate (i) a Eurocentric world, a world with its centre in Europe, and (ii) a unicentric Europe, a Europe with its centre in the West'. The attempt to regenerate Europe reflects the response to the collapse and decline of the individual global empires of the European nation states: 'the "Market" aspect of this new Europe should not deceive us. It is meant to deal in "power units" more than in economic units alone'. It is such new power which will be exercised on the Third World and on Eastern Europe. The latter will increasingly be squeezed between the Community and the Soviet Union until 'Europe becomes split in a much more fundamental manner than by the Cold War'. Comecon is unlikely to be able to countervail this new division of Europe. The Third World contries might, if they mobilise sufficiently determined contervailance on a global scale.[16]

The implicit exaggeration of Galtung's thesis can be seen by reference to the complex factors involved in the association of less developed countries to the Community. It also emerges in the extent to which Galtung neglects the internal dynamics of the EEC, and the inability of its institutions to bridge the gap beween super-power pretension and bureaucratic muddling. His argument on the nature of power in the Community again shares a similar method with the Euro-enthusiasts of the Centre and Right. It is superficially backed by a number of figures and tables indicating the quantitative weight of the Community in global terms, without appreciating the extent to which the quality of power in a real sense is missing from the overall picture.[17] Such power depends on a particular combination of political, state, ideological and economic relations. In the Community sense, as we have argued in earlier chapters, such a combination is missing. Moreover, it is missing not because of insufficient subjective factors (lack of a Community spirit or the will to integrate) as because of objective problems thrown up by the process of integration itself, and its unequal structural, spatial and social distribution.

Fracture Lines

This argument has been well put, in general terms, by Tom Nairn. He cites Galtung's argument that Europe has the ideological edge on America and other global competitors since in terms of 'culture or ideology Western Europe has always remained the centre of the world . . . and the cradle of the major ideologies of conservatism, liberalism and marxism'.[18] Nairn points out that there is an absent guest on the list: nationalism. More importantly, he stresses that the role of the nation-state in capitalism has been two-sided. It both promoted the defence of initial markets in which nascent capitalist enterprise flourished, and then sought to protect them in the arena of the world capitalist economy. National capital outstripped the nation-state, yet also needed and depended on nationalism to protect its global adventures. This was especially true in terms of the uneven development of capitalism itself. Regional disparities in the widest sense have 'sought out and found the old buried fault lines of the [European] area . . . Nationlism in the real sense is never a historical accident, or a mere invention. It reflects the latent fracture lines of human society under strain'.[19]

Nairn points to the fact that the divisions between North and South Europe, stressed by Farhi, represent such major fracture lines.[20] He could have stressed also the emergence of an 'inner' and 'outer' Community in terms of product, income and employment, reflected in Brandt's recommendation of a 'two-tier' Community. Such fractures are scarcely papered over by the Community's regional policy with its outdated assumption that incentives and indirect intervention will equalise the European distribution of economic activity. The regional disintegration of Western Europe which would be formalised by such a two-tier Community is echoed in the regional disintegration of constituent nation-states such as Britain, with a running civil war in Northern Ireland, and devolutionary pressures on a major scale from the Scots through the mid 1970s.

Nairn also seems very much on the right lines in pointing out that, while the major super-powers also have regional problems, they confront them from a much stronger organic base than does the European Community. As he argues,

among the five great power candidates [the Community] alone is not a 'nation' nor likely to evolve into one. Three of the other four are indeed, in very different ways, pluri-ethnic communities occupying great tracts of the globe. But this only reinforces the point. For they have succeeded in imposing a unified nation-state sutructure and a supporting mass nationalism on their heterongeneous basis (more or less as England and France did in earlier modern times). And two of them, of course, have done this in terms of new modes of collective development diverging from the capitalist forms described above.[21]

Moreover, one could argue strongly that the European Community is subjectively perceived as progressive, by its advocates, yet in objective terms is backward-looking. The Schuman Declaration itself, to the effect that the Coal and Steel Community would ensure that another conflict between France and Germany was not only unthinkable but materially impossible, amounted to one of the best ways, after the event, of trying to avoid the past. The idealistic intention to 'overcome narrow nationalism' gained impetus only in the post-1945 period, by which time nationalism and two wars had already *dis*integrated Western Europe as the major force in global politics and economics. By the standard of the United States, where federalism grew organically under virtually ideal conditions, the federalist movement in postwar Europe was 200 years too late. Also, unlike the Soviet Union or Communist China, where decrepit social and institutional systems were challenged and overthrown by a new system, reinforced by a new ideology, Western Europe is trying to integrate in the twentieth century on the liberal capitalist ideology of two centuries ago. It is trying to shape the future by the blueprint of yesteryear.

This is not to say that the Community has no 'supranational' future, nor that it will fail to achieve higher stages of economic integration to a greater or lesser degree. But the ideology and policies of capitalist integration in the Community are unsuited to the real structural needs of the Western European economies. Virtually every reference to the role of the state in the outdated Rome Treaty involves an explicit 'authority' to restrict rather than socialise and democratise state power. The supranationalism intended by the federalists assumes that the working of the market mechanism will equalise social and economic conditions, rather than promote structural, social and spatial inequality. State intervention is held to be necessary at Community level, but only as an indirect and secondary instrument, with mainly negative rather than positive powers.

Thus some Euro-enthusiasts find themselves dismayed when governments in the 1970s have responded to the economic crisis by increasing subsidies and salvage operations rather than embracing economic union. Conceiving the role of the nation-state mainly as 'nationalism', they disguise from themselves the primary role of state intervention in mediating conflicting interests arising from the basic instability and incoherence of capitalism itself. The ongoing force of national interests in mediating the problems of uneven development, and opposing supranationalism, is well illustrated by the failure to make significant progress on common policies since the departure of De Gaulle. For most of the 1960s it was commonplace among the Euro-enthusiasts that if only De Gaulle were to join Joan of Arc in the Elysian fields, others with heads below the clouds could get on with the rational construction of Europe. De Gaulle went, and the heads of government committed themselves to economic and monetary union by 1980. But they then found that the rational construction of Europe was more difficult than anticipated.

In reality, the European Community in the decade since De Gaulle's departure has evolved not one major economic policy of practical significance, i.e. a policy which has been started, is working now and promises to be effective in future. In monetary policy, moneta*rism* imposed primarily at national level what is more prominent than an approach to a binding monetary union. The initial 'snake', or aligned band of currencies, was abandoned twice by France in the early 1970s. 'Son-of-Snake', or the European Monetary System, proposed in 1978, was botched by the initial refusal of Britain to join, and by the delay in agreement of both Italy and France. Not least, the EEC's programme for economic 'recovery' since the mid-1970s has amounted to waiting for 'big brother' in the United States to expand the US economy and thus provide demand for more exports from Europe. For an allegedly economic Community, little could more clearly demonstrate its status as supine partner rather than budding super-power.

Relations of Force

However, one of the *key* respects in which Europe neither is, nor is likely soon to prove to be, a super-power lies in its lack of independent 'relations of force'. This includes the NATO framework as a whole, which literally locks the military capacity of Europe to the United States, with the need for a joint turning of keys before weaponry over a certain 'kill' threshhold can be released. At the Community level, it also involves relations of force in another sense. The Commission has none of the attributes for independent enforcement of any decisions, in particular a policing force. If it were to indict a nation-state in the European Court of Justice, it could not compel the attendance for the hearing of a given national representative. In contrast with the United States, it has no 'national guard' which it can send in when the state authorities disregard its rulings. Respect for these depends on nation-states accepting them, just as invocation of 'an important national interest' (in the phrase of the Luxembourg compromise of January 1966) is up to the nation-state itself.

Of course, De Gaulle not only withdrew temporarily from Community institutions, but also withdrew more permanently from the NATO organisation, and 'went it alone' with his own military and defence programme. For a while, as he pushed massive resources into a nominally independent rocket, supersonic bomber and nuclear arms capacity, it looked as if he might reverse the fate of Britain in cancelling Blue Streak and TSR-2 Also, of course, his 'withdrawal' from NATO did at least cause the latter to move its headquarters from a scenic site on the Seine to a complex of squab structures on the road to Brussels airport. But De Gaulle's 'big push' on an independent 'defence' capacity, and his gestures to NATO have not had the same central effect as his 1965 'empty chair' policy, and in large part because of the different relations of force between the European and NATO communities. The EEC may be no mere paper tiger, but NATO and Soviet missiles have nuclear teeth.

Mary Kaldor has clearly pointed out the interrelation of 'the NATO' question with the difficulties which the European Community has experienced in developing its 'own' defence industries, and thus gaining common policies over a broad range of advanced technology. Of course, there have been joint 'European' defence projects, including the multi-role combat aircraft, which took-off with possibly the unique distinction in some commentators' eyes of performing no single role better than the individual specialised planes it replaced. On the other hand, there is no guarranteed common purchasing policy for European defence products because of the US role in NATO. Nominally, there is supposed to be a 'two-way street' in purchasing policy, from both American and European companies. But, for the vast part, there has been one-way traffic from US suppliers to European buyers.

As Mary Kaldor puts it, the creation of 'European' multinational defence companies 'would mean greater *military* integration . . . In other words, European arms companies imply European defence just as the two-way street implies NATO and American defence'. She stresses that in fact NATO is under strain, in as much as the United States feels that it is not getting a return in economic terms – support for the dollar – for its military commitment in men, materials and hardware. There are also the general fears of European penetration of the US market, even if these are less in some quarters than comparable fear of Japan and South-East Asian exports. But, as she adds, such differences – like those wider dimensions of global struggle between the United States and the Soviet Union – have taken the form of a necessary 'ritual' masking social conflicts within respective spheres of influence. Meanwhile, in her own words, 'at the apex of the integrated NATO command system there are the American troops in Europe'.[22]

Informal Imperialism?

If it is improbable that the European Community will become a super-state or super-power on the US model, it is quite possible that it will provide a framework for what Giovanni Arrighi has called 'the informal empire of free enterprise'. By this he means – in contrast with formal imperialism – not a state above other states, but an area or zone of economic domination. In the nineteenth century, such a domination was established by Britain in a wider area than that of formal empire through the mechanism of free trade, dominated by Britain. In the later twentieth century, with the rise of multinational capital and an increasing trend for foreign investment to substitute for foreign trade, a new informal empire is being established. As Arrighi puts it: 'the specific characteristic of the contemporary phenomenon is not free trade but free enterprise'.[23]

Arrighi admits that the distinction between the two kinds of formal imperialism is not rigid. Certainly, in the EEC, one has seen a nominal emphasis on free trade in the Community Treaties, and an actual dominance of multinational capital over the last twenty years. He has drawn the concept from Hobson, and applied it — with important variations — to a world nearly a century on from that on which Hobson based his analysis.[24] One of the key factors is identification of which state or group of states, behind the informal structure, actually serves ends which cannot, or cannot as well, be served by formal imperialism.

In the European case, the prime candidate is not hard to find. Germany, like Japan, has had a bitter experience of trying to establish a formal empire. Both have achieved more through economic dominance than they gained by attempts to establish political hegemony through military means. It is reputed that Bismarck, in one interview with a lobby from the Pan-German league, who were inviting him to send troops to back trade in Africa, turned to a map of Europe behind him and declared: 'Gentleman, here is Germany and here is her Africa'. Certainly West Germany, from the ashes of defeat and Allied occupation, has risen phoenix-like through economic power, establishing an economic axis from the Netherlands to Austria which makes *Anschluss*, in retrospect, seem like pure military adventurism.

Moreover, in retrospect, the Community framework has served West Germany very well. The initial trade-off between De Gaulle and Adenauer, whereby France would remain in the Community for high farm prices in return for accepting free trade with German industry, has served Germany well on both accounts. With a small-scale peasantry and a self-employed farm population, the Federal Republic has gained significantly on both the agricultural and industrial fronts. More importantly, the combination of a basically undamaged heavy industrial structure, with an undervalued currency through to the early 1960s, plus the facility of a skilled indigenous labour inflow from the Eastern Zone in the 1950s, enabled West Germany to build an export machinery *sans pareil* among Community countries which little save world recession could compromise. By the time that key world currencies faltered against the power of the Deutschmark, from the later 1960s, successive revaluation alone could not qualify the force of German export penetration, and the mounting of massive foreign reserves.

This situation of economic dominance, in contrast to a weak dollar and a perennially weak pound, has given West Germany more than a place in the Council of Ministers. It has given her a dominant position not only within the Council, but also in other councils of world finance such as the IMF. Chancellor Schmidt, whose 'home economics' philosophy of balanced budgets and financial stringency has earned him acceptability in the financial institutions of the Bundesrepublik, and notoriety abroad, has not hesitated to instruct the rest of the world, including the United States itself, on how to run their economies. For weakly structured economies emerging, perhaps temporarily, from the long march out of Fascism, such as Portugal, such insistence on financial disciplines has been disastrous. For others, such as Britain, it has at best suited the inclinations of a government unready to transcend economic crisis through radical measures, and at worst been disadvantageous.

In practice, the success of the postwar West German economy has been virtually unique in Western Europe. But, as with nineteenth-century Britain, which established its dominance through being the first starter in modern industry, postwar Germany expects other countries with different structures and circumstances to follow her economic model. On a monopoly capital base, masked by a liberal capitalist philosophy of *Mittelstandspolitik* and the so-called Social Market philosophy, West Germany flirted only once, and briefly, with anything as progressive as Keynesian intervention, in the late 1960s and early 1970. Since 1974, her economic philosophy has been more rigorously monetarist than that of the United States.

Tragically, in the later 1970s, the Federal Republic is not only in a position to urge different economies to emulate her own unrepeatable postwar experience, but is seeking to impose that model on them through the IMF and the international banking framework. Such imposition, on different systems and societies, of one's own image, is the classic format of imperialism. Even worse, other countries cannot in practice follow the West German model, not only because it is too late, but also because it is literally inapplicable in conditions of world slump. The very 'virtues' of postwar German expansion have been founded on export-led growth. But the structure of her visible exports, since the mid-1960s, has been predominantly — 80 per cent — investment goods and materials for industry. Other countries cannot purchase West German visible exports on a sufficient scale to re-employ her economy without extensive deficit financing and reflation of precisely the kind which the German authorities, in their financial wisdom, abhor.[25]

As a result, West Germany not only is the deflationary state *par excellence* in the European Community, but also is in a position to demand parallel deflation from other countries. The monetarism which underlies such demands is a reactionary philosophy of non-intervention in market forces, by which the strong — whether firms, social classes or countries — seek to help themselves at the expense of the weak, yet lack the perception to realise that only by financing and aiding the weak could they conceivably further help themselves to bigger shares of world markets. Implicitly, the crisis of the West German economy is masked by the extent to which it has exported some 0.6 million 'guest' workers back to their homelands. But, in effect, the crisis is one of domestic under-consumption, and an economy unable to absorb the heavy industrial and investment goods necessary to re-attain full employment.[26]

For anyone familiar with the themes of pre- First World War imperialism, the omens are ominous indeed. In one sense the sheer advance of nuclear technology and global meta-kill may render a repeat of German military ambitions improbable. Certainly she is aware that any military conflict in Europe would be likely to be fought over her own graveyard. Nevertheless, to adapt a well-know observation, for West Germany economics may well prove to be war by other means. The nineteenth-century imperialism, whereby European powers disarmed and neutralised weaker states in less developed countries, has given way to a new form of imperialism whereby West Germany as banker to the Western world fights through credit and finance to prevent any economic armaments which could defeat her export industries.

The EEC clearly provides precisely the instrument suited to her short-term needs. It probably was not mere chauvinism which promoted French planners in 1960s to comment on the Rome Treaty as a formula for tariff 'disarmament'. Monetary union would provide a long-term formula which would establish a Federal German dominance over other EEC states of a kind on which Bismarck could only have speculated. With one strong central economy, and a Deutschmark zone, West Germany would exert a hegemony in Western Europe greater than that of nineteenth-century Britain. The orthodox mechanisms of her dominance would make the gold standard appear positively neutral by comparison. The mechanisms of a European Monetary Fund, dominated by her reserves, would give Germany within Europe what the United States for more than twenty postwar years enjoyed through dominance of the IMF.

NOTES

1. See further J. Fourastié and J.-P. Courthéoux, *La Planification Economique en France*.
2. See, further, Alain Joxe, 'Atlanticisme et crise de l'Etat européen: la crise militaire', in Nicos Poulantzas (ed.), *Crise de l'Etat*, (Presses Universitaires, 1976) part IV, pp. 309—16.

   Cruise missiles based in Western Europe in the 1980s would be supplementary to the inter-continental ballistic weapons, and do not essentially qualify the preceding argument.
3. EEC, *Memorandum de la Commission sur la programme d'action de la Communauté pendant la deuxième étape* (1962) p. 84.
4. Jacques Mallet, 'Les États Unis et le Marché Commun Européen, *Revue de l'Action Populaire* (June 1963).
5. Jean-Jacques Servan-Schreiber, *The American Challenge* (0000) chs 1 and 2.
6. George Lesser, 'Les États Unis ont-ils intérêt à l'élargissement de la Communauté?', *Le Monde*, 13 Oct. 1970.
7. Emile James, 'Les États Unis sont-ils encore favourables a la Communauté européenne?', *Revue Banque* (Paris: July-Aug. 1972) pp. 645—50.
8. See, further, 'L'Unité de l'Europe ne doit pas se faire aux dépens de la communauté atlantique' (report and analysis of the Kissinger declaration), *La Monde*, 14 Dec. 1973.
9. See 'The View from Brussels', *Time Magazine*, 9 Dec. 1974.

10. 'Les Relations Europe-États Unis', *La Monde*, 27 Mar. 1974.

11. Hélène Delorme and Frederic Langer, 'L'Europe des Neuf: Une Dépendence Contradictoire', *Revue Française de Science Politique*, no. 4 (Aug. 1976).

12. Charles Hargrove, 'President Giscard d'Estaing sets confederation and elected Parliament as goal for Europe', *The Times*, 29 Jan. 1977.

13. See, further, R.J. Harrison, *Europe in Question* (1974) p. 188.

14. See David Leitch, 'The Tower of Chirac', *New Statesman*, 21 Jan. 1977.

15. Johan Galtung, *The European Community: A Superpower in the Making* (1973); and Walter Hallstein, *Europe in the Making* (Allen & Unwin, 1972).

16. Galtung, op. cit., pp. 12, 17, 97 and 151–9.

17. Ibid., ch. 3.

18. Ibid., p. 53.

19. Tom Nairn, 'Super-Power or Failure?' in Tom Nairn (ed.), *Atlantic Europe*? pp. 68–77.

20. Andre Farhi, 'Europe: Behind the Myths', in Nairn (ed.), op. cit.

21. Nairn, 'Super-Power or Failure?'.

22. Mary Kaldor, *The Disintegrating West* (Allen Lane, 1978) especially chs 7 and 10.

23. Giovanni Arrighi, *The Geometry of Imperialism* (New Left Books, 1978) pp. 102–8 and 139.

24. J.A. Hobson, *Imperialism: A Study* (Allen & Unwin, 1938).

25. Karl Georg Zinn, in Stuart Holland (ed.), *Beyond Capitalist Planning*, ch. 5 (Basil Blackwell, 1978).

26. See, further, Zinn, op. cit.

Part Five
Associates and Applicants

9 Association or Domination?

Shortly before the signature of the Rome Treaty in 1957, four of the member countries of the now enlarged Community of the Nine were substantial colonial powers: Britain, France, The Netherlands and Belgium. The very impetus towards European integration partly reflected crisis in the old-style imperialism of direct rule abroad. For two of the countries concerned, The Netherlands and Britain, peaceful decolonialisation was under way and would continue, with whatever eleventh-hour disgrace in the case of Rhodesia. For the two others, France and Belgium, the end of the colonial era was forced, fought and traumatic. Mollet was pre-occupied with Algeria, rapidly following the abortive Suez adventure and the defeat in Indo-China following Dien Bien Phu. In Belgium, big-business interests were still determined to support regimes in the Congo open to their influence, to the point of financing ongoing civil war.

Neo-Colonialism and Yaoundé

In the circumstances, it was hardly surprising that the first association agreement of the Six with some of the previous colonial territories of France and Belgium should have been open to charges of neo-colonialism. Since that first agreement at Yaoundé in 1963, association was extended to include special arrangements with Kenya, Tanzania and Uganda at Arusha in 1969 with a further major agreement including other Commonwealth countries, after EEC enlargement, at Lomé in February 1975. The Lomé agreement, even on the Marxist Left, has given rise to strongly differing reactions. Thus Johan Galtung has seen it as neo-colonialist, while Bill Warren has claimed that it represents 'a major and path-breaking step forward for the under-developed countries and for their relationship to the advanced economies'.[1]

The issue is important, not only for the millions of undernourished, underemployed and underprivileged in the countries concerned, but also in terms of determining whether the European Community has already played or can undertake a progressive international role. It also relates to the question whether the Community can in fact fulfill some kind of super-power role. If so, this raises a further paradox: how can it play a super-power role in external affairs without amounting to such a power internally? Is the pattern traceable in association an exception, or does it represent writing on the wall for the future, despite the disarray of the Community in such an area as reaction to the oil crisis of the 1970s.

There is no doubt that the first Yaoundé agreement was dominated by the ex-French colonial territories in Africa.[2] There also are strong grounds for claiming that the link by which many of them remained bound to France represented – in itself – a closely neo-colonial relationship of domination.

This was partly due to the continuation of the so-called 'franc zone' and partly to the smallness and poverty of some of the main countries concerned. In scale and role, the franc zone could not be compared with the sterling area. In the early 1970s, in fourteen African countries, it amounted in volume terms to less than 3 per cent of the francs circulating in France. This partly reflected the poverty of countries such as Chad, Upper Volta, Mali and Niger, with among the lowest income per head in the world. In this sense, Paul Fabra has questioned whether one should talk of a franc zone rather than a poverty zone.[3] But the charge of neo-colonialism also related to the terms on which the French government was prepared to underwrite the currencies of the respective countries and allow them to run deficits with France. These included maintenance of a fixed exchange rate with the French franc and the establishment of the head office of some of their central banks in Paris. Under such conditions, it was hardly surprising that there should have been close political leverage in terms of French trade and technical assistance.

On the other hand, while France's ex-colonial territories dominated the first Yaoundé agreement, its formal terms appeared quite advantageous to the associates. The basic principles were simple enough. The Community undertook to reduce its tariffs to zero on goods coming from the associates. Despite qualifications, this was crucial to the latter in as much as several of their primary exports would otherwise have faced the common external tariff. Inversely, the associates were required to reciprocate by allowing duty-free access for Community exports, and to abolish quantitative restrictions on imports. The *formal* safeguards which the associates could in principle employ unilaterally to protect themselves were considerable. Thus Article 10 of the Yaoundé Association stated explicitly that three of the earlier main Articles concerning the liberalisation of trade, tariffs and quotas

> shall not preclude prohibitions or restrictions on imports, exports or goods in transit justified on the grounds of public morality, public policy, public security, the protection of human, animal or plant life or health . . . national treasures . . . or industrial and commercial property.[4]

In effect, one did not need a Sorbonne degree in sophist philosophy to find a loophole sufficient to adopt protective measures for the associated country.

Of course, form and substance differ. First, a weak partner with a strong legal argument may not be able to stop himself from being robbed with impunity. In the case of the French associated territories, the franc zone and the lack of an independent national currency spoke volumes for a dependent relationship against a few sentences of formal independence in the Yaoundé agreement. This reality of domination coloured French agreement to the specific terms of association. Second, the formal reciprocity of the association veiled the fact that most of the trade concerned was complementary rather than competitive. The pre-industrial economies of the associates were sending both France and other EEC countries primary products which they anyway needed, on cheap terms. Third, the terms of trade in the 1960s were moving dramatically against the African associated territories, especially in their trade with the EEC, where they *halved* between the first and second Yaoundé agreements against a deterioration, still severe, of a quarter in their world trade.[5] This degree of unequal exchange substantially offset the nominal value of the aid and technical assistance which they gained from the Community's Development Fund for associated territories.[6]

Second Best and Renewal
The fact that the associated territories chose to renew the Yaoundé agreement in 1969, and the fact that Kenya, Tanzania and Uganda negotiated association, has been taken as evidence that the original associates saw themselves as benefiting from association, with the new associates also reading such benefits into their applications. Thus Jean-Louis Giraudy wrote in 1973 that 'over ten years the associated territories have freely chosen to renew their links with Europe'.[7]

But in fact both the freedom and the choice were in question. The freedom for the nominally ex-dependent French territories was substantially qualified by their continuing dependence on France for support of their currencies, their deficits, and such substantive aid as happened to back the formalism of their French-modelled five-year plans. The choice was a real one, but for the second best of association rather than isolation in an increasingly hostile world economy where aid agencies could not avert crisis in development, and where alternative real support lay under the unwelcome shelter of the US or Soviet super-power. Even in the case of the Tanzanian flirtation with Chinese technical assistance, the authorities seemed aware that the best alternative to being beaten by the EEC Association was to join it. Tanzania, with Kenya and Uganda, saw two British applications for EEC entry in the 1960s and read their real future options clearly.

The 'second best' option is well enough illustrated by the comment of Torelli and Valaskas that in reality 'there were few attractive alternatives to the renewal of Yaoundé'.[8] It is supported also by a report of Philippe Lemaitre on the state of mind of the associated territories in the approach to the renewal of Yaoundé 2, or the Lomé Convention, entitled quite simply 'The Associates are Afraid'. The associates wanted to protect the special access which they had on the export side to the EEC, whatever the import costs, and to avoid 'its dilution and weakening in a more general framework'.[9]

This was directly in contrast with the declared aims of the British Minister for Overseas Development, Judith Hart, and the renegotiation position of the Labour Party, which was aimed precisely at breaking down the exclusiveness of the previous association agreements by extending its application rather than limiting it mainly to the ex-French colonial territories. On the other hand, Judith Hart also wanted to increase the effective aid component in the Community's Development Fund. The case for a wider world agreement was expressed by Jan Tinbergen. He argued that, while limited liberalisation arrangements such as Yaoundé could be interpreted as restricting freer world trade, they could also constitute a possible step towards world liberalisation, to which he hoped they would in due course lead.[10]

Whatever the apparent similarity of approach between Judith Hart and Jan Tinbergen, their views of the aim of transforming Yaoundé into something more global differed when it came to the question of means. For Tinbergen, devoted to the ideal of a harmoniously competitive market, the globalisation of Yaoundé took the form of extending the market mechanism in a world in which, he also hoped, price competition would be equal. By contrast, Judith Hart was concerned to bring the *least* developed Commonwealth countries into association with the EEC, and to do so on trade and aid terms which gave them a chance of pursuing their own paths to socialist development if they so chose.[11] This involved confrontation with the explicitly capitalist philosophy of 'development' as pursued at the time by the West German authorities, who were happy to facilitate German private investment in countries whose infrastructural costs had been paid for by the French or the British.[12]

New Deal at Lomé?

There is little doubt that Judith Hart's efforts to widen the global range of the previous association agreements played a significant role in Lomé. In such an effort she had considerable support from Claude Cheysson, then Commissioner for Development Policy, and Jan Pronk, the Dutch Minister for Overseas Development.[13] All three were strenuously opposed by the French and German governments.[14] Their success appears to have stemmed partly from the soundness of their case in global, *ideological* terms against the narrower interests of the ex-French colonial territories, plus specific *political* factors at that juncture in the history of the Communities. Which bring us to the division of opinion between Marxists such as Warren and Galtung on the significance of Lomé, as well as to the specific terms of the agreement itself.

The Lomé agreement involved four new departures *vis-à-vis* the previous

Yaoundé arrangements. First, the associated countries now did not have to undertake 'reverse preferences', i.e. reciprocal concessions on exports from the Community in return for their exports to it. Second, they were allowed to give preferential treatment to other developing or developed countries in terms of access to their markets. The third departure was a special deal for sugar, including not only the Caribbean associates, for whom it was crucial, but also India, who was otherwise excluded. Fourth, Lomé involved an export revenue stabilisation scheme — STABEX — which covered exports of key primary products and raw materials.[15]

The first provision could be seen in one sense as formalising the exception clauses already noted in the original Yaoundé agreement. But this would understate its significance. In practice, it made the exceptions which were difficult to implement unilaterally into a new general rule. It also abandoned the formal fiction of a free trade area between equal partners when in reality the Associates were weak and the Community member economies were strong.

The second provision on preferential treatment to other developing or developed countries, if the Associates so chose, was important in two respects. It recognised the importance for Associates of establishing links with countries at a similar level of development, and thereby implicitly admitted that specialisation and division of labour alone would not assure them gains from trade with the more developed countries.

The third provision, on sugar, was the only arrangement in the Lomé Convention to make specific guarantees on price and access for a given commodity. It provided for total annual imports from the countries concerned of 1.4 million tons for an indefinite period (though with a review after seven years), with the price linked to the internal EEC support price for beet production (in 1975/6 some £150 a ton). In this way, despite an overall quota, the Associate sugar suppliers secured treatment similar to that of the Community's own sugar producers.

The fourth provision, the STABEX scheme, was entirely novel. It covered key exports of thirteen main groups of products from Associates to the EEC, including coffee, cocoa, tea, cotton, timber, palm nuts and products, coconut oil, groundnuts, bananas, sisal, copra, hides and iron ore. In total, at the time, it covered some £1000 million of exports by Associates to the Nine. The stabilisation formula was based on reference levels by individual country. It meant that if earnings fell below 7.5 per cent of an average for previous years, and only 2.5 per cent below such an average for the twenty poorest of the forty-six countries, they would get a subsidy. Payments from the fund would be outright grants to the least-developed associates, and repayable over five years for the others if they exceeded their reference levels during five years.

In addition to these features of Lomé, the European Development Fund, available for Associates, was renewed at a level of some £1.5 billion, slightly more than the *per capita* funds provided under the second Yaoundé convention. The Associates were to have more control over the fund than before. Moreover, crucially, any signatory country could opt out of Lomé if it so chose.

Scope and Limits

The reactions to Lomé, as has already been indicated, were mixed. Bill Warren commented not only that if must be considered 'a major and path-breaking step forward for under-developed countries and for their relationship to the advanced economies' but added that 'there are no snags (even if the Associates don't get everything they want)'. He claimed that it could not 'be convincingly argued that the more vigorous development of the associated economies along these lines would be a barrier to socialism in Africa', and judged that 'the agreement of the European Community to a system so favourable to its associated under-developed countries can only be explained as conscious promotion, as a far-sighted strategy for these countries.[16]

Johan Galtung admitted that in terms of 'the scope of operations it must be one of most extensive . . . trading and marketing arrangements . . . in the world's history', affecting some 500 million people (more or less equally divided in population terms between the EEC and the associates. He also agreed that there was no inbuilt obstacle in Lomé to the construction of socialism in the associated territories. However, he pointed out that the STABEX scheme varied widely in its incidence between countries, affecting more than 90 per cent of exports in some cases and less than 9 per cent in others. He also argued that, granted the regimes in the countries concerned, the very negotiation with capitalist countries in the EEC was likely to reinforce capitalism rather than Socialism.[17]

By the standards of Yaoundé and the ties between France and its former colonial territories, it is difficult to interpret Lomé as neo-colonialist. To do so, the agreement would have to have bound the signatories to certain conditions which they in fact not only escaped, but managed to rebut as general principles such as reverse preferences for industrial goods from the EEC. The scope for associates to extend individual preferences irrespective of the agreement itself meant that they were not tied to the EEC and could develop special relationships with Socialist countries such as China if they so chose. The sugar agreement gave parity treatment to associate and EEC producers, even if on a quota, and thereby at least countered unequal exchange. Also, the STABEX scheme clearly favoured the least-developed signatory countries by its different threshold level, thereby offsetting its different incidence on their total overall trade.

Some of the major limits of Lomé are indicated by the range of less-developed countries to which it does *not* apply. As Brian Walker, Director of Oxfam, wrote in April 1975, its 'benefits will apply to only one tenth of the people of the developing world'.[18] In negotiating the agreement, Judith Hart, as British Overseas Development Minister, had sought to secure a division of Community aid on at least a 50:50 basis between associates and non-associates. After the agreement, and during the referendum debate on British entry, she stressed that the failure to establish this should be seen as qualifying the advance which, in itself, Lomé had represented. This appears to have underlain the statement by the dissenting Ministers in the 1975 referendum on British membership of the EEC which stressed that absorption of Britain into a regional bloc in Western Europe would hinder rather than help 'our ability to cooperate with the 2,700 million people who live in the six continents of the world.[19] Nevertheless, even a critic such as Brian Walker granted that 'the great importance of the Lomé Convention is that it has changed the rules and set precedents which all future trade negotiations will be expected to follow and expand'.[20]

From Strength or Weakness?

So how can one assess the significance of Lomé in the context of the global relations of the EEC? Was Lomé an exception indicating new forms for Community action on a global scale? Did it represent the force of progressive internationalism over neo-colonialism? Was it a new international initiative by the Community, or a major concession wrested by the less-developed countries?

Tom Nairn argues that

> Lomé hardly makes sense if interpreted as the tightening grip of an aggressive new super-power. It does not present a picture of a strengthening state imposing a new imperialist stranglehold, [and that] were this the case it would be very hard to understand why states like Tanzania or the new revolutionary regime in Guinea-Bissau had chosen to sign. Rather, the impression given is that of the relative advantages which a group of less developed countries can extract *from a weak capitalist state*.[21]

To clarify the factors involved, it is useful to relate them to the main elements in the distribution of power which we have used before: i.e. politics, the state, ideology, capital and labour. There is no doubt that the Lomé negotiations took place in political circumstances which exposed the Commission and the Community to considerable pressure. A Labour Government in Britain was in the process of renegotiating membership, with explicit hostility to the previous terms, and especially their impact on less-developed countries. The Government Minister responsible for Lomé happened to be an ardent and highly able advocate of the progressive internationalist ideology which gained some success in Lomé. In this she also had considerable support from the Commissioner responsible for development policy. This combination of circumstances did not so much imply that the Commission had state power and was weak, as that state interests, and the need for some success items on the renegotiation agenda of the

Labour Government, reduced the obstacles to pressure from three sides (Britain, the Commission and the less-developed countries) for a new Convention embodying some advance for the less-developed peoples concerned.

To this extent, Lomé indicates that any major advance by the Community in this or other areas will depend on a specific combination in the distribution of power at the political, ideological and economic levels. Progressive policies need able advocacy at the political and state level, otherwise they will not see the light of day, far less change events. But they are a necessary rather than sufficient condition for success. No one event, or policy, such as the Lomé Convention, tells of the shape of things to come.

NOTES

1. Johan Galtung, 'The Lomé Convention and Neo-Capitalism', in Tom Nairn (ed.), *Atlantic Europe*? (Transnational Institute, Amsterdam, 1976) Chapter Part IV; and Bill Warren, 'The EEC, the Lomé Convention and Imperialism'. in ibid.
2. In May 1956 France had made association of her (at the time) dependent overseas territories a condition of her membership of the EEC, and thereby influenced the Fourth Part of the Rome Treaty (Articles 131–6) and the establishment in the Treaty of the European Development Fund (designed to channel aid to the associated territories). Yaoundé formalised the relationship between the now independent ex-colonies and the Community. It covered eighteen countries, including Burundi, Cameroon, the Central African Republic, Chad, Congo (Kinshasa), Congo (Brazzaville), Dahomey, Gabon, Upper Volta, the Ivory Coast, Madagascar, Mali, Mauritania, Niger, Rwanda, Senegal, Somalia and Togo, plus Surinam, The Netherlands Antilles and the French overseas territories and departments.
3. Paul Fabra, 'Zone franc ou zone de pauvreté?', *Le Monde*, 2 Dec. 1972.
4. Royal Institute of International Affairs, *The EEC and the African Associated States: the Convention of Association* (Oxford University Press, 1963).
5. M. Torrelli and K. Valaskakis, *L'Association CEE – l'Afrique Noire: Phénomène de Domination*? Centre de Recherches en Dévelopment, Table 28; *Economique* (October 1973) table 28.
6. The unequal exchange argument, based on labour theory of value, is well put in an analysis of Senegal by Samir Amin, *L'Afrique de l'Ouest Bloquée* (Éditions de Minuit, 1971) and in more general terms of Aghiri Emmanuel, *L'Exchange Inégal* (Paris: Maspero, 1968).
7. Jean-Louis Giraudy, *La Commission européene veut renforcer l'Association Europe-Afrique*, 30 Jours d'Europe (Brussels: May 1973).
8. Torelli and Valaskas, op. cit., ch. 2.
9. Philippe Lemaitre, 'Les 'Associés' Ont Peur', *Le Monde* (undated) in Communautés Européennes, *Les Grandes Problèmes Européens* (Brussels, 1976).
10. Jan Tinbergen, 'L'Association des États Africains et Malgache et L'Economie Mondiale', in Institut d'Études Européenes, Université Libre

de Bruxelles, *La Renouvellement de la Convention de Yaoundé* (Brussels, 1972).

11. See, further, Judith Hart, *Aid and Liberation: A Socialist Study of Aid Politics* (London: Gollancz, 1973).

12. For a faithful account of German official support for association as a field for profitable private foreign investment, see Hans Mahnke, 'De nouvelles Cibles pour les Investissements Étrangers', in *Les Grands Problemes Européens*.

13. Claude Cheysson, (Interview) *L'Accord de Lomé*, 30 Jours d'Europe (Mar. 1975).

14. See, *inter alia*, Philippe Lemaitre, 'La France et l'Allemagne tentent de retarder le Versement de l'Aide des Neufs aux Pays Sous Developpés, *Le Monde*, 26 Sept. 1974.

15. See, further, in detail, Overseas Development Institute, briefing paper, *The Lomé Convention* (Mar. 1975).

16. Warren, op. cit., pp. 97 and 99.

17. Galtung, op. cit., pp. 103, 108–9.

18. Brian Walker, '*A New Economic Order*', Letter to *The Times*, 10 Apr. 1975.

19. See 'Dissident Ministers Issue Statement on EEC, *Financial Times*, 24 Mar. 1975.

20. Brian Walker, *A New Economic Order*, op. cit.

21. Tom Nairn, 'Super-Power or Failure?' in Nairn (ed.), op. cit., p. 77.

10 Applicants or Supplicants?

In September 1977 the EEC Commission met at La Roche in the Ardennes to consider two major dimensions of Community policy: economic and monetary union, and enlargement to include Greece, Spain and Portugal. Sceptics might well deem the two objectives incompatible. Economic and monetary union, scheduled originally for 1980, had been indefinitely postponed because of the clear disunion of exchange rates during the 1970s. In itself this reflected the difference between strong and weak currencies, with major disparities emerging between the French franc, British sterling and the West German Mark. But it also threw the Common Agricultural Policy into disarray, i.e., the very policy which would be most strained by enlargement of the Community to include the new applicants.

At a minimum, it might be held that the EEC should put its own house in order before enlarging it by including three new countries. Certainly the report on enlargement which the members of the Commission considered at La Roche was sceptical of any rapid transition period, such as that undertaken by Britain – within five years – earlier in the decade. It made reference to membership of the new 'three' within ten years, stressed the difference between the level of development of the 'three' and the main countries of the Nine, and argued that 'it would be illusory to think that such a gap could be overcome within the space of a transition period of ten years'.[1] Thus the welcome, in principle, to the three new applicants, was relatively lukewarm. With ten years in which to consider their membership, and a transition period of another ten years or more, the applicants might find themselves full members of the Community only in the twenty-first century.

Obstacles to Enlargement
The reasons for the qualified welcome were clear enough. They included not only the disarray of the Community itself, but also the major structural problems of adjustment which would be entailed both for the applicants, and for the key Community policy; the CAP. The problems were viewed with particular acuity by the main beneficiaries to date from the CAP: the French. In a debate in the French Senate in June 1977, the former EEC Commissioner, Edgar Pisani, made plain the touchstone of the CAP in stating that the policy had enabled France to become a permanent exporter of agricultural products. But, he added, the picture was not so

positive if one considered the implications of enlargement to the three applicants, especially in the 'strong areas' of the Mediterranean agricultural economy: fruit, vegetables and wine. Producers in the applicant countries, he claimed, would penetrate the French market and undermine the security and standard of living of French producers who were already challenged by Italian produce.[2]

Pisani's comments, amply echoed by other contributors to the debate on enlargement in France, were particularly interesting —and relevant — granted his previous responsibilities in the Commission. Critics of the Community as an inward-looking rich mens' club might well take his claims in justification of their case. Yet, form the perspective of the European Left, it is relevant enough to point out that Pisani, a Socialist Party Senator, was expressing the fears of many members of the Socialist Party that their own supporters in farming regions and constituencies would be undercut or ruined by competition from the would-be applicants.[3]

According to Roy Jenkins, the President of the Commission at the time, the question was relatively simple. The enlargement of the Community to include Greece, Spain and Portugal would 'cost us all a lot of money' but was politically 'unavoidable'. To give an indication of the scale of expenditure involved, Mr Jenkins asked Ministers of the Nine in October 1977 to suppose that it was decided to raise the resources available for the three applicant countries to 60 per cent of the average available on a *per capita* basis to the enlarged Community as a whole, which would put them halfway between the present support costs for Ireland and Italy. Such sums, he claimed, would be equivalent to double the present fiscal resources of Portugal and about a quarter as much for Spain and Greece. But they would be necessary to secure an adequate standard of living in the applicant countries, and a Special Fund should be established for this purpose.[4]

Several questions are raised by such an approach to enlargement. One of the most basic is whether the Community should have a common agricultural policy in the first place. The structural disparities between the nine present members are startling enough, without enlargement. Most notably, there is the disparity between Britain, where the working population in agriculture totals less than 3 per cent, and Italy, where it still amounts to 17 per cent, while in the Republic of Ireland some 1 in every 4 workers is employed in agriculture. By contrast, in Greece, Spain and Portugal some 30 per cent, or virtually 1 in 3 workers, are employed or underemployed in agriculture: specifically, over 34 per cent in Greece, and 28 per cent and 23 per cent respectively in Portugal and Spain. For the EEC Nine as a whole, only 1 person in 10 is now employed in agriculture.

The addition of the three applicant countries to the Community would represent an increase of agricultural production to be convered by the CAP of only one-fifth, but an increase in cultivated area of one-third, and of the number of agricultural workers of nearly two-thirds relative to those of the Nine. Moreover, agricultural productivity measured in terms of output per hectare is sizably lower in the applicant countries than in France (taken as a key Community producer). For wheat, such productivity in Greece is only a half that of France, and one-quarter to virtually one-fifth that of France in Spain and Portugal. In barley, the ratios are a half, two-fifths and less than one-sixth for Greece, Spain and Portugal respectively in relation to France, while even in wine production, output per hectare in Spain and Portugal is only about half of that of either France or Italy.[5]

Such quantitative disparities of course reflect profound qualitative differences between the nature of agriculture in the three applicant countries and the main economies of the present Nine. The contrast is not simply between peasant and capitalist farming, as for instance *between* Greece and Britain, but also between capitalist and neo-feudal forms of ownership and tenure *in* countries such as Portugal and Spain. In southern Italy, the *latifundia* of absentee landlords and the *mezzadria* or share-cropping system are already notorious, but relatively exceptional. In the Iberian peninsula the *latifundia* are dominant, with 1 per cent of farms representing more than half the agricultural area of Portugal.[6] In Spain, with some reason, the Communist Party has based its agricultural policy on an anti-*latifundist* stratery, with proposals for the reform of large land-holdings and the establishment both of greater democratic management of agriculture and new producer and distributive co-operatives.[7]

Enlargement versus Development?
In their own way, these issues illustrate the limited relevance of Community integration policy to major sections of the workforce in the applicant countries. It is strongly arguable that Spain and Portugal, in particular, less need integration of their existing agricultural structures into the CAP than a transformation of the structures themselves and their integration — at nation level — into a different mode of development.

In a system of share-cropping, and other pernicious forms of land tenure in Spain, Portugal and parts of Southern Italy, the most meaningful 'liberalisation' would be a freeing of tenant peasants from forms of holding which, in some cases, were abolished in France with the revolution of 1789. Similarly, the most meaningful 'support policy' would be income support for the agricultural working population itself, on social justice grounds, rather than price support for owners and controllers of land whose role is classically parasitic and exploitative. Only such policies would 'integrate' the tenant agricultural working population of these countries, in a significant way, into the social structure of their own economies and countries. Capitalist integration through the CAP would largely leave them as dependent, peripheral and marginal in the EEC as before.[8]

Apart from this, it would be naive of the advocates of enlargement of the existing Community to expect that the reduction of working population in the applicant Three would parallel that of the main economies of

the original EEC Six through the postwar period. The main outlines of
this dramatic reduction in agricultural working population in the Six,
from an average share of 1 in 3 to 1 in 10 workers in agriculture from
1950 to the late 1970s has already been illustrated. Even if it were paralleled in the applicant three countries, it would take until the middle of the
first quarter of the twenty-first century before Greece, Spain and Portugal
as a whole achieved the present proportions for the agricultural labour
force within the total working population.

Besides, such a reduction in parallel with the original Six members of
the Community is most unlikely. It took Britain most of the nineteenth
century to reduce agricultural labour as a share of total working population
to the present levels of the original Six members of the Community: i.e.
to around one-tenth of the total labour force. This was with a major
demand-pull for labour in urban industry, and against the background of a
long-standing supply-push of labour off the land through the extension of
capitalist production in agriculture, dating from the enclosures of common
land in the sixteenth and seventeeth centuries.[9] In Germany, France and
Northern Italy, the emergence of industrial capitalism from the mid- and
late nineteenth century occurred without a comparable reduction of agricultural labour. It was only the period of sustained demand for labour
after the Second World War which effected the major shift in the distribution of labour between agriculture, industry and services already noted
above. Even with this remarkable demand for labour from agriculture – in
practice the effect of young people not entering agricultural employment
– Italy still has nearly one person in every five working in argiculture.

Moreover, the bulk of the outflow of labour from agriculture in the
original Six members of the Community occurred in the 1950s and early
1960s. It depended on a specific combination of factors during the period
of postwar reconstruction, when labour demand in industry was accompanied by both capital deepening and widening: i.e. both more capital
per worker and more workers overall in industry.[10] There is little doubt
that such labour availability – in Marxist terms drawing a reserve army of
labour into the active labour force – made possible the super-growth
phase of postwar development. But its role was secondary rather than
primary: it depended on industrial demand for labour of an exceptional
kind whereby labour displaced by machinery in some sectors of industry
was by and large re-employed in other sectors of industry – or services –
where employment was expanding.

Virtuous to Vicious Circles

From the later 1960s such a combination of virtuous-circle effects were
giving way to more classic vicious circles. While the immediate twenty
years of the postwar period had seen the rise of entirely new industries,
or the extension of existing industries on a new scale through rising real
incomes, this virtually Schumpeterian boom of innovation peaked out,

with investment increasingly taking the form of replacement of existing
plant and equipment by less labour-intensive techniques.[11] Technological
unemployment, which the more superficial commentators ignored, crossed
the European industrial horizon. Through the 1970s it has come closer,
reinforcing the cyclical unemployment caused by the deflations imposed
by governments in desperation following the OPEC oil and other commodity price rises.

If there were a chain of entirely new Schumpeterian innovations in
sight, capable of creating entirely new industries or services which could
replicate the postwar boom in the Six, the applicant three countries might
be able to offer attractive locations, at relatively low labour costs, for at
least a high share of the new industrial employment. But nothing as yet is
even in view. What is on the agenda is a series of process rather than
product innovations of a kind which threaten major technological unemployment not only in industry, but also in services. Micro-processors are
but one such example. They are likely to replace white-collar office
workers, who at present use electronic calculators or electric typewriters
by processes which displace both operations on a major scale.[12]

Apart from this, while Greece, Spain and Portugal are geographically
peripheral to the rest of Western Europe, European capital – as previously
noted – is not expanding its circle of operations in a semi-circular manner
through Southern Europe. While favouring some parts of Iberia and the
Attica region in Greece for some of the time, it has made what amounts
to a quantum leap in location since the mid 1960s, when falling growth and
rising wages have made it more cost conscious in the main EEC countries.
Since the mid-1970s it has increasingly favoured Brazil rather than Portugal
(partly for political reasons), and Singapore and South Korea rather than
Southern Italy or Spain. So long as such countries offer labour costs one-
fifth or less than those of Southern Europe, there is a real likelihood that
the applicant countries to the EEC will be as marginal to European industrial capital as is their agriculture in relation to capitalist farming in the
more developed countries of the Community.[13]

As a result, there is unlikely to be the demand-pull for labour from
agriculture, paralleling the postwar process in the main EEC countries in
the twenty years after the Second World War. On the one hand, the
location of relatively labour-intensive production by the new multinationals
has moved entirely outside Europe, while capital in modern European
industry is increasingly displacing indigenous labour. At the same time, the
fiscal crisis of the main EEC countries during the 1970s, when they have
insisted on subsidising profits rather than reshaping and reflating public
demand, has diminished their capacity to absorb an increasing share of
labour in public services. On such grounds it is possible, but unlikely, that
the applicant three countries will see their agricultural labour force decline
on the lines of Trend C in Fig. 2.1. More probably it will be slower and
on the lines of Trend D. Even without fatalism, or the capacity to fore-

cast trends with accuracy over the long term, the analysis suggests that the applicants may not achieve current EEC levels of working population in agriculture until towards the mid-twenty-first century.

Enlargement and Disintegration?

Such factors indicate the kind of strain which could be posed for the Community if it enlarges to a total of twelve countries without profound changes in both the nature of the Common Agricultural Policy and the nature of those policies which concern and affect the distribution of income and employment: i.e. Industrial, Regional and Social Policy. Such strains conceivably could disintegrate the Community as we at present know it.

Certainly, there is not class or pressure group within the Nine which is pressing for enlargement on the grounds that without it capital and industry will lack the labour for expansion. One of the ironies of the creation of the initial Community of the Six was the fact that demand for Italian labour (or its response to industrial employment opportunities) fell from the early 1960s, and gave way to the immigration of predominantly Portuguese, Spanish, Greek, Yugoslav and Turkish workers. Thus, quite apart from the fact that there is currently a major employment crisis in the Nine, capital has been able to attract and employ non-Community migrant workers as and how it chooses.[14] Inversely, during the present crisis, the key Community employer of migrant labour – West Germany – has neatly expelled more than 0.6 million such 'guest workers' since the beginning of the recession in 1974.

If the three applicant countries were to become full members of the Community, such 'guest workers' from Portugal, Spain and Greece would have the same rights to permanent residence and social security benefits as present Community nationals.[15] By the ideals of a Community in any genuine sense, such rights would represent a common policy without respect to country of origin or nationality. But, in practice, it would qualify the power of capital to command and dismiss labour in relation to its dictates and its needs.

The implicit obstacles to enlargement thereby include not only the support and adjustment costs for agriculture, but also the support costs for those unemployed or non-employed in industry and services. Karl Georg Zinn has shown that if the 0.6 million 'guest workers' who left West Germany from 1974 had been German nationals, or had enjoyed equivalent social security rights, this would have increased total registered unemployment in the Federal Republic to nearly two million – and with it the public expenditure costs for unemployment benefits.[16]

Again, if EEC integration were based primarlily on social and political grounds, with explicit admission of the need to establish equal rights to welfare and income on a European scale, the extension of support costs for agricultural labour and would-be workers in industry and services should be not only thinkable, but also desirable. But it would in itself mean a transformation of the present basis of Community policies, and with them a transformation of the present relations between capital, labour and the State within the Community countries.

Put differently, it would mean a social policy which was based on principles of social justice, rather than on the practice of meeting the retraining costs of unemployed workers in some industries. It would also mean an agricultural policy which was based on income support for those who worked in agriculture, rather than price support and subsidy for those who owned land and controlled agricultural production. Further, it would need a regional and urban policy capable of adjusting the supply of employment, income, jobs and housing to the social choice of those who preferred particular locations. In turn this would entail a transport and environmental planning policy far outstripping present Community perspectives. But it would also mean policies for economic planning which changed the future, rather than simply forcasted scenarios of the undesirable, in the manner of recent Commission and Community reports.

In essence, particularly in view of the major structural slump of production and employment, such change would amount to a new mode of development, rather than the attempt to enlarge a Community whose present modes of growth is not only in question, but in crisis.

The present scenario for enlargement has of course been strongly influenced by two factors. On the one hand the loss of momentum in integration which the supranationalists lament and which they first, vainly, hoped would be overcome by admission of the United Kingdom, Denmark and Ireland. On the other hand, there is the more laudable concern to recognise the new parliamentary democracy, or its re-establishment, in three formerly Fascist countries. Yet if the advocates of an enlarged, formally democratic Community wish to see their vision fulfilled, they will need to face more basic issues than the arithmetic of higher support costs for agriculture in the event of Greece, Spain and Portugal being admitted to membership. As many children in the applicant countries could tell them, the multiplication of zero by Twelve gives a result similar to multiplying Nine by zero. Alternatively, an almost empty vessel is not filled by adding further empty vessels to the shelves. If the Community is to be more than an expanded map reproduced by the Commission's Information Division it will need to recreate itself on new principles and new lines involving qualitative change rather than mere quantitative expansion.

In practice, unless there is a change in the mode of Community integration itself, enlargement could weaken even the present drift of common policies, and inhibit supranationalism in a manner which might not be unwelcome to many of those who view the present Community with misgiving. In effect, a partial enlargement of the Common Agricultural Policy as at present operated, with a two-tier system in favour of initial and new members, could further qualify the impetus to integration as such, and result in a confederation of Western European countries loosely related through one of the least efficient policies devised by international bureaucracy. Such an arrangement would confirm the worst principles of integration on the Community agenda to date, and represent a Community of an industrial free trade – for those strong enough to face it – with uncommon agricultural markets. Such a formula of GATT plus CAP may not have been what Jean Monnet had in mind, nor what a more genuinely international Europe could achieve in relation to its less-developed Continental partners.

The Association Alternative
But in any case, there is a clear option for the applicant countries which could serve their economic interests better than full membership: association.

As has already been seen from analysis of the Yaoundé and Lomé agreements, there is at least doubt whether these have clearly disadvantaged associate countries, and in some quarters approbation for their openness. The very principle on which such association agreements were based is relevant to would-be members of the present Community: i.e. admission of unequal levels of development and the need for different policies to tackle them.

While admitting that there are important differences in the level of development between the applicants themselves, the structural problems faced by a country such as Portugal clearly are not going to be aided in a significant sense by full membership of the Community.

For instance, since the military and political revolution of April 1974, several Governments in Portugal have fallen as a consequence of the imposition of deflationary terms for IMF loans. Despite the fact that one-third of Portugal's trade deficit in the mid-1970s was in cereals and food items, rather than consumer or luxury goods, and despite the fact that Portugal needs major public investment in both industry and public services if her long-term economic and social structure is to be secured in a democratic framework, the IMF imposed conditions (backed especially by West Germany), which were not even appropriate to the more developed countries in which they were conceived and first applied.

Ironically, when West Germany has an export structure where four-fifths of visible export trade is in investment goods and materials for industry,[17] such policies of deflation are not even in the donor's interest. There is a limit to the number of machine tools which can be consumed by any Wuppertal householder. In export terms, jobs in the Ruhr are best served by German-backed credit for industrial expansion and development in countries such as Portugal, Spain and Greece.

Thus the refusal of significant credit, on expansionary terms, to such would-be members of the Community is not even in the interests of the strongest member of the Community itself. Such a basic contradiction is closer to the formal imperialism of the classic model – in the sense of external intervention in the domestic affairs of another state – than to Arrighi or Hobson's 'informal' variants.[18] As with the initial Commission proposal that support aid to the new members should be less than two-thirds of the average *per capita* for the *whole* enlarged Community, it augurs ill for the applicants.

From the two-tier Community which Willy Brandt recommended in the Nine (an inner core proceeding to monetary union, with the rest tailing along), it is clear that a Community of Twelve would represent a three-tier Community with the outer periphery lagging at a pace dictated by the competence and incompetence of the inner hegemonic bloc. This now is, and would be, dominated by West Germany within a Deutschmark zone (whatever the *maquillage* of its chosen name, such as ECU) and ruled by the iron fist of a European Monetary Fund – a Euro IMF – which would itself be dominated by the monetarism of the Bundesbank and its pre-Keynesian ideology.

In such a context, for the applicants, full membership of the EEC would amount to a formula for dependent development, rather than genuine integration.

NOTES

1. Philippe LeMaitre, L'adhésion de la Grèce, L'Espagne et du Portugal ne devrait intervenir qu'après une longue transition', *Le Monde* 18–19 Sept. 1977.

2. 'La Grèce doit entrer dans la CEE, *Le Monde*, 2 June 1977.

3. See, further, Jacques Grall, 'Le débat au l'élargissement de la CEE', *Le Monde*, 12 Sept. 1978.

4. Michael Hornsby, 'Mr. Jenkins says enlargement of the EEC will be expensive', *The Times*, 19 Oct. 1977.

5. See, further, Christian Heimpal, 'The Cooperation of the European Community with Southern Europe', in Fundacao Gulbenkian, *Conferencia Internacional sobre Economia Portugesa* (Lisbon: 1977).

6. Stuart Holland, 'Dependent Development: Portugal as Periphery', in Dudley Seers (ed.), *Underdeveloped Europe* (1979).

7. PCE, *Manifesto Programa del Partido Comunista de Espana* (Colección Ebro, 1975) pp. 118–21.

8. The occupation of the *latifundia* of southern Portugal, most notably in the Alentejo, following the events of 25 April 1974, was a more notable social advance – currently threatened with reversal – than anything likely at present in Portugal through the CAP.

9. See, further, Karl Marx, *Capital*, I, Chapter 25; and Stuart Holland, *Capital versus the Regions*, chs 2 and 4 (Macmillan, 1976).

10. A point stressed by Charles Kindleberger in *Europe's Postwar Growth: the Role of Labour Supply* (Oxford University Press, 1967).

11. Both Andrew Shonfield in *Modern Capitalism* (RIIA and Oxford University Press, 1965) chapter 3, and M. M. Postan in *An Economic History*

of Western Europe 1945—64 noted the speeding up of innovation and its virtuous effects. But both authors wrote and published shortly before the turn of the virtuous circle.

12. See, *inter alia*, Michel Bosquet, 'L'âge d'or du chômage', *Le Nouvel Observateur*, no. 734 (December 1978): Such an employment crisis through new processes is of course reinforced by the crisis of technological unemployment in basic industries such as steel and chemicals, and the undermining of shipbuilding and textiles production by Asian countries.

13. See, further, Seers (ed.), *Underdeveloped Europe* (1979).

14. See, further, Russell King, 'Long-Range Migration Patterns in the EEC: An Italian Case Study', in Roger Lee and Philip Ogden (eds), *Economy and Society in the EEC*, ch. 6 (Saxon House, 1976).

15. Even this was challenged by West Germany in December 1978 during the negotiations on Greece's membership.

16. Karl Georg Zinn, 'The Social Market in Crisis', in Stuart Holland (ed.), *Beyond Capitalist Planning* (Blackwell, 1978).

Index